RUSSIAN TALK

RUSSIAN TALK

Culture and Conversation during Perestroika

NANCY RIES

Cornell University Press

ITHACA AND LONDON

First published 1997 by Cornell University Press
First printing, Cornell Paperbacks, 1997

Printed in the United States of America

Cornell University Press strives to use environmentally responsible suppliers and materials to the fullest extent possible in the publishing of its books. Such materials include vegetable-based, low-VOC inks and acid-free papers that are recycled, totally chlorine-free, or partly composed of nonwood fibers. Books that bear the logo of the FSC (Forest Stewardship Council) use paper taken from forests that have been inspected and certified as meeting the highest standards for environmental and social responsibility. For further information, visit our website at www.cornellpress.cornell.edu.

Library of Congress Cataloging-in-Publication Data

Ries, Nancy, b. 1955
      Russian talk : culture and conversation during Perestroika / Nancy Ries.
          p.   cm.
      Includes bibliographical references (p.) and index.
      ISBN 0-8014-3385-1 (cloth : alk. paper). —ISBN 0-8014-8416-2 (pbk. : alk. paper)
        1. Language and cultural—Soviet Union.   2. Oral communication—Social aspects—Soviet Union.   3. Perestroika.   I. Title.
   P35.5.S65R54   1997
   306.44'0947—dc21   97-10136

Cloth printing   10 9 8 7 6 5 4 3 2 1

Paperback printing   10 9 8 7 6 5 4 3 2

For my mother, Frances Kiernan Ries,

in memory of my father, William Alfred Ries,

and for Natasha, invaluable friend.

Contents

Acknowledgments

Many hurdles had to be crossed in order to do fieldwork in Russia in the late 1980s. It is now hard to recall how it was then, when permissions were hard to secure, funding agencies were skeptical, and urban Russia was not seen as an appropriate subject for anthropology. Many people and institutions provided crucial help in navigating a range of difficulties. First among them is Carol J. Greenhouse, then in the Anthropology Department at Cornell University. There is no way I can thank Carol enough for all of the doors she has unlocked for me over the years, both intellectually and logistically. It is no exaggeration to say that this research would never have been possible without her help.

Other members of the faculty at Cornell provided valued guidance. Along with steady encouragement, P. Steven Sangren provided crucial direction for this work; these pages hardly do justice to Steve's theoretical models, which have been not just inspiration but revelation. Billie Jean Isbell sparked me to consider a number of key ethnographic issues. Michael Scammell, then in Cornell's Department of Russian Literature, has been both valued teacher and cherished friend; the challenges he has offered have been crucial intellectual guideposts.

The main period of this research, nine months in 1989 and 1990, was made possible by a grant from the Ploughshares Peace Fund and by a Foreign Language Area Studies (FLAS) HEA-Title VI Dissertation Research Fellowship, administered through the Graduate School of Cornell University. Many thanks go to Mary LeCron Foster and Robert Rubinstein of the Committee for the Study of Peace of the IUAES, who were instrumental in getting me into the field. I am most grateful to Valerii Aleksandrovich Tishkov, director of the Institute of Ethnology and Anthropology of the Academy of Sciences, who facilitated my research in Moscow in a number of ways.

Both the Graduate School and the Anthropology Department at Cornell University supported me during writing with fellowships and teaching assistantships. Two preliminary trips to Moscow in 1988 were supported by funds from the Peace Studies Program and the Center for International Studies at Cornell. Research time in 1992 was made possible by support from Colgate University. Postdoctoral research in 1994 and 1995 was funded by a grant from the Joint Committee on the Soviet Union and its Successor States of the Social Science Research Council and the American Council of Learned Societies with funds provided by the State Department under the Russian, Eurasian, and East European Training Program (Title VIII).

Friends and colleagues have provided intellectual sustenance as well as critical reflections on this work over the years. I am particularly grateful to Jane Balin, Susan Buck-Morss, Julie deSherbinin, Bruce Grant, Michael Peletz, Judy Rosenthal, and Stacia Zabusky for their incisive insights and for the crucial support they have offered. Many thanks are due as well to Marjorie Mandelstam Balzer, Philip Bennett, George Chialtas, Paula Garb, George Gibian, David Holmberg, Wendy Kohli, Kathryn March, Alice Nakhimovsky, Rosemary Nossiff, Marc Novak, Slava Paperno, Dale Pesmen, Walter Pintner, Dick Sylvester, Cathy Wanner, Thomas Wolfe, and the participants in the 1993 SSRC Summer Workshop in post-Soviet Sociology and Anthropology for advice, ideas, and inspiration along the way. Michael Connolly, Laurence G. Jones, and Natalia Sadomskaya, my intellectual mentors long ago at Boston College, planted seeds which they may find bearing fruit in this work. Henk Newenhouse provided gifts of mentoring, friendship, and possibility which have both spurred and sustained me. As readers for Cornell University Press, Marjorie Mandelstam Balzer and John Bushnell gave extremely constructive comments and suggestions, for which I am most grateful; I also greatly appreciate the editorial wizardry provided by Carolyn Pouncy and Teresa Jesionowski. From our very first meeting, I have benefited enormously from the enthusiasm, insight, and creativity which Fran Benson, editor-in-chief at Cornell University Press, has brought to this project. For use of their marvelous photographs, I am most grateful to John Einarsen and Robert Kowalczyk.

My mother, Frances Ries, and my late father, William, nourished my intellectual efforts with faith and confidence. My sisters, Susan Barnes and Margaret Ries, and their families have been encouraging, interested, and helpful in ways they cannot even imagine. My dear friend, Cara Durschlag, has seen me through two decades of wandering and writing, and she, more than anyone else, knows what it is all about.

The largest debt of gratitude is owed to my friends, colleagues, and acquaintances in Russia. Many people opened their lives to me, shared their stories, answered my questions, and tolerated my intrusions and early efforts at cultural interpretation. I particularly thank Marat and Sasha Akchurin, Alexei Didurov, Inna Kabysh, the Khanin family, Sasha Mazaev, Ira Sandomirskaia, and Vladimir Vishnevskii for sharing their interesting points of view and warm friendship. The members of the Sector on America of the Institute of Ethnography have been unfailingly generous and welcoming over the years. Two colleagues, Tamara Vladimirovna Ravdina of the Institute of Archeology and Sergei Serov of the Institute of Ethnography, both now deceased, contributed in very different ways. Dmitry Khanin always patiently and elaborately answered my questions about Russian language, ideology, and society; I appreciate his continuing generosity as both friend and informant (or, as he says, "specimen"). My deepest affection and most profound gratitude go to Natasha Kulakova, Volodia Ravdin, and Natasha Ravdina, who epitomize for me the warmth, wisdom, and sanity of Russian family life. Natasha, my colleague from the Institute of Ethnography and anthropological exchange partner, has been a true friend, my best cultural guide, and most trusted critic; she has helped me in a hundred different ways, but most of all I cherish our long conversations, through which a different world has become meaningful for me.

N. R.

A Note on Transliteration and Translation

I have used the Library of Congress system of transliteration throughout this book, with the exception of certain well-known terms and names which have been anglicized in a different way. I have, for instance, rendered "glasnost" without its final soft sign; I refer to Dostoevsky, Jakobson, Mandelstam, Sinyavsky, and Yeltsin (rather than Dostoevskii, Iakobson, Mandel'shtam, Siniavskii, El'tsin), following either the most common way of anglicizing a name or the author's own chosen way.

Translations are my own, except where otherwise noted.

RUSSIAN TALK

I am falling in love with Russian fairy tales. . . . In language that brooks no contradiction you are told about a talking dog, a holy old man, a centaur, in a field of oats or an aspen wood, and other miracles—hey, presto, there you are! On and on and on it goes like this! . . . without end. What joy! And Ivanushka will never extricate himself from the adventure that begins at the crossroads.

—Andrei Sinyavsky, *A Voice from the Chorus*

Anyone interested in how a view of the world is shared, recognized, maintained, or socialized within a community must attend to language made public and socially compelling, must attend to talk.

—Michael Moerman, *Talking Culture*

Introduction

Ethnography begins, write Keith Basso and Henry Selby (1976: 3), in "a disciplined attempt to discover and describe the symbolic resources with which the members of a society conceptualize and interpret their experience." The interpretive tradition in anthropology impels us to explore the ground-level processes through which shared meanings are transmitted and performed, the day-to-day local systems, whether of ritual, discourse, or practice, which express a "distinctive manner of imagining the real" (Geertz 1983: 173).

Based as it is in personal encounters, observing the lives of individuals and their interactions in small groups, and attending to the ways people describe their worlds, the ethnographic project is an "artisan task of seeing broad principles in parochial facts" (Geertz 1983: 167). The bridge from parochial facts to broad principles is a hermeneutic one, requiring much weaving back and forth between isolated threads of meaning until some kind of pattern becomes visible and articulable. Though we usually call such patterns "culture," that term is merely shorthand for the complex, indeterminate, and ever-shifting sets of symbolic codes that people deploy to express and assert themselves, singularly or collectively.

On my first trip to Russia in 1985, the first person with whom I conversed was Dusia, a woman who shared my sleeping compartment on the trans-Siberian express, headed west toward Moscow. A beautiful woman in her early sixties, with sapphire eyes and golden hair, Dusia was traveling from her home in Yakutsk to a small village four hours north of Krasnoyarsk—a journey of about 3,500 kilometers each way, which would take her a week on a variety of trains and buses. In the village that was her destination her mother had been buried in 1944, and Dusia was making her annual pilgrimage to visit her mother's grave on the anniversary of her death. After she placed some plastic flowers on the grave and paid the cemetery tender for his attentions, Dusia planned to return to Yakutsk. Although full of questions for me about life in the United States and other parts of the world, she was not inclined to answer any questions about herself, or to speak of politics or Soviet life. As it turned out, most of our talk about the Soviet Union centered around manifestations of weather in Siberia.

In 1995 the first person I interviewed on a research trip to Yaroslavl, a city north of Moscow, was a mafia gang leader. As a kind of practical joke, an acquaintance set up a lunch for me with Alesha, who he said was a businessman. A handsome man in his early thirties, Alesha surprised me when I asked him what kind of business he was in. "I am a gangster," he said, smiling and enjoying my shock. Over lunch he answered many of my questions about mafia practices in the "new Russia" and told me some amusing stories about his recent stint in prison; then he invited me to drive around with him for the rest of the day as he called on his "clients," several of whom were former communist bosses, now members of Yaroslavl's business elite.

These brief descriptions of two encounters, separated by ten years and thousands of miles (both literal and symbolic), illustrate the kinds of communicative exchanges on which the ethnography at hand rests. While these and many other encounters with singular individuals hold enormous significance for me personally, they are also full of meaning in an ethnographic sense: they can be "read" or interpreted from various angles; they are like small doorways into a complex system of meanings and values, ideologies, identities, and life strategies. Dusia's near-silence in 1985 and Alesha's bravado in 1995 reveal many things: about gender and the ways it can be performed or expressed, about life histories and their power to shape practice, about different kinds of social commitments and strategies, about the relationships between individuals and the state systems in which and in reference to which they operate, about the enormous transformation in a society over a decade of revolution.

These encounters also illustrate the specificity (and perhaps the peculiarity) of ethnographic practice and representation. There are certain inescapable degrees of arbitrariness and accident in the positioning of any individual ethnographer within a society—especially an immense one such as Russia. I met Dusia and Alesha through different forms of happenstance; the one merely because we were assigned to the same compartment on a train, the other because of a quite attenuated sequence of relationship (he was the friend of an acquaintance who was the friend of a cousin of a close friend of mine) and because I had expressed interest in meeting members of the local business community.

Over the years that I have been working in Russia (primarily in Moscow, though with stints in Yaroslavl and journeys to other places), I have made choices about what I wanted to study and decisions about how best to gather the kinds of "data" I sought; I have pursued contacts with particular kinds of people, who I thought might provide valuable insights or perspectives pertinent to the topics that interested me. Ultimately, however, the ethnography I have produced here is the product of the specific and often somewhat random encounters I managed to have. My analysis or interpretation has entailed the hermeneutic task of locating within the conversations and narratives I heard and the observations I made certain kinds of patterns: parallels, regularities, common juxtapositions and oppositions, habitual remarks, recurrent arguments, and so on. While every conversation or experience involves the unique dynamics of a particular moment with distinct individuals, these encounters are also ripe with cultural values and meanings, as well as with intercultural misunderstandings, maskings, and misrepresentations.

In this book I present a selection of the narratives and observations that I gathered, primarily during nine months in Moscow in 1989 and 1990. By choosing these texts, I am suggesting that they exemplify something "cultural" rather than being purely idiosyncratic, that however ephemeral and personal they may be, and however much they were affected by my own presence, they are nonetheless typical of prevalent types of Russian expression in the later years of perestroika.

My aim in this book is not to provide a comprehensive sociology of the permutations of culture and expression in Russia during and after perestroika. If such an undertaking were possible, it would be outdated even before it was fully written. Instead, I try to illustrate something of the complex intervocality of various historical and human vantage points, as expressed through the daily narratives and practices of Russians themselves, and to tease out and abstract from these narratives the social and ideological orientations they convey and reproduce.

The primary theoretical argument that I make here is that spontaneous conversational discourses are a primary mechanism by which ideologies and cultural stances are shaped and maintained. Furthermore, I contend that the discursive world does not merely reflect the world of more obvious social action, but also helps to construct it; that in talk, various conceptual patterns and value systems are encapsulated in narrative, even mythic form, comprising models for life as much as models of it (Geertz 1973: 93; Rosaldo 1986: 134). The types of stories, jokes, and complaints that circulated in Moscow in the perestroika years were not just reactions to the events of the day; they were, as I hope to demonstrate, a significant constitutive aspect of the events themselves. *Talk*—in all its forms and manifestations—is a key ingredient in the production of social paradigms and practices, and in the reproduction of what has often been called "Russianness."

Of course, as the accounts of my meetings with Dusia and Alesha illustrate, there are countless different ways to be Russian, and the major social changes of the past years have produced diverse and fascinating permutations in the realms of cultural identity and practice. Nonetheless, there are distinctive and enduring semiotic codings which are a crucial aspect of the discursive production of culture; these can be traced and studied.

This does not mean that these codes are culturally or socially determining; as Dmitry Shalin put it in his introduction to a collection of brilliantly insightful essays on Russian culture, "although human understandings form a system, the latter is never devoid of inconsistencies and contradictions" (1996: 5). I would make this point even more strongly and suggest that the semiotic or discursive codes that we call culture are *always* being resisted, contradicted, and undermined on many levels and in many ways. The years since 1985 in Russia have entailed (as Shalin also stresses) a profound shifting and challenging of modes of discourse, and that very fact means that any represention of contemporary Russian discourses will probably be somewhat "ethnohistorical" by the time it is published.

However much life in Russia has been altered by the reforms since 1985, though, it is also vital to understand the continuing durability of many institutional systems, social practices, and—central to this ethnography—modes of discourse. The interplay of continuity and change, the dialectics of social reproduction and revolution, and the strategies that people employ to deal with these are thus other theoretical issues addressed here. I have found remarkable the degree to which my Russian friends and acquaintances have kept up with the transformation of their society, how calmly they have adapted to changing circumstances and learned new modes of action, how smoothly they have incorporated into their stories and anecdotes all the novel material thrown up by the processes of transition. In this book I suggest that the extraordinary changes in Russian society have been negotiated, in large part, through the continual exchange of stories about those changes; furthermore, I maintain that the stories people tell follow certain durable narrative conventions, and that these conventions ensure a certain degree of cultural (and probably psychological) continuity, despite massive restructuring.

The narratives I present here to illustrate these issues are not, however, the final object of analysis. One of my objectives is to suggest some of the complex and dynamic (and often paradoxical) effects that certain kinds of discourse may have had within Russia during the perestroika years. Many of the conversations I had and the stories I heard implicitly or explicitly addressed the structures and practices of power in Russian (Soviet) society, and decried the vast gaps between the world of those with power and those without it. But, as I hope this work shows, in certain ways the particular logic of power and powerlessness in Russia was reproduced by the very lamentations and narratives that denounced it.

The existential question that inspires my own work is the same question I heard a thousand times in Moscow: Why is Russian experience so full of suffering and misfortune? Taking one of many conceivable approaches to grappling with that profound (and probably unanswerable) question, this book examines the possibility that the regular posing of such key rhetorical questions helps sustain the kinds of social and cultural institutions which perpetuate that "suffering." This, then, is an interpretation of cultural texts that keeps one eye on other things: social structures, power relations, modes of resistance and reproduction, the difficulties of democratization, and the paradoxes of and potential for societal transformation.

Ethnographic Scope and Methods

This study is necessarily narrow in terms of both time and social range. It is like a small set of cultural snapshots taken at a particular historical moment and focused on certain kinds of expressions produced by a relatively small number of people in Moscow. I made a concerted effort to speak with people who would represent a variety of views and experiences, although, because of the ways in which my research evolved, many of those people would be considered members of the Moscow intelligentsia. Though *intelligentsia* is an inherently slippery term, here I use it in the broadest sense, as referring to relatively well-educated persons in intellectual, professional, or semiprofessional lines of work. In other words, my informants were members of a sort of urban "middle class," though that label is highly problematic in the case of Soviet Russia (see Balzer 1996 for intriguing discussions of this issue). In the course of fieldwork I spoke with relatively few manual laborers or rural workers, on the one hand, and I had only two acquaintances among the "highest" Moscow elites, on the other.

My colleagues at the Institute of Ethnography and my other friends, acquaintances, and interviewees often helped me widen my understanding of their world by introducing me to *their* friends and acquaintances in casual settings or by arranging more formal meetings with people they knew. In this way, I conversed my way through different personal networks. Many of my friends expressed special concern that I meet the "real Russian people"—the *narod*—and they thus often brought me into contact with those whom they claimed were their "truly Russian" acquaintances: factory workers, rural people, and the like.

This brings me to the crucial question of ethnicity, a question many of my informants themselves raised when asking me about my research topic. The ethnic backgrounds of the people I spoke with were varied; while many defined themselves as "pure Russians," many others identified themselves as "fully" Jewish, or as having, for instance, partly Russian and partly Armenian, Georgian, Azeri, Uzbek, Bashkir, Kazakh, Buryat, or Latvian ancestry. Although other studies might privilege the important theme of ethnic identity and how it is negotiated and contested through narrative, I was more inclined to seek out commonalities in narrative style and reference and the relationships between personal, local discourses and more broadly shared ideological frameworks. Proclaimed ethnic differences were often less vividly marked among my Moscow informants than shared linguistic conventions; whether this is more the result of common socialization via language, similarities in the effects of Soviet systems and pedagogies, or situational choices about "how to speak" is hard to judge. One friend who described herself as Armenian, for example, produced narratives that were generically identical to those produced by "pure" Russians. In fact, as my time in the field went on, I started hearing myself produce Russian-style narratives and litanies, although I have not a "drop of Russian blood" (to use a metaphor common to Russian and English) in my ancestry.

My informants ranged across age groups and across political, economic, and social spectrums: I interviewed party functionaries and well-known dissidents, state planners and figures in the then-sprouting business class, patriotic veterans and absurdist writers, communist philosophers and liberal journalists. Among my friends I counted people with obvious status and the luxuries that status conferred—fine apartments, automobiles, and dachas—as well as some who had no special privileges and who lived in one room flats in crumbling apartment blocks, took the Metro, and spent their summers in the hot city. My networks connected me to approximately one hundred people, although since I came to know many in the contexts of their familial or professional circles I had contact with several hundred more in the course of my fieldwork. In line with long-standing ethnographic practice, I have disguised the identity of speakers whom I cite here in several ways in order to protect informants' anonymity. Names have been changed and in several cases professional and other identifying features have been altered.

When I set out for Moscow in September 1989, it was to study local constructions of "Russianness" and how these might manifest themselves in and inflect political and economic discourse and decision making, especially as U.S.–Soviet relations and the cold war were concerned. It was impossible to imagine that within two months the Berlin wall would come down and with it so many of the political and social edifices of the cold war. As it happened, those momentous historical events in November in Berlin proved a tremendous help to me, for I had begun to understand, within only a few weeks of beginning my fieldwork, that there really *was* no Russian "cold war culture," that, indeed, the kind of consciousness of the nuclear arms race that from 1945 on inspired Western war fantasies and peace movements, and their thousands of cultural productions, had hardly taken shape in Russia. The fall of the Berlin wall and the subsequent rapid unraveling of most remaining cold war tensions gave me the opportunity to indulge in a little joke—"Well, I came to Russia to study the Russian view of the cold war, but it just ended"—and then to converse on different themes with my informants and interviewees, who were much more interested in other topics in any case. Although it is true that those other topics also centered around apocalyptic visions, these were not visions of nuclear apocalypse; they were, instead, immediately compelling images of the dissolution of local worlds. The bulk of conversations I had concerned perestroika and how it was affecting people's lives and images of their country and its history. That was what people were talking about, and as ethnographers often do, I decided to let my informants guide me to the heart of their concerns.

Finding myself in the field with a collapsed ethnographic agenda was beneficial, because it allowed me to recognize the importance of the issues that I discuss in this book. I never completely left off pursuit of my nonissue, partly because that was my official reason for being in Moscow; my visa and my institutional support on both sides had been obtained so that I could do my research on discourses concerning war and peace in the nuclear age. Because of this official purpose, I interviewed people with whom I might not have spoken had my subject been "narratives about power and suffering." Yet these official interviews (with military personnel, veterans, journalists, political elites, party spokespersons) themselves provided valuable material for sketching out some of the texts and contexts of the discourses I heard.

Perhaps one-third of the material presented here was gathered in formal, planned situations, set up for the explicit purpose of conducting an interview; most of these conversations were tape-recorded. The rest comes from notes about informal conversations with a variety of people, often over tea and sweets in someone's apartment, at meals, during long strolls in parks or shared rides in the Metro, at evening gatherings, birthday or holiday celebrations, or while visiting someone's modest dacha outside of the city. While I sometimes had the audacity to pull out my tape recorder or note pad on these occasions, usually I did not, because they so inhibited conversation. Immediately after leaving someone's company, if at all possible, I jotted down notes to myself about the talk that I had heard.

Living and Working in Moscow

Moscow is a place of contrasts as great as the city itself. The majestic product of centuries of planning, engineering, and construction—a modernist metropolis, the national hub of high politics, manufacturing, science, and culture—it is also, as visitors have noted for centuries, an "overgrown village"—organic, sprawling, irregular, and uncontrolled, offering countless oases for private and, in some ways, almost provincial living. It was both a thrilling and a tiring place to live; thrilling because of the grandiosity of its attractions and oddities (its megalithic buildings, its impossibly broad boulevards, its phenomenally large and baroque Metro), and tiring for exactly the same reasons, because it is not really a city on a human scale until you get into the quieter rhythms of its neighborhoods and some of its ancient, crooked, obscure little streets.

The setting for the most dramatic mass rituals of the Soviet state, Moscow is also, like any city, host to all the unrehearsed, unofficial, and sometimes rather illicit rituals of day-to-day existence. In the perestroika years, it was, of course, also the site of many of the momentous rituals of democratization, that helped set the stage for the Soviet Union's demise.

As an ethnographer, I tried to take part in or observe the different rituals of Moscow life, including the rather dry official rites of the Soviet state and the emotion-filled democratization rallies of the perestroika years. Most free time was taken up, however, with more spontaneous rituals: strolling with friends—a key ritual of urban life beautifully described by John Bushnell (1988); sitting for hours, talking or reading, on benches in the forests that surround the city or, more often, in the untamed woods that thrive in apartment courtyards; browsing the state shops and kiosks just to be amazed or amused by what was there—or what was not; gawking at the glitzy foreign cosmetics stores or poking into the narrow, new cooperative shops that began to appear in the late 1980s (see Boym 1994: 227, on this practice); taking the Metro to see what strange goodies might be on sale in particularly interesting stores like "1,000 Little Items" (*Tysiacha melochei*) or "Russian Gifts" (*Russkie suveniry*); walking along the

"Love in the Metro" (Photo by John Einarsen and Robert Kowalczyk)

Arbat or down Gorky Street (now reverted to its prerevolutionary name, Tverskaia ulitsa); visiting museums and exhibit halls—often less to see what was on display than to do some serious people-watching, get warm, and enjoy a cup of Turkish coffee (the cafes in museums were usually the most comfortable in the city).

On Tuesday or Thursday afternoons I often dropped by the Institute of Ethnography to visit my colleagues for conversation or to take care of some bureaucratic matter. After sitting for a while in the small office shared by ten or so people, working or talking quietly one on one, at a certain moment word went around: *"Chaiku pop'em?"*—"Shall we drink a little tea?" and the organization fell into place: someone took the old electric kettle to fetch water; someone else pulled out the motley assortment of chipped china cups, and a third person cleared a space on a table or desk. Often, someone pulled a small treat from purse or briefcase, maybe home-baked, maybe something purchased at a shop along the way to work, maybe even something novel, such as an edible gift from abroad. Whatever was brought was shared equally, although the women with small children might be coaxed into taking an extra piece home. Meeting with my *sektor* at the Institute was one of the most important rituals of my week, giving me a sense of belonging and close participation in a work-place environment. My friends there always seemed interested in what I was up to, and they provided a wonderful sounding-board for my ideas and reflections; the regularity of these visits also gave me a crucial way to keep up with the pulse of change in Moscow, and conversations frequently turned into solemn, hushed discussions of the new woes that social changes were bringing.

Another ritual of my fieldwork was made up of the visits I paid, almost religiously (in several senses of that word) to Masha, a young poet I met in 1988. In her mid-twenties, Masha lived with her mother, Anna Aleksandrovna, in a Krushchev-era apartment on the third floor of a six-story walk-up, a short bus ride from Metro station Tekstilshchiki on the southeast side of Moscow, fairly far out from the center; (like most medieval cities, Moscow has grown in ever-larger concentric rings around the Kremlin and thus the logic of the city is one of center and periphery, in both physical and metaphorical senses).

Their two-room flat was spare but orderly, a prototypical Moscow apartment. Whenever I visited, we invariably spent the whole time (3 to 4 hours) in the tiny kitchen, where they fed me meals of borshch, rye bread, cabbage or beet salad, fried potatoes and sour cream, followed by tea or instant coffee and homemade cookies and preserves. Everything in their kitchen had its place, and there was never a bit of grime, never a single unwashed dish. In the fall, a line of jars of home-preserved apples and currants ran along the back of the counter, and on top of the refrigerator sat huge jars full of salted cucumbers and home-stewed whole tomatoes. In a large metal bucket in the corner, sat the salted cabbage Anna Aleksandrovna put aside for winter consumption; it was possible to buy this cabbage at the private markets throughout the winter, but Anna Aleksandrovna scoffed at people (like me) who don't make their own.

Masha and her mother always wanted to know everything I was doing and everyone I had met. They got a great thrill out of my mistakes in pronunciation and my strange way of thinking or doing things. Sometimes Anna Aleksandrovna would get an inspiration, and cajole Masha into joining her to sing some of the Ukrainian folk songs she had grown up with in her village near Kiev; the haunting, sad harmonies of this traditional women's music filled the small kitchen and sent chills up my spine.

After spending some time with us, Anna Aleksandrovna always retired to her room to let Masha and me talk by ourselves. Masha regaled me with stories of her life or accounts of her friends' lives, and all these were as poignant, and often as tragic, as episodes from a Russian novel, or as peculiar and enchanting as fairy tales. I heard about how a gypsy woman put a curse on her when she was a child because she gave the woman one of her precious apples instead of a monetary handout; the curse caused her periods to stop, and was lifted only when a Baptist priest gave her mother holy water to put in Masha's tea and sprinkle on her underwear. I heard about Masha's father, an architect who had been killed by a trolley-car when Masha was young.

I heard about Masha's former husband, a poet like herself, who at age fourteen had left his seriously alcoholic family in a tiny village in Siberia and come to work as a night watchman in a Moscow factory, earning barely enough to survive. She told me that though she still adored him, she had had to leave him because at age twenty-five his poetry—"the only thing that mattered to him in the world"—had begun to dry up, and he became morose and impossible to live with. One week Masha told me that her new lover's father had just killed his wife with a knife during a drunken fight and was now in jail awaiting trial. Another week she described how a mutual friend, an older poet, gave all his money away to help younger artists, while he himself lived as meagerly as could be, surviving on bread and tea in his room in a communal apartment.

Often Masha retold significant passages from Russian literature or history, using these to shed a certain light on contemporary life in Russia. She almost always recited her new poems for me and spoke about how poetry was her highest value, how she felt it was her calling to express in verse the tragedies and absurdities of Russian existence. I sat enraptured as she spun out her stories and poems; it was impossible to tell where the stories left off and the poetry began. Along the way, I began to think of her as my shaman, that singularly perspicacious individual who through mythic narrative guides those who listen to notice the deeper patterns of meaning in a culture. Masha's stories were often larger than life, indeed her *life* was larger than life; but her narratives cast some of the cultural orientations and symbolic codes that certainly existed beyond her kitchen table into bold and visible relief. My afternoons with her helped me see and hear things I might otherwise have missed.

I had another guide to Moscow in the person of my friend Olga; we too had our ritual of regular meetings, usually seeing each other several times a week: doing errands together, meeting at the Institute of Ethnography, sitting in her apartment for conversation and tea, attending political rallies. She always invited me for family outings, special events at her son's school, weekends at their simple hand-built dacha, dinners with friends or relatives—so that I would get a taste for the typical routines of Moscow life.

Olga lived with her husband, Misha, and their eleven-year-old son, Petr, in a one-room apartment in an old, central section of Moscow. Their one room was like a nest, lined in several layers of the family's possessions, which had gradually squeezed all movement into a small central area.

Olga had moved into this apartment with her parents when she was twelve; before that, her family lived in one room in a Moscow barracks, sharing a kitchen and bathroom with fourteen other families—a typical situation in the postwar years. When she married, her parents managed to buy a cooperative apartment for themselves and gave this apartment to Olga and Misha. At that time, the young couple had been lucky to get an apartment of their own, although by the 1980s the three of them had quite outgrown its small space.

When I visited, we two sat at the kitchen table crowded with books and papers, knick-knacks and tools, and Olga fed me fried or boiled potatoes with sour cabbage from the market and thin slices of bread from a brown rye loaf—her family's standard supper, which has become my favorite meal when in Russia. After this we always sat talking for hours, drinking tea with spoonful of raspberry or apple preserves.

Olga was quite a different kind of shaman—the wisely ironic kind, the kind who listens politely to the anthropologist's endless theorizing about culture, her interpretations of the stories she has heard, or her generalizations about Russian ways of being, and who then in a superbly chosen word or two contradicts much of what the anthropologist has said, setting her straight, showing her what she has missed in her assessments of Russian mentalities, providing ample evidence of the profound individuality of each informant. Over a period of years, this shaman has tried to coax her stubborn anthropologist to a more subtle and respectful perception of Russian society.

I tried to conduct my life as other Muscovites did, eschewing taxi cabs and foreign-currency stores and relying instead on the Metro and state stores or *kolkhoz* produce markets—although as state shops became less and less predictable, I began to use the new foreign shops as a source for wine, chocolates, or then-exotic treats (canned pineapple, Western-style cookies, or liqueurs) for gifts when I was going for a meal or a visit. Entering these stores was always a shock to my system; in the early 1990s they were still rare enough to seem very strange—bright, efficient, and overflowing with goods, in contrast to Moscow's standard shopping venues.

Although I was officially housed in the Hotel Akademicheskaia at Metro station Oktiabrskaia, after a couple of months, with the help of a string of friends, I managed to rent a small furnished apartment—unofficially—on the other side of the city, a short bus-ride from Metro station Sokol, which is three subway stops out from the center. I would stop by my hotel room every few days, muss up the bed, and greet the floor-attendant; she would smile at me ironically, but never said a word to me about my disappearance.

Having an apartment gave me the opportunity to live in a standard-issue, Brezhnev-era building in a typical residential neighborhood, to get to know the shops and services in the area, and to purchase onions, carrots, beets, or bundles of fresh dill and cilantro from the old women (*babushki*) who sat on wooden crates in front of the Metro peddling their garden wares. With a kitchen (instead of only a hotpot and the awful buffet in my hotel), I was able to cook real meals for myself and, on special occasions, for my friends. I started doing more serious food shopping, which not only taught me some of the complexities of provisioning in Moscow at the time, but also helped me feel a part of the exchange loop, since I could keep an eye out for things I knew my friends might need while on my own shopping quests.

Most people relied on unofficial and informal networks of family, friends, colleagues, and acquaintances to acquire the goods, services, and paths of access they needed to manage the gaps in the official distribution system. While such reciprocal bonds characterize relations of families and friends in most industrialized societies, the degree to which these exchanges provided a basis of material security in Russia (and the entire Communist world) is notable. Most of the exchange relationships that I observed had such long histories that people did not really talk about them; this pattern of relations was largely invisible to my informants until they were questioned about it.

Foreigners were often drawn into exchange networks because of the special kinds of access and favors we could provide (or people thought we could provide). Such favors could be as simple as carrying letters out of the Soviet Union for mailing abroad or as complex as the possibility of organizing an international visit for an academic or entrepreneur, a favor many people in Moscow were seeking during perestroika, as restrictions on foreign travel were lifted. When setting up ethnographic interviews and meetings, I was always prepared to be asked for a favor (small or large, doable or not), and I regarded this as part of the normal flow of exchanges, a practice that in fact helped me to secure a kind of belonging within my own networks. It was sometimes difficult for me to convince people that the only favor I wanted, as a partner in exchange, was to talk with them, or, more important, to listen as they talked, to be invited for tea or a family gathering, where I could see how they lived and listen to their stories, debates, joke-telling cycles, and (most commonly) their litanies of complaint about the disappointments of perestroika.

There was often a profound intensity in the way that people spoke with me and with each other. Whether we were walking arm in arm along the parkway near Pushkin station, squeezing together in a painfully crowded subway car, or perching on wobbly stools at a tiny formica kitchen table, the space created by conversation seemed to be a sacred one, a closed circle beyond which everything vanished for the moment and the vividness of the images being shared was all that mattered. Although it may seem melodramatic or clichéd to say so, talk was what mattered most for many of the people I knew in Moscow; it was the context in which souls could emerge and artifices fall.

Whether conversation is maintaining its centrality in the escalating hustle of post-Communist Russia is a difficult question; as a young artist said to me in Yaroslavl in 1995, "nobody has time to talk anymore, we are all just trying to survive."

During perestroika, however, talk was energetic, fervent, and full of vivid images and emotions. People wanted to be heard, listened to, acknowledged, and understood. I hope that I have managed in this book to portray accurately even a little of what they told me. I want those people who opened their lives to me to understand the admiration, passion, and concern for Russia with which I have undertaken the present account. More than anything, I want them to find ways to prosper, on and in their own terms.

CHAPTER ONE

The World of Russian Talk
in the Time of Perestroika

Why are we destined to live like this, when in all the other countries of the world, you can
go into any store and buy ten different kinds of sausage and as much sugar as you want?
—Russian woman's lament, Moscow 1990

In the late years of perestroika, the city of Moscow echoed with profound but unanswerable questions. Conversations overflowed with bitter examinations of the sacrifices made in the name of Communism and apocalyptic projections of the future. Appalling historical revelations competed for attention with graphic images of contemporary crime. Laments about the absurdity of Soviet life were trumped by tales of bizarre changes in the local world wrought by Gorbachev's reforms. As the shelves in state stores grew emptier and emptier, talk grew more and more fervent.

Over a nine month period (September 1989–May 1990), I watched as my friends and acquaintances struggled with the problems of living in a collapsing state system and listened as they talked about their own and their society's predicaments. A cluster of tragic, paradigmatic questions, variously phrased, were circulating widely in private conversations as well as in the media. One was both question and lament: *Why do we live like this?* Why, after so much sacrifice, suffering, toil, and hope, are our lives so difficult? As one woman put it during an interview, "Why is everything so bad with us?"

Another central question, "Where are we going?" seemed to cast Soviet society as an unguided vehicle rushing down all the wrong roads and heading toward disaster. A passage from the weekly magazine *Ogonek* (Sept. 9, 1989: 1) illustrates this:

> "Where are we going!"—Today these words are more and more often pronounced not in an inquiring, but in an exclamatory key. In them are inlaid, to put it mildly, bewilderment at the fact that perestroika is bringing re-

sults that are the opposite of what was expected: instead of a profusion of goods—a total deficit; instead of a high productivity of labor—strikes; instead of stability—ethnic and social conflicts.

Increasingly, by the late fall of 1989, many people were lamenting that the road their society was on seemed to lead only to a dead end (*tupik*); with this metaphor they signaled their feelings of hopelessness, their sense that the horizons that seemed to beckon for a brief time during early perestroika had disappeared.

Declarations such as these about Russian suffering and the futility of reform movements seemed to me at first just natural, normal responses to the real travails of the past and present and the threatening array of possible futures. By 1989 the promises of perestroika had worn out for most people; the utopian visions of a free and prosperous society that characterized the early perestroika years (roughly, 1985–88) seemed to have evaporated; the demise of Soviet power was under way (although the speed and drama with which the Soviet Union eventually collapsed in 1991 were hardly imagined). Party leaders had failed from the beginning of perestroika to set rational policies of reform, and they were equally failing to react in dynamic or just ways to the unexpected consequences perestroika wrought.[1]

Even as people faced immediate material challenges—the growing scarcity of basic foodstuffs and household supplies, the gradual decline in public services, and new layers and forms of bureaucratic obstruction and obfuscation—they also had to cope with the psychological stresses of social transformation. Although people were enjoying ever-expanding freedom of expression and access to information, the unrestrained delegitimation of the social ideals and practices under which they had always

---

[1] The concept of perestroika was first introduced by Gorbachev in the April 1985 Plenum of the Communist Party Central Committee. As Gorbachev intended it, perestroika was to usher in a period of industrial acceleration and modernization. The broader social processes of glasnost and democratization, introduced in the January 1987 Plenum, were intended to bring "openness" to the entire management structure. "The essence of perestroika," wrote Gorbachev, "is that it unites socialism with democracy" (1987: 35). There is a wide range of opinion among political scientists and social critics, East and West, as to whether it was ever possible to combine socialist state planning with market mechanisms. I am inclined to agree with those, such as Lewin (1988) and Kerblay (1989), who asserted at the time that there was a moment of opportunity and that a rational combination of socialist and market systems could have occurred. Looking back on the system after its collapse, we can see that because of contradictory ideological positions and the entrenched force of the bureaucracy, the leadership failed to effect meaningful structural changes, and their backsliding and confusion led the populace to resent the economic changes that had such negative effects on their lives. See Aslund (1989) and Goldman (1992). It is also clear, however, as Lewin (1995), Jowitt (1992), Moskoff (1993), and many others have argued, that structural, social, and cultural factors all played key roles in the process of collapse, and present continuing obstacles to the development of post-Soviet democracies.

lived was disorienting. Even more disorienting, perhaps, was to have to face the future with no clear idea of what that future would resemble or whether it would bring increasing prosperity for all or civil war in the streets. It was clear that strategies for living would have to change, but it was unclear to what extent; and many sensed that great pains would have to be endured—individually and collectively, physically and spiritually—in the process of transformation.

It was no wonder that people amply articulated their frustrations and fears. It was not surprising that the stressful conditions of life were the main topic of discussion. I wondered, though, what I could learn about "political culture" from the long narratives about poverty, suffering, and absurdity which made up so many conversations. It seemed hard to escape from the endless litanies of hopelessness and cataclysm, to turn people toward what I thought would be more productive ways to cope with the present and imagine the future.

The fact that many of the examples of talk I collected came from members of the intelligentsia was of crucial importance. The Moscow intelligentsia has always been a key voice in the country, and this was especially so with the advent of glasnost. In a period of profound social revolution, this voice was loud with lamentation, alarm, cynicism, and despair. How could reasonable social evaluation and reformulation occur if the very people who had the ability to evaluate the problems and possibilities facing Russia in a rational and sober way were instead crying out—and thus spreading—their hopelessness, outrage, and fear? As Moshe Lewin writes, "The contribution of some of the media and many of the intelligentsia to a panicky view of things is undeniable. They have played a role in an extremely dangerous loss of credibility of even the new institutions of state power introduced by the reforms. . . . In fact, they almost talked themselves and the country into having those calamities that they so assiduously predicted" (Lewin 1995: 302).

For me as an American, with my own culturally molded (and perhaps unwarranted) confidence in citizen empowerment, it was confusing and frustrating to hear cataclysmic discourses[2] from my friends and infor-

---

[2] My use of the term "discourse" follows from Joel Sherzer's seminal (1987) essay. "In my discourse-centered approach," he writes, "discourse is the broadest and most comprehensive level of linguistic form, content, and use. This is what I mean by saying that discourse and especially the process of discourse structuring is the locus of the language–culture relationship. . . . Since discourse is an embodiment, a filter, a creator and recreator, and a transmitter of culture, then in order to study culture we must study the actual forms of discourse produced and performed by societies and individuals, the myths, legends, stories, verbal duals, and conversations that constitute a society's verbal life" (Sherzer 1987: 306). Sherzer's work, and Urban's influential (1991) study of Shokleng (Brazil) talk and myth, provide crucial methodological frames for using discourse, which is concrete and recordable, to ground discussions of "culture."

mants at a time when there seemed to be extraordinary opportunities to reshape society in positive ways. Finally, however, it was my own continual experience of frustration over the communicative gap I felt with my friends—our radically different ways of conceiving and communicating the problems facing Russia—that alerted me to look at precisely those discursive moments which triggered my frustration as ethnographically instructive and significant.

Gradually, I began to realize that the expressions of hopelessness and despair I was encountering were paradigmatic; that is, they seemed to follow generic patterns and they regularly deployed a fairly narrow stock of symbolic referents. Constantly exposed to these modes of speaking, I felt compelled to explore their provenance and cultural meanings, to wonder about their various and often paradoxical social effects, and to consider the role of language in social reproduction more generally. Instead of judging these discourses critically, as I had at first, I started to think of them as part of a larger cultural *ritual*, at the crux of a set of revolutionary ritualistic processes perestroika had engendered, expressing in an often mythic idiom the unresolvable contradictions and tensions of Russian social life.

The realm of such ritualized discourses was hardly separate from the more obvious realms of politics, economics, and law, in which major structural transformations were being negotiated; rather, the ritual laments of the perestroika era informed and influenced these processes, challenging them in subtle and often not so subtle ways. The discourses of the intelligentsia during the perestroika years had a significant cultural impact. Through the talk of Moscow intellectuals, the issues of the time were processed and their spread and meaning was intensified. Furthermore, in dialogical fashion, the voice of despair fueled the propagation of rival voices, those that rejected fatalistic stances and romantic populism and instead imbued zealous self-concern with an almost inviolable legitimacy (a stance that seems to have developed rapidly along with the new wealthy classes).

One of the most important ideological operations that perestroika narratives and laments performed was to highlight the conflicts among a variety of social groups, seeking in these conflicts (whether material or metaphysical) explanations for the tragedies of Russian/Soviet existence. These narratives might contrast the stupidity, selfishness, and sadism of those in power (at whatever level: institutional, local, regional, or national) with the innate wisdom, generosity, and goodness of the people. They might contrast the shameless materialism of the newly sprouted business class with the spiritual virtues of the intelligentsia. Alternatively, they might blame the backwardness and stubbornness of the masses for the seemingly unchangeable conditions of Russian economy and society,

lamenting the powerlessness of the Soviet intelligentsia to overcome supposedly inherent qualities of "Russianness."

Personal narratives constructed an archetypal world in which, for instance, an honest and decent writer, excluded from the glamorous halls of
the Writers' Union, suffering from a lack of decent food and housing, deprived of access to his own culture's greatest literature, still remained true
to his highest values and his aesthetic; a world where mothers, though
worked to exhaustion, never failed to sacrifice themselves for home and
family, their labors ultimately supporting a whole nation; a world where
poor peasants, reduced to their last potatoes, still shared whatever food
they could muster with wanderers in even greater need.

As melodramatic as they may seem, such narratives symbolically rehearsed an ideology about the natural or inescapable dichotomies between high and low, rich and poor, powerful and powerless, Them and
Us, elites and people. Presenting themselves and their acquaintances,
friends, colleagues, relatives, and neighbors as Russian allegorical characters (Lavie 1990), Moscow storytellers fashioned for their own imaginative habitation a romantic, tragic, but also darkly amusing land out of
materials borrowed from "the real world"—the realm of painful, difficult,
material experience.

Personal narratives served as the grounds for people to perceive and
promote themselves (individually and collectively) as important, even
when they lacked concrete power or status. This social power was gained
through often subtle discursive inversions of the values, plans, and representations of reality promulgated from above, from the realm of Communist authority. The narratives I was hearing thus seemed to be key to
the maintainance of a symbolic hierarchy of value which was the inverse
of the utilitarian value hierarchy promoted in Russian socialist (and, increasingly, Russian capitalist) discourses. The chilling irony of men's jokes
and quips and the solemn tragedy of women's laments harbored a kind of
resistance to internalization of the official ideals and standards that structured many of the patterns of daily life (and of life trajectories) and caused
people so much trouble. Listening for such symbolic inversions with sen-
sitivity to their deeper logics and effects might, I imagined, provide some
understanding of the wider social contexts in which the political discussions and conflicts of the day were grounded.

Discourse and Social Reproduction

In this book, I focus on Russian discourses as a crucial field for the production and negotiation of cultural meanings and value, arguing that language is a primary facilitator of both hegemonic authority and resistance

to it. "Discourse is a site of struggle. It is a terrain, a dynamic linguistic and, above all, semantic space in which social meanings are produced and challenged" (Seidel 1985: 44). This view has been well articulated in social theory (see Austin 1962; Hymes 1974; Giddens 1984; Hanks 1987; Gal 1989; Bauman and Briggs 1990). As Peter Burke argues: "speaking is a form of doing . . . language is an active force in society, a means for individuals and groups to control others or to resist such control, for changing society or for blocking change, for affirming or suppressing cultural identities" (1993: 26).

How, after all, was the entire Soviet project constructed, shaped, promoted, maintained, and challenged, if not through *talk*: discussion, argument, cajoling, and declamation? In any culture, people (whether peasants, workers, academics, bureaucrats, businesspersons, or national leaders) do not just act, they act in particular ways because discourse makes these forms of action meaningful, appropriate, and valued.[3] Conversely (a point crucial for understanding the Soviet/Russian case), they are able *not* to do things, to resist (in whatever form), because the world of talk—however subtly—creates and ratifies an "intersubjective, mental world" (Giddens 1984: 83) in which their inaction (or perverse action) makes sense, and what is more, makes *value*.

By the term "value" I do not mean an abstractly codified religious or quasi-religious standard or continuum of morality; rather, I use it to denote what is actually an unruly, contingent, multidimensional field in which evaluative oppositions and significations are in perpetual play, negotiation, and exchange (Smith 1982). As Munn (1986: 8) puts it, "value in this sense is general and relational rather than particular and substantive"— in other words, there is no absolute value referent, but rather a constant assertion and negotiation of positive and negative value which takes place via the symbolic dimension of all the practices of day-to-day living, and which is intimately tied to the creation of selfhood and collective identities.

My earliest ethnographic observations led me to consider talk an especially meaningful arena of value production and negotiation among Russian-speakers. Whereas in other societies the production of social value may seem to occur more prominently in other types of practice, such as the exchange or destruction of valued objects (Weiner 1976; Munn 1986; Kan 1990; Bataille 1985: 116–129), through distinctive consumerism

---

[3] We should not underestimate, for example, the role of discourse in the creation of value around new "business" identities. People have been able to reconstruct themselves in an entrepreneurial vein in part via discursive media (both oral and written) through which the core ideologies of business—capitalist efficiency, careful management, optimism, and profit-making—have been promoted, valorized, and made familiar.

(Bourdieu 1984), ritual participation (Sangren 1991), hospitality (March 1987) or in a host of other ways, in Russia talk in all its manifestations is a markedly significant domain of value creation—perhaps, in part, because other domains of action have been so restricted. This is to say that Russian talk is not just an activity during which value creation is described, but one in which, during which and through which value is actually produced.

While talk is a central locus of value production in all societies, in Russia it has long been highly marked; consider, for example, the constant references to the "kitchen" as the most sacred place in Russian/Soviet society. There, over tea or vodka, people could speak their minds, tell their stories, and spill their souls openly; see Pesmen (1995) on the sacredness of all these communicative forms of collective interaction. The Soviet state was, of course, a critical agent in the continuous sacralization of private talk, since only in these quiet communicative exchanges did most people feel free to communicate honestly and openly; however, it would greatly oversimplify the dynamic relationship between local cultural worlds and the vast state apparatus to say that private talk was valued only because it provided a space of freedom from the state's vigilance.[4]

Although the Soviet leadership strived systematically from the 1920s onward to establish and control the symbolic frames and codes of Soviet society (Clark 1977; Dunham 1990; Lane 1981; Hellberg 1986; Tumarkin 1991) and the cultural patterns of Soviet citizens (Mead 1951; Redl 1964; Mikheyev 1989; Attwood 1990), these efforts were only partly successful. No matter what totalitarian discourses ensnared a person, she or he was still the product, the possessor, the reproducer, and the user of the ineluctably diffuse resources of culture and language. It matters little whether this person was a collectivized and industrialized peasant, a top scientist or dissident writer, or a national leader (McAuley 1984: 30–34). Indeed, neither Communist leaders nor Russian citizens could avoid communicating in (and thus reproducing) the vernacular of Russian, with all its metaphors, tropes, key symbols, folkloric referents, generic structures, and stylistic norms. The fact that the Soviet leadership tried so hard to change these linguistic systems through the poetics of revolutionary iconoclasm (Stites 1989), terror, repression, rote pronouncements of propaganda, and endless pedagogy signals the leadership's understanding of the critical role of language as a political resource.

[4] Other important domains where social value in Russia is produced are dress and domestic maintenance among women (Dunham 1990) and mischief making among men. I will discuss these further in Chapter 2, but it should be remarked here that even in these domains, talk *about* these practices (lamenting, storytelling) is the principal medium through which the value of these practices is elaborated and performed.

As must be clear, I am partisan to the argument that Communist culture—even Stalinist totalitarian Communist culture—never replaced or erased Russian culture, but was itself permeated, patterned, and structured by it.[5] "What the scholarship of comparative communism has been telling us," notes Gabriel Almond, "is that political cultures are not easily transformed. A sophisticated political movement ready to manipulate, penetrate, organize, indoctrinate, and coerce and given an opportunity to do so for a generation or longer ends up as much or more transformed than transforming" (Almond 1983 in Brown 1984: 7).

Robert Daniels has argued consistently in his works (cf. 1962; 1985) that Communism in the Soviet Union was Russified through and through. Among other Sovietologists, Robert C. Tucker has been an articulate and insistent proponent of the view that what emerged from the 1917 revolution was "some sort of amalgam of the prerevolutionary culture with the sociocultural innovations that the revolutionary regime has succeeded in implementing" (Tucker 1977: xvii). Tucker observes that during the most profound revolutionary changes, any new system will "incorporate into itself elements of the national cultural past, as Soviet Communism did, for example, when in 1924, on Lenin's death, it established an official Lenin cult, replete with the mummy in the mausoleum on Red Square, which struck some protesting Communist revolutionaries at that time as a revival of the Russian Orthodox Church's old custom of preserving the bones of saints for display to the faithful" (1977: xvii).

The sphere of public events and rituals in Russia demonstrates this persistence of or reformulation of the old in the culture of the new. It is in day-to-day language, however, that we can observe (or hear) the operations of the most diffuse—and, arguably, most powerful—mode of cultural reproduction.

This focus on language as a key mechanism of cultural reproduction should not lead readers to assume that I am seeking to locate some essential, ancient, prerevolutionary "Russianness" in the discourses of the present era. In any case, there is no such thing as an essential "Russianness," nor could there be. Cultural systems are semiotic rather than essential. A culture is a "web of significance" (Geertz 1973: 5) that is constantly woven and rewoven, continually integrating all sorts of historical changes and

---

[5] See Bourdieu's general comments on the limits of totalitarian institutions (Bourdieu and Wacquant 1992: 102). Mikhail Epstein (1991: 72) identifies the various strands of Soviet ideologies, showing how instead of being a hegemonic system, they are actually a pastiche of sundry (and seemingly incompatible) doctrines: Marxist–Leninist, Enlightenment, Slavophile, populist, utopian, and so forth. A highly insightful critique of oversimplified versions of the relationships between "official" and more diffuse cultural ideologies can be found in McAuley (1984). See also Burant (1987).

innovations. Any bits of linguistic or other "cultural" expression observed in Russia today are thus products of an infinitely complex set of influences and causes, some national–historical, others local, familial, or idiosyncratic. To determine where they come from in any absolute sense is nearly impossible. As Sangren has noted, it is "very difficult to describe the complex matrix of social and cultural institutions that structures the ways in which 'effects' are fed back (to borrow a metaphor from systems theory) and converted into causes" (1987: 6).

Communication is always in process; any moment of talk, for instance, arises in response to the complex influences of the past, but it is also a particle of meaning, structure, and value which can inflect the future (Bakhtin 1981; Ochs 1992: 338). Social life is, as Giddens says (1984: 3) a *"durée,"* a "continuous flow of conduct" in which every action (including every utterance) is part of an unending play of productions having both intentional and unintentional, consciously chosen and culturally reflexive dimensions (Hymes 1964: 22–23).

For an example, when Gorbachev spoke of Soviet society using kinship terms, as he often did, was he borrowing intentionally from Soviet-era propaganda, meant to inculcate a sense of familial relations among Soviet peoples (Clark 1977), or did he pick up this metaphor from its diffuse use in Russian vernacular? Did he employ this trope to reinvigorate those kinship attitudes among his listeners, or to reassert his own paternal position in Soviet society? Did such metaphoric invocations merely promulgate that trope in Russian speech, or might they have served to foster the patriarchy-resistant rebelliousness of non-Russian nationalists or heterodox Russian politicians?

In my research, I was not interested in measuring the degree of intentionality or the immediate effects of any particular utterance (a futile enterprise in any case). Rather, I wanted to understand, on the one hand, the general cultural meanings and discursive structures that were engaged in certain kinds of utterances, and, on the other, some of the larger social and political sources and resonances of those underlying meanings and structures.

The political, economic, and social activities of the middle years of the Gorbachev era were woven across the warp of stories, fables, anecdotes, secular prayers, and sacred questions. One way of analyzing the conflicts, problems, and outcomes of perestroika is to attend to these discursive acts and their inherent structures, meanings, and power.

The units of discourse and the patterns of behavior that I outline here are both the products of and the producers of Russian identity and (Soviet) Russian society and have to be examined in both of these valences. Through their continual expression of stories about themselves and their world, Russians collectively have helped to reproduce the very hierarchies and oppositions of value which seemed to be the inherent, "natural" (Bourdieu 1977: 167–171; Giddens 1984: 25) and immutable structures of that world. An understanding of the past structuring and present restructuring of that world must, therefore, incorporate an awareness of the ubiquitous discursive practices through which that world is produced and reproduced. Ethnography affords a proven set of methodological and interpretive tools for gathering and analyzing those discursive practices.

So far, despite growing attention, East and West, to the local practices of family and work as sites of social reproduction (Yanowitch 1985; Field 1987; Millar 1987; Buckley 1992; Edmondson 1992), the rhetoric of politicians (Urban 1994; Anderson, Chervyakov, and Parshin 1995), and to the problem of "public opinion" in general (Lewin 1988: 75–78), there have been few analytical explorations of day-to-day Russian talk or personal narratives. For the most part, such talk has been examined only anecdotally; the stories that Russian people tell about themselves and their society have been largely overlooked as objects of analysis. There is only a fairly small (though growing) ethnographic record of contemporary Russian "voices" or interpretations of the meanings and structures of Russian lives (Wierzbicka 1989; Ries 1991 and 1994; Dunn 1992; Pilkington 1994; Tumarkin 1994; Dickinson 1995; Pesmen 1995; Cushman 1995; Lempert 1996).[6]

Focusing on talk as an agent of cultural reproduction obviates such intangibly mystical notions as "national character" while validating one of the underlying aims of that concept, to account for the reproduction of human regularity within societies across time and space.[7] Because the ele-

---

[6] A number of volumes refer to the "voices" of glasnost—but one finds that these are rarely voices from the population at large. Instead they are usually the voices of the intellectual or artistic elites. See, for example, *Voices of Glasnost*, which turns out to be "Interviews with Gorbachev's Reformers." Nina Tumarkin's nuanced and quite moving study of "the cult of World War II" in Russia (1994) and Stephen Kotkin's social history of Magnitogorsk (1991) are two of the few scholarly works of recent years that encompass the narratives of all kinds of people. See also David Mandel's fascinating interviews with workers in the post-perestroika era (1994). Journalists have collected (though not analyzed) interviews with a range of people; see Parker's *Russian Voices* (1991), Gray's (1989) interviews with Soviet women, and Einarsen's *Kyoto Journal* interviews.

[7] The decisive drawback of the studies of Russian national character is that they fail to account for or even adequately theorize the modes of transmission and reproduction of the qualities (values, attitudes, and so on) which they summarize, relying instead on vague and ethereal concepts such as "mentality," as Dmitry Mikheyev does (1989). Beginning with an appropriately critical glance at the geographic, climatic, religious, and swaddling explanations of the Russian national character, Mikheyev muses that, if combined, they might yield a "key for understanding the Russians" (1989: 635). But then he proposes the idea of mentality as the explanatory key. "Mentality," he writes, "is largely determined by the basic perceptions of the environment, life and time, which are formed in early childhood, in an

ments of stories people tell about their lives and their worlds have a certain familiarity (like folktales, they follow particular structural lines and rely on a stock of conventional details), the categories people employ with regularity (such as "the Russian people," "the Russian woman," "the Russian character," or "the Russian soul") are experienced as natural and essential, both to the users of those terms and to others who hear them.[8] This constant and ubiquitous discursive naturalization of socially constructed categories accounts, in large measure, for the perception that ethnicity is biologically, genetically, or even climatologically (Pipes 1974) reproduced. The irony is that the very acts of talk that naturalize or essentialize cultural reproduction are themselves much more the actual mechanisms of that reproduction than biological factors. In this way, Russian talk effectively disguises, mystifies, and alienates (Sangren 1991) its own culturally reproductive power. This may, in fact, be one reason that casual, quotidian Russian talk has never been an object of investigation or interpretation.[9] In subtle ways, talk deflects attention from its own agency.

Local Ideas about Culture, People, Language, and Character

It is difficult to grasp the frames of Russian discourse or the particular contents of Russian talk without recognizing the multiple implications of certain fundamental but often very slippery concepts. Although they strenuously objected to my use of the term "Russian culture," claiming that Russian culture had been utterly destroyed after the 1917 revolution,

---

almost genetical fashion, and persist throughout the rest of life." He uses the passive tense throughout his essay when referring to the formation and transmission of mentality and this allows him to avoid entirely the question of how this mentality is formed and reproduced or of what it consists. By the time his essay concludes, he has made mentality itself the causal agent. This kind of tautology is the common problem of "national character" discussions (see Dicks 1960: 637 for a good example of such tautological reasoning). Other studies of Russian national character in English are Bock (1980), Glazov (1985), Goldman (1950), Gorer and Rickman (1950), Hingley (1977), Kluckhohn (1962), Likhachev (1981), Mead (1951); and Mead and Metraux (1953).

[8] This naturalization of what are actually arbitrary symbolic elements is a critical part of the reproductive power of stories. See Bourdieu (1977: 164–167). It strikes me that all the references (both serious and ironic) that Russians make to their character have motivated a common journalistic and occasional scholarly reification of that concept.

[9] Both Russian and Western specialists in Russian folklore, literature, and linguistics have largely inscribed their way around this space of daily talk without entering it, despite the many truisms about live Russian talk (it is, for example, said to be very emotional, dramatic, committed to deep spiritual and philosophical matters, and so forth). Moreover, as Maureen Perrie (1989: 119) has pointed out, folklore too has seldom been mined as a source for understanding Russian mentalities (Gibian 1990 and 1991 and Sinyavsky 1984 are exceptional in this regard).

my informants themselves often interjected references to "the Russian people," "the Russian person," "the Russian soul," or simply to "we Russians"; these native categories were posited to stand without explanation or elaboration, as essential natural categories eminently observable and thus objectively real.[10] Use of such key terms encapsulated and seemed to render unmysterious for my informants the continuity and substantiality of Russianness (Hymes 1964: 12; Bourdieu 1977: 164–171).

Such key categories are subsumed within a broader native concept, variously termed "Russian history," "Russian life," or "the fate of Russia." All these take place on a territory with both real and legendary status: "the Russian land." The routine invocation of these expressions, preeminent clichés of Russian talk, suggests an underlying cultural ideology of national relations based upon narrative rather than organic metaphors. In other words, Russian national identity is often conceptualized in terms of a common history or tale. The dissident (émigré) writer Vasily Aksenov, writing in *The New Republic* (April 16, 1990) about his return to his homeland after many years in the West, utilizes this trope of the tale: "I merely wish to know this: is there, behind all the tragicomic turns of our Russian tale—all the revolutions, counterrevolutions, Stalinisms, neo-Stalinisms, revisionisms, thaws, freezes, perestroikas, glasnosts—is there, behind all this, some enchanted playwright, some divine author who knows how the story ends?" (cited in Slobin 1992: 257).

Alongside the trope of a common story, more essential bases of ethnic belonging are often referred to in conventional speech. Blood is frequently invoked as the medium of Russian commonality, as are genes and bones. However, attention to the deployment of these bodily metaphors in Russian conversation demonstrates that it is the body's experience or endurance of the Russian story that metaphorically imbues the blood, genes, or bones with Russianness. In local terms, then (Geertz 1983: 55–70), Russianness is an organic quality that precipitates from the experience of the Russian story. Among other things, however, the Russian story is often described as bloody (*nasha krovavaia istoriia*), so the influences seem to flow both ways, from the story into the body and from the body into the story. In this way, as a freely exchanged metaphoric substance, blood is frequently posited as the medium of enculturation in Russia, while it is also a symbolic substance within the "difficult" and "complicated", but also "rich" Russian story.

This raises the question of whether Russians see individuals as born

---

[10] See Wierzbicka (1989) and Pesmen (1995) on the Russian concept of soul; Cherniavsky (1961) on *narod* and Wierzbicka (1985: 165) on the similar Polish use of *narod*. These kinds of terms are ideologically rich posts of reference which help to anchor what Benedict Anderson (1983) refers to as "imagined community."

Russian or as becoming Russian through life experience. The answer seems to be: both. Born into the context of the many-layered, fantastically embroidered, epic tale that is Russia, individuals also to greater or lesser extents embody that tale in the personal narratives they fashion from the materials of their own lives and, in so doing, assert their cultural identity and belonging. I realized this during fieldwork in Moscow in 1992 and 1994, when, in subtle ways, people characterized those who emigrated, held positions of power, or, as in the perestroika period, moved away from their relative poverty by joining business ventures as negating their Russianness in the process; "those people are not Russian, not ours," was a refrain I often heard. Such people, in effect, symbolically contradicted the narrative structures of the Russian story or "wrote themselves out" of it. Those whose narratives fit in as appropriately structured chapters, verses, or even footnotes to the epic saga of Russia, asserted themselves to be part of that saga and produced from it the stuff of their own social value.[11] While these patterns of identification began to shift as many people made their moves away from the story of suffering, poverty, and powerlessness, the orienting framework of the patterns did not. Although new ways to be Russian have developed in the post-Soviet environment, these are still widely disparaged by those who identify themselves with a mystical concept of Russianness. In part, of course, this is because such discursive strategies allow people to defend, justify, and extol the value of their own identities and their lower socio-economic status in the face of the self-valorizing stories of the Moscow *nouveaux riches*.

Narod: The Key "Key Word"

There was a certain Russian word which I could bring myself to pronounce only with difficulty in my conversations with friends and informants. This was odd, as the word was one of the most common in Russian talk, a key word, important and useful. But I always felt sheepish trying to use this word; it was like borrowing someone else's slang, or, more accurately, like saying someone else's prayer. The word was *narod*: people, populace, folk. In Russian, the word *narod* is employed in a variety of ways; it can mean "people" as connoting "the citizens of a nation"; "ethnic group," as in "the Soviet Union is made up of many different peoples";

---

[11] For comparison, Michael Peletz (1997: 51–54) describes how Malays protect their local and personal identity as Malay by not resisting (discursively or otherwise) the Islamic resurgence movement, since that movement has insinuated itself into the very fabric of Malaysian identity and to contradict it is to contradict one's own identification as Malay (as well as to incur political reprisal).

and simply "people" as in "there are many people here" ("it's crowded"). But its most significant usage, perhaps its most common—yet often most sacred—use is to mean "the Russian people." While it can be modified as *"russkii narod,"* the *"russkii"* is not really necessary in most contexts. To say *"narod"* is to pronounce a metaphor; *narod* in this usage is a word which refers not to any literal demographic entity as much as to a mythical conceptual one, with a wide range of implications and metaphoric ramifications.

In prerevolutionary Russia, *narod* was used both derogatorily and reverently, depending on the speaker's own social position, to designate the peasantry and budding proletariat in contrast to the aristocracy, the merchant class, and the intelligentsia. The late nineteenth-century populists (*narodniki*), themselves mostly from the aristocracy or intelligentsia, elevated *narod* to a sacred term (Frierson 1993), and it was thus employed through the revolution and the Soviet period, though there was often a slight redolence of condescension in official Soviet uses of this term, and often a great degree of irony, and disdain in the intelligentsia's use of it—although in contexts where they asserted their attachment to the "suffering masses" members of the intelligentsia might include themselves in its positive connotations.

Narod can thus refer to many different fields of encompassment. In certain uses, *narod* conditionally embraces both populace and leaders, as in a phrase used during World War II: *"narod-geroi"*—"heroic people." Most often, however, *narod* implies "the people" as distinct from those who have power, or, as has been heard often in recent years, those with wealth—the new business classes. *Narod* always suggests by implication its opposite—all those who have power over, exploit, and do not take care of or appreciate "the people." *Narod* may mean "the heroic people" but it more commonly stands for "the victimized people."

In its positive valences, the mere invocation of the word, without any adjectival qualifiers, can suggest the following attributes: faithful, devout, brave, simple, modest, honest, innocent, solid, strong, self-sufficient, all-enduring, long-suffering, and much deserving. *Narod* suggests an uncomplicated lifestyle, an unpretentious diet of potatoes, cabbage, bread, sausage, apples—with the added succor of beer, vodka, and tobacco. It invokes hard work, familial closeness (and conflict), somewhat rough (though tender-hearted!) men and big, strong, strict, but generous women. It implies a nation of people tired of politics, expecting little but the worst from above.

While *narod* invokes the extraordinary energy and creativity of the Russian folk tradition—song and dance, stories and rituals, poetry and art—

it also automatically conjures an entire history of war and famine, obedience and abuse, poverty and endurance, suffering, loss, and death. During perestroika, the word was frequently articulated with a tone of wounded pride, signaling a sense that once again the people's suffering was being ignored.

All this symbolic content was what made it so difficult for me to use the term *narod* when referring to the Russian population. To say *narod* is not just to refer to a denotative category, but to invoke an entire story, a sacred epic—and to invoke that saga is to claim not only its personal meaning but indeed one's own identification with *narod* in that saga, an identification that seems disingenuous for foreigners to make.

A paradigmatic example of the way that *narod* is deployed and how it resonates I found in a late 1992 brochure advertising subscriptions to the Communist paper *Molodaia gvardiia*: "*Molodaia gvardiia* is an uncompromising conversation with readers about the fate of the *narod*, about our much suffering motherland, already ruined by "democrats," about the history and future of our fatherland. The rebirth of governability, spirituality, and the culture of the Russian *narod* and all of the peoples of our multinational Union . . . that is the general theme and pain of our authors."

This little bit of ad copy contains all the preeminent metaphors of *narod* identity: the metaphor of the timeless, long-suffering motherland (*rodina*), the history-associated fatherland, and the "child"-*narod*. I asked one friend, a philosopher, to comment on the relation of these terms. He said: "Of course, *Rodina* is habitat, nature, soil—but it's a very *fermenting* thing. Upon or within it history takes place; legends, values are born. *Narod* grows out of these two things. *Narod* is like . . . the spirit of these two things together. It isn't local, though. It too spans the generations and becomes an energy source."[12]

What, then, I asked, was the character of the relationship between individual and *narod*, how were these two things articulated? My friend thought for a moment, and then said "they are connected via *dusha*—the soul." Well, then, I asked, what is *dusha*?

Dusha is some kind of inborn ability to feel what is right and what is wrong and to repent somehow. In Russia there is this notion that people from the *narod* have this ability more developed than people who are already not part of the *narod*, who disassociated from *narod*, became intellectuals or whatever. The *narod* lives *en masse* and keeps its traditions and customs,

---

[12] This narrative was spoken to me in the flawless English of this Russian (Jewish) informant. All the other texts quoted in this book were spoken in Russian.

while people who are separated from the *narod* come to be more on their own, feel that those rules and regulations are not obligatory for them, so they can do whatever they want but they will not feel the burden of this awareness; they might realize they are doing wrong but it will not affect them as deeply as someone who stays in the *narod*. Also, *dusha* is some ability to feel very deeply. So you feel deeply, first of all nature, the beauty of nature, the oneness, your own oneness with nature, and this whole feeling of being at one with the landscape means that you are part of the landscape, and that the landscape expresses the same kinds of feelings that you experience yourself. The Russian people think they have soul and they doubt that anyone else has. Russians have *dusha* because they are moral. Being moral—it is not just to be kind, generous, it is basically some kind of connection between individual and community and nature. So there is a feeling that you yourself are not that important, but you are important through the community of which you are a part, and through nature, and this always made Russian soldiers so good, because they thought nothing of sacrificing themselves for their motherland. So even though the feeling of individual value is weakened, the feeling of community is completely strengthened . . . so that is *dusha*, which is the mechanism of this. *Dusha* is basically a mechanism of involvement, maybe not direct involvement, but a mechanism of association of oneself with a broader set—*narod*.

This text captures some of the complexity of Russian ideas about Russian *being*, and the confidence that people could have in the wealth of their identity. Although members of the intelligentsia might scorn the entire concept of *narod* as a loaded, overused, ideological construct (not unlike "intelligentsia" . . .), although they might vehemently denigrate the *narod* as backward, ignorant, uncivilized, filthy, and so on, or bemoan the negative effects that *narod* sensibilities and practices presumably have on Russian high culture and civility—still these same individuals might resort to this term and identify themselves with it in a number of contexts.

Language as Wealth or Power

My informants frequently proclaimed their language to be their most important resource. "We may be poor compared to you in the West, but our Russian language is richer than rich," was how one historian described it during a conversation about the economic travails of Russian existence. Well-cultivated national pride (defiance, even) mixes with an echo of economic self-vindication in comments formulated this way. Such discourses about the wealth of Russian begin with the eighteenth-century scholar Mikhail Lomonosov, whose patriotic aphorisms about the Russian language adorn schoolroom walls even in the present.[13] Whether this idiom, which is part of a broader ideology about the glories of Russianness, existed before Lomonosov publicly venerated the language is unclear. It has, in any case, a certain historical pedigree, and may be seen as an example of what Alan Dundes (1972) terms "folk ideas."

When I heard people exalt the wealth of Russian, they seemed generally to have in mind three facets of their language: first, its intrinsic structural features, such as lexical precision, noun and adjective declension, and syntactic flexibility, which make Russian both manipulable and generative; second, its poetic or lyrical qualities, which are partly structural (parallel declensions and conjugations often rhyme) and partly intonational; and, third, its seemingly inexhaustible stores of *parole* (Saussure 1959).[14] The first two aspects of the language, abetted by the high value given to linguistic creativity and play—to what Mikhail Bakhtin (1981: 273) termed "heteroglossia" (*raznorechie*)—have lent themselves to the constant development of the third, and Russian can be described as a fertile and playful language.[15]

Along with all this received (and beloved) *parole*, Russians value the particular nuances of feeling and understanding communicated through their language, that bath of orally transmitted cultural material which provides a warmth of familiarity and belonging. Avidly mixing their metaphorical substances, Russians often say that they drank in all this stuff (lexical, emotional, and ideological) "with their mother's milk"—an apt

---

[13] "Karl V, emperor of Rome, used to say that he would use Spanish for speaking with God, French with friends, German with enemies, and that Italian most befits conversations with those of the female sex. But had he been exposed to Russian, he would have added that Russian suits all the above situations, for he would have found in it the magnificence of Spanish, the liveliness of French, the power of German, the tenderness of Italian, and on top of all that the wealth and expressive precision of Greek and Latin" (Lomonosov 1952: 391).

[14] By *parole* I mean basic lexicon, as well as all the metaphors, tropes, similes, sayings, proverbs, maxims, charms, curses, obscenities, fables, fairy tales, epic tales, songs, ballads, poems or parts of poems, ditties, jokes, riddles, tongue-twisters, slang expressions, lines from plays or films, official slogans and subversive parodies on them, and so on, which Russians come to know and rely on as they grow up.

[15] The recording of the products of the Russian linguistic imagination, and the scholarly analyses of these have a long, abundant, and often eminent history. In the 1800s, V. Dal', A. Afanas'iev, and D. Sadovnikov were three luminaries among the hundreds of eager Russian collectors of popular proverbs, sayings, stories, riddles, songs, laments, and jokes. Early in this century the development of Russian formalism inspired structural analysis of these popular texts, and the insights of Vladimir Propp (1968) underlie much subsequent analysis of folktales. In the postwar period Russian folklorists produced hundreds of collections of various aspects of Russian verbal production. This field includes lexicographies of a wide range of vernacular and slang. Russian literature, the presumably more "refined" cousin of Russian folklore, has, of course, been vastly surveyed and intensively scrutinized. The study of Russian linguistics (and Slavic linguistics more generally) also has a distinguished tradition.

metaphor for the physical and conceptual internalization of culture. Russians themselves, I would argue, metaphorically allude to this liquid conveyer of cultural essence—talk—which I consider the fundamental vehicle of cultural reproduction, as the primary medium of cultural transmission and national interrelation.

There is social significance in the metaphor of language-as-wealth. To unveil this metaphoric significance, we must ask: What kind of wealth is it? On the one hand, there is the kind of linguistic wealth that can be transformed into literal, material bounty or into special access, status, glory, fame, and so on; this kind of wealth has long been enjoyed in Russia by poets, writers, and bards. There is, as well, the related kind of power that politicians can manage to accrue through their particular kind of verbal art. In this sense, the ability to wield language in ways that resonate appropriately amounts to one of the kinds of symbolic capital on which many have focused (Bourdieu 1977: 186–187; 1991; Hanks 1987; Brenneis 1988; Fairclough 1989; Grillo 1989; Irvine 1989; Burke 1993).

But while there is as much linguistic elitism in Russia as anywhere else, there is also a manifest linguistic egalitarianism—a widely expressed assertion not only that the language belongs to (and is enriched by) all who speak it, but also, reflexively, that being a speaker means one is included in a special kind of national community (Anderson 1983).

A recent text by Tatyana Tolstaya, a well-known contemporary writer, exemplifies these cultural ideologies about language. At the same time disparaging and celebrating (and reproducing) the idea that language is the most important form of power, she writes:

> This is a wonderful point of view. It proclaims the primacy of literature over life, of dreams over reality, of imagination over facts. It says: Life is nothing—a fog, a mirage, a Fata Morgana. But the word, whether spoken or printed, represents a power greater than the atom. This is an entirely Russian view of literature, without parallel in the West. And everyone in Russia, it seems, shares it: the czars and the slaves, censors and dissidents, writers and critics, liberals and conservatives. He who has articulated a word has accomplished a deed. He has taken all the power and responsibility on himself. He is dangerous. He is free. He is destructive. He is God's rival. (1992: 34)

Genres of Russian Talk

Having, a few pages ago, invoked a native Russian trope that relates language to milk, I must now stress that the liquid of cultural meaning does

"Conversation over Tea" (Photo by John Einarsen and Robert Kowalczyk)

not flow freely, but comes in its own particular cultural containers. Like literature or folklore, talk is constrained not only by the range of syntactical or lexical possibilities of a language but by a range of appropriate and familiar genres.

Every society has its own system of speech genres, as Dell Hymes (1964) Gary Gossen (1972), and Joel Sherzer (1983: 8–14) have argued. One way to analyze the linguistic resources and practices of societies is to examine the generic patterns that structure, organize, and characterize that society's way of speaking. Mikhail Bakhtin, of course, argued throughout his long writing life for the importance of an "ethnography" of speaking genres (even commenting on the importance of the estranged perspective of outside observers).[16]

As much as morphology, grammar, syntax, lexicon—shape and structure actual speech productions at the level of sentences, so genre shapes the broader units of discourse; speech genres provide customary conversational forms and inflections. The structures of discursive genres are not as rule-like as grammatical structures (as Fairclough 1989: 31 reminds us, we should not assume any mechanical relationship between discourse types and particular discourses); they are, rather, conventions and patterns, profoundly entrenched through widespread reiteration. As Charles Briggs and Richard Bauman define them, "genres may be seen as conventionalized yet highly flexible organizations of formal means and structures that constitute complex frames of reference for communicative practice" (Briggs and Bauman 1992: 141).

One problem in the analysis of speech (or folklore) genres is that of deciding which aspects of speech forms to use in structuring a classification system: as Briggs and Bauman ask, "What feature(s) constitute a sufficient or adequate basis for defining a genre: morphological structure, content, belief, function, and so on?" (1992: 137). Ruth Finnegan, for example, outlines various features through which genres can be classified: stylistic or formal traits, subject matter, occasion, role and context, performative characteristics, local terminologies and taxonomies, and specifics of time, place, and environment (1992: 143–144). She points out "the possibility of conflicting but equally tenable classifications" (145). She also warns us that "the target is sometimes a moving one: new genres arise, old ones are developed, manipulated, or reinterpreted" (175).

My own generic classifications of Russian speech in the time of perestroika are deliberately flexible; that is, my classification of genres is based

---

[16] Bakhtin himself never undertook such an ethnography as far as oral speech is concerned, though his insights are extremely valuable; see especially "The Problem of Speech Genres" in Bakhtin (1986).

simultaneously on thematic, formal, stylistic, and performative characteristics, as well as on the contexts in which these emerge. This is because
Russian genres are themselves blurry, unfixed, protean, and inter-
penetrating.[17] This does not mean, however, that genres are not powerfully constitutive and constraining patterns in the overall production of
speech acts. In oral communication as much as in literary, genre is form-
maintaining; like cell walls, genre serves to corral and contain the various
elements of culture, ideology, and value. It is one of the first of many em-
bedded structures for the protection and reproduction of cultural pro-
priety; gender norms, power and status appropriateness, and other marks
of identity are maintained through the correct deployment of the genres
of speaking (Ochs 1992). Arjun Appadurai remarks on the importance of
this kind of formal characteristic in studying culture when he writes that
"societies do manifest certain configurations because they have come to
be shaped in certain ways, not just by values and beliefs, but by styles and
genre conventions" (1991: 18). Indeed, values and beliefs are well pro-
tected and effectively transmitted through culturewide observance of the
basic protocols of genre—an observance which is automatically socialized
as part of the acquisition of language.

Moreover, it is clear that as much as the cell walls of genre protect cultural material, so they also serve to exclude alien material. Non-native
ideologies and values, themselves encapsulated in their own generic containers, do not easily traverse cultural boundaries to penetrate native discourses. Just as improper or odd grammatical constructions would call
forth the criticism, "that is not Russian," so might unusual discursive
genres seem to be "not Russian." I had the experience many times of having my remarks during conversations completely ignored, or met with
strange looks, as if I had mangled pronunciation or syntax. This is what
Terry Eagleton refers to as "closure" (1991: 194), "whereby certain forms
of signification are silently excluded, and certain signifiers 'fixed' in a
commanding position." The more I learned and practiced not just proper
language but proper *genres*, the more I was able to participate fully in
conversations with Russians and the more I was able to belong. This does
not mean, however, that I was able to communicate everything I wanted

[17] Scholars in folklore studies, from whom anthropology took its inspiration to study generic classification in speech, have made numerous caveats regarding the problematics of
classification in the study of folklore genres (Finnegan 1992). Many have questioned the
hegemony of traditional genre designations. Dan Ben-Amos (1976) has critiqued the search
for universal genres, arguing for a culture-specific designation of genres. Alan Dundes's
work (1980) characterizes this open-genre approach. Sandra Stahl's (1989) genre of the "personal narrative" and her in-depth interpretations of the spoken texts she collected is close to
my own approach.

to say. My adoption of Russian speech genres meant putting aside certain key attitudes, ideas, and approaches to life which American speech genres supported and contained, but which Russian genres did not.

One particularly American genre of speaking to which I was inclined could be termed "practical problem-solving." [18] For example, in conversations about food shortages (a very popular topic, since shortages kept getting worse and worse at this time), I tended to ask questions about how Soviet food-distribution systems are operationally structured, assuming that it would be interesting to try to imagine (although, of course, in very crude ways) how these might be improved. I eventually realized that my Russian interlocutors did not find my question appropriate for discussion. They seemed more interested in impressing and astonishing each other with increasingly dire accounts of shortages and tales of how difficult it was becoming to buy anything. My genre not only did not fit in with theirs—in fact it contradicted their genre and threatened to deflate it if they engaged it seriously; this they managed to avoid by ignoring it altogether in ritualized speech settings. In more prosaic contexts, of course, my Russian friends were far more expert than I could ever be at devising intricate and ingenious solutions to the problems of everyday existence. In a sense, their lamentation of structural challenges allowed them simultaneously to celebrate their own highly developed but impromptu coping skills.

While a few of the speech-units I discerned in Russia fall into the basic slots of traditional folklore forms (like proverbs and jokes), the majority do not reflect the genres of scholarly folkloristics, nor do they fit into the generic categorizations that students of Russian folklore use. For most of the texts I present in these pages, a Russian native speaker would have no generic label. Nonetheless, these unclassified verbal performances are distinguishable and generalizable as generic and thematic patterns, patterns that constrain and reproduce cultural structures, emblems, stances, and values every bit as much as do more traditional mythopoetic genres. Furthermore, these speech genres seem to be related to traditionally recognized genres in several ways (i.e., morphologically, metonymically, genetically). Although often in disguised or lacunary form, traditional folkloric structures, logics, elements, moods, devices, characters, and themes permeate contemporary Russian communication (both oral and written) to such an extent that the meanings inherent in Russian verbal production and performance cannot be elucidated without reference to their folkloric ancestors and cousins.

---

[18] See Dundes's interesting comments on this American ideology—he calls it a "folk idea"—that "all problems can be solved" (1972: 100).

Table 1. The Russian talk world during perestroika: a schematic representation

"Official" power (high social status genres)

Deliberate silence

Communist rhetoric

Pedantry   Doxology   Cant

Imprecations   Orders

Scolding   Didactic proverbs   Slogans

Female   *Male*

The Russia tale

Poignant Proverbs

Blaming   Cursing

Superstitious warnings   Threats

Envy tales   Danger of men tales

Laments   Bragging

Shopping tales   Mischief tales

Husband tales   Sexual or drinking epics

Rumors   Male self-mocking

Perestroika horror stories

Complete disintegration tales

Lamenting questions   Perestroika jokes

Litanies of suffering   Litanies of absurdity

Litany of "The dead end"

Saints' lives

"Unofficial" power (low social status genres)

The above is a schematic diagram of the Russian talk world I encountered during perestroika. This diagram is arranged along two axes that
skeletally define the relations of Russian conversational units: a horizontal
gender axis and a vertical power axis. The situation of any genre of talk
along these axes is only approximate, since the specific themes,
stances, and contexts of actual speech-acts could serve to situate a genre
differently. Still, as a rough sketch of the basic relationship of forms it may
help to provide orientation in a complex system.

At the top of the chart are the discourses of "official" power, discourses
still heard widely in perestroika times. Below that is a layer of "unofficial"
power genres: proverbs, imprecations, scolding, threats, and so on. Not
everyone could wield "power" genres (either official or unofficial); such

genres were proper only to certain categories of people or within certain contexts. At the same time, individuals who learned to manage them astutely created power and privilege for themselves in the very process of iterating these discourses (and few gained power who could not wield them). This is not to say that the wielders of power genres were not invested with other forms of social capital that made their social positions objectively powerful relative to other positions; obviously many other factors are engaged in the consititution of status and authority. Talk was not necessarily the most important determinant of these, but it was a key component in the assertion of power and position (cf. Urban 1994; Anderson, Chervyakov, and Parshin 1995; Brenneis 1988; Grillo 1989; Hanks 1987; Irvine 1989; Fairclough 1989; Bourdieu 1991).

The horizontal axis is structured by the gender marking of various speech-forms. It was unusual, for example, to hear overt litanies from men (male litanies were disguised as philosophical speculations or in other ways); women told jokes, were poignantly facetious, and used other such ironic forms less often than men. There was, indeed, a prevalent opposition in the world of Russian talk between male genres (humorous, nonchalant, exhibitionist), and female genres (serious, involved, moralistic). Male talk tended to include more ironic genres and female talk, more solemn ones. It must be stressed, however, that this pattern was constantly inverted; I knew men who seemed always to be lamenting, and women who made bawdiness their business (the singer Alla Pugacheva and her many clones exemplify an archetypal version of the latter). Nonetheless, an opposition between the inflections of irony and solemnity could be generically characterized at its extremes in the gulf between (male) obscenity and (female) sorrow. In other words, gender and tone are two parallel, or indexed (Irvine 1989; Ochs 1992), systems of differentiation. The importance of the relationships between gender and genre will become apparent in Chapter 2.

Genre, Resistance and Reproduction

Cultural or ideological oppositions, such as those inherent in constructions of gender, power, status, and value, are both resisted via acts of speaking and reconstituted through them (Willis 1977). Any type of talk can be viewed as accomplishing several tasks at once with reference to the overall system of speech genres: first, it asserts and constructs itself and defines its own position in the structure of genres; second, it subverts the value of other positions or resists the claims of other positions; and, third, it reasserts the structure of the system as a whole (the relations among various genres). Since all these things seem to occur concurrently when people talk, I do not want to privilege one aspect—self-creation, resistance, or reproduction—over another.[19]

In stressing the presence of a resistant dimension in reproduction and a reproductive dimension in resistance, I situate myself in a particular place in the ongoing anthropological discussion of resistance. While it would be comforting to celebrate unequivocally the resistance offered by many Russian discourse forms, empirical observation shows them to be caught up in a net of reflexive and often contrary effects. Furthermore, as Sherry Ortner argues in a brilliant essay on historical studies of resistance, fully resistant discourses are probably rare, since, "in a relationship of power, the dominant often has something to offer, and sometimes a great deal (though always of course at the price of continuing in power). The subordinate thus has many grounds for ambivalence about resisting the relationship" (1995: 175).

In Russian talk, for instance, the genres of male mischief—joking, irony, sex tales, and violence tales—were at one level a mode of the construction of certain types of Russian masculinity, a way men had of creating themselves as men. At another level, however, these genres were deployed in resistance to other positions in the structure of genres: i.e., power genres and solemn female genres. At this level, male mischief genres resisted or more directly subverted several things at once—representations of the Russian world as either "important" or "tragic," ideologies about the appropriate behavior of men (or of "Soviet" men), and social (or official) judgments that asserted that men's value is created through serious dedication to work and family. At yet another level, however, the genres of male mischief provided fairly stable positions against which other genres could assert themselves; in other words, male mischief genres gave power genres (or wifely nagging genres) the material against which to assert their authority or level their complaints. At this third level, discourses within a particular genre thus contributed to the constitution of and particular structure of the system as a whole.[20]

Likewise, the more commonly female genres of suffering—litanies and saints' lives—resisted or contradicted power (and the pain of reality) by discursively transforming suffering at the hands of power into a status

---

[19] See Bourdieu and Wacquant (1992: 79–83) and Giddens (1984: 289–297) on this debate; see also Kleinman's (1992) sensitive discussion of pain and resistance and Harvey (1993) on the dialectics of the reproduction of rural poverty in the United States.
[20] While this description of the relativity of genres may appear Bakhtinian, it developed out of ethnographic observation rather than from theoretical reflection. It does, however, fit in with Bakhtin's concepts of utterance, dialogue, and intertextuality (1984; 1986).

higher than power can achieve. These genres operated by inverting existing hierarchies of value, rather than subverting or mocking them as did male mischief genres. In paradoxical ways, however, as I shall show in Chapters 3 and 4, these resistant genres to some degree unintentionally valorized or empowered the very structures they subverted.

Finally, even "powerful" discourses did not merely express and exercise their own powerfulness; they also constantly and actively subverted and resisted the demands and claims (the subversion and resistance) of other discourses, and thereby also served to reify the structure of interactions. While it may seem to abet the interests of those wielding power thus to recapitulate the existing structure of relations among genres, in fact this often backfired. Gorbachev's way of speaking is a case in point. While Western listeners were impressed with Gorbachev's rationalism and intelligence, native Russians, having heard many hours of his expatiations, reacted strongly against the pedantic stance the Soviet leader took. As one friend commented, "he is didactic, like a rural teacher." This didacticism, combined with Gorbachev's provincial accent, made him the target of laughter and mockery; by 1989, people expressed annoyance at Gorbachev's mode of discourse rather than approval of (or even reasoned disapproval of) the things he was saying.[21]

That consequence was not merely personal, however. The particular relationship between authoritative didacticism on the one hand and ironic response on the other was one of the many structures of Russian (Soviet) society that, arguably, needed to be rearranged if perestroika was to succeed.[22] Rather than further democratic engagement and collective problem solving, the dialectics of pedantry, irony, lament, and doomsaying contributed, as Lewin put it, "to blocking the mainsprings of recovery" (1995: 309). The question of how this circuit might be altered—how dis-

---

[21] Clearly, there would have been far less disdain for Gorbachev's orations had his reforms actually improved people's economic and social situations; since the reforms had the unintended effect of making daily life *more* difficult rather than less, people were understandably aggravated at his rambling, televised sermons.

[22] Comments I heard (and read) widely during my fieldwork such as "we Russians have to become different kinds of people," or "we have to transform ourselves" spoke poignantly of the vague sense my informants had of the role their own ways of thinking (talking) played in the failures of perestroika. See Eagleton (1991: 200) on the space discourse leaves for imagining an "emancipatory politics" despite the blindly reproductive power of ideologies. Lewin (1995: 293–332) describes the Moscow intelligentsia's penchant for replacing discredited ideologies and discourses with new ones (among them nationalism, negationism, westernism, catastrophism) instead of with reasoned analysis, though he also rightly points out the "many impressive acts of courage and works of intellect and integrity by these or other parts of the same intelligentsia."

course genres that better support and nourish democratic structures and social relations might become more prevalent—is an immensely challenging one. Of course, the problem of encouraging the replacement of ideologized discourse with critical thinking and discourse is one which any progressive social movement, in any society, must address.

CHAPTER TWO

"Our Fairy-Tale Life":
The Narrative Construction of Russia,
Women, and Men

Clichés are the signposts of art, its milestones. By following them life, hardly noticing as it does so, turns into a fairy-tale or a legend.
—Andrei Sinyavsky, *A Voice from the Chorus*

Our food stuffs merely
make our tastebuds happy now,
But we should get ready in advance
to live without our ham and sausage.

Without bakery sweets!
Without cabbage! Without mushrooms!
Without noodles! Without vermicelli!
Everything will vanish. Get ready.
—Part of a poem by Timur Kibirov

At a small gathering over tea one afternoon in 1990, conversation turned to "the complete disintegration" (*polnaia razrukha*) of Soviet society. As people traded examples of social chaos and absurdity back and forth, and the conversation reached its climactic pitch, Volodia, a writer, turned to me and delivered a punch-line, with a sardonic glee typical of certain kinds of Russian pronouncements: "You know what this country is, Nancy? This country is *Anti-Disneyland*." He was justifiably proud of his precise symbol for Russia, one that described quite well the sense of inhabiting a mythical land where everything was geared toward going wrong: a gargantuan theme park of inconvenience, disintegration, and chaos. Indeed, the most popular thrill of the day seemed to be wondering, aloud, "How bad can it get?" and spinning wickedly frightening but fascinating scenarios about the dissolution of order. This was precisely what we around the table had been doing when Volodia tossed in his metaphor.

His idea of Russia as Anti-Disneyland also conveyed Volodia's impression that Russia and America are inherently opposite kinds of realms, based around opposite cultural fictions. If Disneyland celebrates a mythic American prosperity, if it is conceived around the ideology that life can be a boundless magical realm of cheerfulness and fun, then Anti-Disneyland is fashioned around a spectacular commitment to poverty, humorlessness, and travail. The one is captured in the image of a high-turreted fairy castle; the other is represented by the image of a grungy, overcrowded communal apartment where everyone fights for access to the bathroom.

His image also aptly hinted at the inventedness of the Russian world, which often seems like a fairy-tale land to insider and outsider alike, a product of mythic imagination. Zara Abdullaeva recently declared: "The fabled realm inhabited by this nation is indeed enchanted: the most common things go astray here, while extraordinary ones come to pass. Cause–effect connections have been severed for good, common sense casually defied, and some impenetrable magic rules that fools smart people and gives fools a break" (1996: 209).

Russians regularly use the phrase "our fairy-tale life" (*nasha skazochnaia zhizn'*); referring to the October revolution, one journalist lamented: "This fairy tale was popular for so long."[1] Satirical writers from Saltykov-Shchedrin to Sinyavsky have expanded this type of conceit into whole sagas of the fantastic and absurd. Many of these literary sagas take advantage of the fantastic, mythic, always huge and often monstrous productions of the state. There has long been much to parody in these utopian attempts to invent and secure a fantasy reality (attempts that occurred regularly well before 1917).

But there is a distinctly fairy-tale quality to the reality conveyed through average, day-to-day conversation as well. A conventional inventory of generic forms, images, themes, and figurative devices supplies the collective imagination with the materials to create magically charged narratives within daily talk and gossip. These narratives, in turn, help to fashion the cultural realm which is Russian "fairy-tale life." Certain meaningful symbolic keys serve as a discursive frame for the constant recreation of the Russian life-world. In his essay "Blurred Genres" Clifford Geertz refers to these structures when he writes of "the repetitive performance dimensions of social action—the reenactment and reexperiencing of known forms" (1983: 28) and to "reiterated form, staged and acted by its own audience" (30).[2]

---

[1] *Ogonek*, September 2–9, 1989.
[2] Geertz is, however, strangely silent about informant narratives and discourses and the roles these play in "social drama," preferring to focus not on words but on form enacted

All this pivots around the creation of self or selves. The structures that mold a social world inhere first in the person; local worlds are, as it were, by-products of people's productions of themselves. As Barbara Myerhoff writes, "One of the most persistent but elusive ways that people make sense of themselves is to show themselves to themselves, through multiple forms: by telling themselves stories; by dramatizing claims in rituals and other collective enactments; by rendering visible actual and desired truths about themselves and the significance of their existence in imaginative and performative productions" (Myerhoff 1986: 261).[3]

Much of the examination of Russian talk that follows focuses on the modes of production and representation of the Russian "characters" who inhabit, as subject and object, the Russian "Anti-Disneyland," and who often seem to have stepped out of the rich fairy-tale land of Russian epics and tales.

The Perestroika Epic: "Complete Disintegration"

One evening in March 1990, at a festive dinner with some friends, tales of "complete disintegration" circled the table almost to the exclusion of other topics. "Did you know that by now everything in Kaluga Province is under rationing?" "My parents in Kiev have planted their own potatoes." "I heard they are now selling sausage so contaminated with pesticides, hormones, and radiation from Chernobyl that you should not feed it to children—but still people are buying it, so starved are they for meat." "What we are seeing is complete ruin." "Yes," said one young man who works for the transport system. "At work we heard, some Japanese came, inspected our rails—and said that they had never seen such a nightmare, the rail beds are crumbling and the rails are in terrible condition—they said we will have terrible crashes, especially on the busy Moscow–Leningrad line." "Yes," said another man, "complete disintegration." At one point in this litany of ruin I naively tried to interject the question: "Well, what can be done to remedy these problems?" My question was

---

bodily. In the Russian case (and, one suspects, in other cultural milieus as well) talk is a crucial medium for the reiteration of form. Ortner's concept of "key scenarios" (1973: 1341) seems to embrace both discursive and bodily performance. Bourdieu's *habitus* is likewise a product of (and producer of) discourses and bodily practices (although his earlier work is also heavily inclined towards emphasis on the reproductive power of physical rather than verbal practices).

[3] The long-term Soviet project (involving myriad social and scientific resources) to create the "New Soviet Man" (Bauer 1952; Attwood 1990: 32–66) can be seen as an attempt, however befuddled by conflicting ideologies and the totalitarian means engaged to realize it, to create a new world by refashioning the standard self.

"We Are Building Communism" (Photo by John Einarson and Robert Kowalczyk)

met with silence; I had failed to understand the ritual nature of this kind of repartee.

The phrase "complete disintegration" and similar phrases such as "complete breakdown" or "collapse" (*polnyi razval, raspad*) resounded through many of the Moscow conversations in which I participated. *Polnaia razrukha* was an abbreviated reference to everything that was supposedly disintegrating in Russian society at the time: it was a discursive signpost which embraced the escalation of crime, the disappearance of goods from the stores, the ecological catastrophes, the fall of production, the ethnic violence in the Caucasus, the "degradation" of the arts, the flood of pornography, and other signs of immorality which some people saw everywhere. Though these tales had their basis in the social concerns and changes of the time, the animated performances whereby people circulated them—vividly embroidering them with personal details, experiences, and emotions—functioned to create a very specific, local sense of that reality. *Polnaia razrukha* became a folkloric genre: it manifested a particular structure (litany), took a particular approach to the subject (portentous), focused on certain subjects (the gorier and more horrible, the better), and it maneuvered its audiences to a desired response (alarmed astonishment). More than this, however, these stories helped to fabricate a sense of shared experience and destiny.

In the late 1980s, a frenzy developed in the mass media to portray the kinds of horrors that were the main and driving ingredients of the *polnaia razrukha* genre. The tabloid news broadcasts that became a regular feature on Soviet television in these years were almost ritualistic inversions of the utopian portrayals of Soviet life that had been a staple of the preperestroika media. The December 17, 1990, broadcast of the popular TV show *Completely Secret* (*Sovershenno Sekretno*) featured a segment on the awful conditions in the morgue of a hospital; interspersed with interviews with doctors and workers were shots of a room full of human corpses— several rows of decaying bodies sprawled on tables. The workers reported that the temperature and sanitary controls were very bad, and that rats regularly nibbled the corpses, a comment that was followed by a shot of rats scurrying along the decaying floor of a corridor.

In March 1990, the popular television show *Vzgliad* did a piece on the Moscow zoo. The punchline was a comment by a zoo worker who reported that he overheard parents saying to their kids: "Look what nice meat there is on that animal." This was followed by a story about a home for the aged where some criminals were sent to live and subsequently spent their time beating and robbing the elderly. There was a panoramic montage of scenes of old people lying in bed, and a mood of intense pathos was established by the music used and the images chosen. Nobody said the words "total disintegration" but the implication was clear. At the end, one announcer intoned: "This is where we are going, friends."

One *polnaia razrukha* tale combined the typical litany of horrors with a tone of moralistic cant: a TV news piece (December 11, 1989) about frost-bitten alcoholics displayed the scarred, bleeding, and skinless hands, noses, and lips of drunks who had passed out on the street during bitter cold days. The interviewer asked, "How did this happen to you?" in order to deliver a message about the immorality and pathos of alcoholism, then added, portentously, "This is what we have come to" (implying, rather disingenuously, that such problems had never occurred before perestroika).

The social horror stories fetishized in the media helped greatly to fuel the growth of a sense of cataclysm in day-to-day narratives. Topics featured in broadcasts were quickly drawn into private conversations where they could be related to actual personal experiences, and one effect of this dialectic was that national problems came to seem very immediate, while personal or familial woes were made epic, invested with historical resonance.

In one conversation I had with a friend while waiting for a bus, the *polnaia razrukha* tale began with empty shelves and circled round and round the various crises of the day all the way to an envisaging of the future destruction of the world at the hands of terrorists with access to the USSR's nuclear weapons, ending with a chorus of "How awful," "What a nightmare," and "What are we going to do?"

Typical incidents of urban disorder—fist-fights, drunks careening along the street, people butting in line or using obscene language openly in public—could stimulate exclamations of "complete ruin." So too could the private vending activity on busy streets or outside metro stations, which during perestroika began to evolve into a huge cultural and economic phenomenon, with dozens of older women standing side by side holding up their wares—a pack of cigarettes, a dried fish, a bottle of vodka—commodities that they had stood in line to purchase from state stores and sell for higher prices to passersby; this kind of activity was snarlingly referred to as "speculation," but the epithet *"polnaia razrukha"* drew it into the broader picture of social disintegration. All these phenomena were construed as proof that the Soviet Union was collapsing into chaos and anarchy (both favorite words of the perestroika period).

One irony here is that many of the people with whom I spoke did not express concrete anxiety about the possibility of personal suffering; there seemed to be more exhilaration stimulated through the sharing of these stories than there was anxiety. It was primarily older people who expressed great alarm at these developments, in part because they recognized the vulnerability of their social position, and in part because the events of the perestroika years completely contradicted all their expectations; for them, perestroika brought a collapse of their whole cultural world. Younger, less immediately vulnerable people, raised on the ubiquitous and only somewhat underground spirit of irony of the 1970s and 1980s (and inexperienced in war or famine), were much more likely to speak in a idiom that expressed their fascination with possible danger. As if from morbid curiosity, such people often said, "How far do you think we will go?" and then went on to try to imagine how far, competing with one another through their various fantasies of ruin.[4]

The situation in stores, however, was the favorite topic of *polnaia razrukha* tales, as it had the most immediacy in people's lives. During the long Brezhnev period known as the era of stagnation (it is enough to say that one word in Russian to invoke the entire period, which only ended with the coming of Gorbachev), economic growth was low, but the Moscow stores were usually stocked with the supplies routinely called for in daily existence, though lines to purchase them could be long. During "stagnation" there were sometimes shortages of particular items, and most people tried to keep an extra supply of certain things on hand. Matches, lightbulbs, soap, toothpaste, toilet paper, salt, and sugar were commonly hoarded. During perestroika, the economic system heaved a great nationwide sigh—and instead of stagnation there were suddenly odd and unnerving patterns of shortages of every kind. This was basically the result of the combination of wage inflation, on the one hand, and declining production, on the other: people had more money to purchase fewer goods. This led to cycles of panic buying and hoarding (on both individual and regional levels), further depleting the availability of goods in the stores. As part of the policy of economic "shock therapy," designed to increase production, the government announced that the prices of basic foodstuffs—including bread—would be raised in the late spring of 1990; this increased hoarding, and, worsening matters still further, caused enterprises to hold back shipments in anticipation of receiving higher prices for their goods after price freezes were lifted.

As Moscow stores became emptier than they had been, and as crucial commodities (sugar, dairy products, meats) vanished from state stores

---

[4] These kinds of agonistic storytelling sessions are a phenomenon well known in many cultures. They could be compared quite readily to more formal types of narrative competition such as those of various Pacific societies (cf. Brenneis and Myers 1984 and Brenneis 1988). They seem to follow the logic of what Luthi (1976), referring to folk tales, calls "intensification"—whereby, with every telling, the gruesome details of a story become exaggerated. Ong's remarks on the agonistic features of oral cultures (1981; 1982: 43–45) are also pertinent.

one after another, people began to speak with real agitation. When, in the spring of 1990, internal passports proving Moscow residency were required to make certain food purchases, the *polnaia razrukha* tales became quite intense. It seemed to me, then, that at the same time that these developments made them quite anxious, my interlocutors were electrified by this intrusion of economic calamity into their personal lives; having to show their passports (and then being able to tell about it) gave them a sense of connection to the more abstract turmoil of larger social levels. And this, I daresay, made them feel personally part of the intense Russian drama widely described as being an interminable cycle of chaos, calamity, and ruin.

One afternoon in April 1990, I passed an acquaintance in the corridor of an office and asked how she was doing. "Everything is alright," she reassured me, "but what a time we are living through!" She went on to tell me the following tale, whispering the whole time as if letting me in on a mystery. "Everything is alright, but it is becoming such a nightmare trying to buy anything!" she said.

> Every store you enter is empty. This is the end, I do not know, maybe we have come to the point of complete ruin. A friend of mine told me about a store he went to, a supermarket, where they were selling nothing but one kind of canned fish, and not just canned fish, but fish of such an awful quality that even drunks would not buy it to go with their vodka. But some enterprising managers, and clerks, having nothing else to do, of course, had carefully arranged all of these thousands of tins—and so there were Eiffel towers of canned fish, and pyramids, and Great Walls—a whole world, the seven wonders of the world, constructed from—sardines.

She finished her depiction of this fairy-tale place by adding the following fairy-tale phrase: "Such a thing is only possible in one country—here, in Russia."

The story itself was quite probably true—the Moscow supermarkets, never super to begin with, in 1989 and 1990 did become like fairy-tale places. One spacious store that I wandered into was selling nothing but half-kilo boxes of salt, and although their display had fewer architectural pretensions, the store clerks had made some effort to display the cardboard boxes attractively throughout the place. If there were nothing else to do, if there were nothing to sell and nothing to buy, shop clerks and shoppers alike could use the materials at hand (or the material lack at hand) to build—from whispered words or from boxes of salt or from tins of fish—"tales" that drolly and adroitly commented on the very lack of consumable substances.

But such tales, whether communicated by means of visual or verbal media, were more than simply commentaries on the situation in the stores. They all served, more generally and more durably, as chronicles of the fabulous–terrible conditions of mythical Russia, Volodia's "Anti-Disneyland."

I would argue that this "Anti-Disneyland" carries as much positive cultural value for Russians as "Disneyland" does on the other side of the world. Obviously, this is not an unambiguous value (as "Disneyland" representations of the United States of America are far from being unanimously appreciated). But the fact remains that many of the Russians I spoke with communicated a construction of their country as an opposite kind of place, an anti-utopia, a "through the looking-glass" kingdom; indeed, one common phrase used ironically for Russia/the USSR was *strana chudes*—"land of wonders." In the same vein, *strana durakov*, or "land of fools," was often heard. This particular symbolic construction—with its own epistemic tradition, its thousands of reverberations in art, poetry, and literature, and its countless unrecorded but nonetheless accretive folkloric (oral) transmissions—was a valued genre of both life and language, to which contributions were always welcome and always enjoyed. I call this genre "the Russia tale." Even when they had tragic elements, such tales were appreciated for their fascinating, appalling, amusing, astonishing, aesthetic elements. Something a noted theater critic said to me during an interview in 1994 supports this interpretation of such discourses. "On the one hand," he said, "in foreign countries [Russians] are afraid to identify themselves as Russian, but, on the other hand, within themselves they are all very proud that they are Russians, that they come from such a country, which has such a strange history."

Stories about the absurdities of Russia triggered complex emotional responses from listeners. It seems to me that these responses were engendered, in part, by the very familiarity of the genre of "the Russia tale." Generic repetition produces an effect of harmonization both personal and social, key to the connection of the personal and the social. As Pierre Bourdieu puts it: "One of the fundamental effects of the orchestration of habitus is the production of a commonsense world endowed with an *objectivity* secured by consensus on the meaning (*sens*) of practices and the world, in other words the harmonization of agents' experiences and the continuous reinforcement that each of them receives from the expression, individual or collective (in festivals, for example), improvised or programmed (commonplaces, sayings), of similar or identical experiences" (Bourdieu 1977: 80).

The common-sense world may be represented as an absurd, nonsensical place. Is it possible, though, to imagine that even nonsense and absurdity are comforting and valuable to the extent that they resonate as forms, of narrative and of society, both personally familiar and culturally distinctive?

To argue that point would be to suggest that Russians, like all people, have been to varying extents stuck inside their genres—their ways of speaking about and constructing themselves as enduring, mischievous, sober or wild, their ways of constructing their *narod* as brutal and brutalized, their ways of constructing this thing they call Russia as an upside-down, sorrowful domain. These genres of personal and national construction were (and remain, to a great extent) a key facet of Russian talk, the concrete mechanism by which a general sense of the social world has been constructed, maintained, and reproduced. Genres like "complete disintegration" and "absurd tales" comfortably (and amusingly) mediate Russian utopian dreams and Russian reality; they provide a descriptive frame for absurdity, making it possible to think, act, and survive within that absurdity.

The "Russia tale," an epic absurdist genre, with boundaries flexible enough to admit all kinds of novel material, was a form of narrative familiar and widespread enough to provide a mode of cultural connection among vastly different people; it is one key thread in a web of communicative exchange and transmission. The endlessly rich Russian tradition of absurdist writing constantly facilitates the weaving of this web in daily conversation, as Russian speakers both explicitly and implicitly cited the parallels between their own absurd experiences and the absurd images made famous by Gogol, Kharms, Bulgakov, Voinovich, and countless others.

Belonging to the web means regularly fashioning personal narratives that embed the self in the larger, ongoing tale. It means keeping certain basic types of stories, anecdotes, absurdisms, and laments "in the air," more or less, not stopping the performance or altering its inherent morphology (the details, as Propp insisted, are optional and variable). The text is, in many ways, the context. In the next section, I discuss the generic ways Russians had of discursively inserting themselves into the "Russia tale"—or, to be more specific, into that epic story's perestroika chapter.

Tales of Heroic Shopping and Female Self-Construction

> Gender ideologies are socialized, sustained, and transformed through talk, particularly through verbal practices that recur innumerable times in the lives of members of social groups. . . . Mundane, prosaic, and altogether unsensational though they may appear to be, conversational practices are primary resources for the realization of gender hierarchy.
> —Elinor Ochs, "Indexing Gender"

In response to the rapidly increasing shortages of consumer goods arose one of the top genres of the period: "tales of heroic shopping." As would be expected, people were actively trading their horror stories about the situation in the stores.

Masha described how she traveled all over Moscow looking for a certain medicine for her ailing mother. She named the far-from-center metro stations in different regions she visited in hopes of getting this specialized medicine:

> First, way up to Medvedkovo, there was nothing. Then down to Lenin-gradskii Prospekt, they also had absolutely nothing, then I finally tried Tushinskaya, just as the pharmacy was about to close. They had one pack of tablets left. I got it, thank God, but I was practically dead from exhaustion and frustration, running around the city from one end to the other. This is our life now, scouring the city, here and there, there and here, wearing ourselves out to get every little thing.

In the telling, because of the dramatic tone she adopted, through long pauses which conveyed suspense, and through her invocation of the distant (unfamiliar, unfriendly) neighborhoods of Moscow, the episode became an ordeal, a quest, a mythical search. Stories like this were extremely familiar. The more poignant ones centered around searches for crucial medicines, items for children, a bottle of champagne for a birthday, butter, meat, tea, detergent. The narrative structure of this tale and others like it that I heard often seemed to follow a fairy-tale pattern and to partake of a fairy-tale toolbag of details and aesthetic devices. A second tale illustrates this quality even more clearly.

This tale was told me by an American colleague, Julie deSherbinin, who spent the fall of 1991 in Russia. She told it as a paradigmatic story about shortages, to illustrate the degree of difficulty in contemporary Russia; Russians tell such stories habitually, on one level, as a way to measure social conditions.[5] But this story can also be read as a paradigmatic tale that illustrates the cultural operation Sinyavsky described—life being turned into legend through the continuous operations of cliché.[6]

[5] This American's emotive retelling of this tale incidentally shows the process by which non-Russians who live for any period of time among Russians may begin to employ Russian speech genres. The more time I spent in Russia, the more I found myself echoing Russian discourses in my own narration of events.

[6] The use of conventional linguistic elements and clichés is not an automatic mark of banality. As George Gibian writes: "the Russian still trusts proverbs, and does not think he is being a parrot when he chooses to pick out of his memory a ready-made folk formula and applies it to a given situation" (1990: 38). The central figure in a certain intellectual circle which I frequented was a respected scholar who always articulated a proverb, joke, or poetic

Julie was staying with a family in Leningrad. One cold December day, the family's *babushka* (grandmother) went out very early in the morning, string bag in hand. By late afternoon she still was not home. "Where is *Babushka*?" somebody enquired. "She went out for sugar and never returned!" came the reply. Finally, late in the afternoon *Babushka* appeared—her string bag bulging with a kilo of sugar. The elderly woman had stood nine hours in line, then turned her ration card in at the end to get her kilo of sugar. All that evening and all the next day, the American guest heard this story narrated repeatedly over the phone; the other family members told it again and again to their friends and acquaintances: "*Babushka ushla i ne vernulas'*" (Grandmother went out and did not return").

Through this tale's telling and multiple retelling, *Babushka* was sacralized—and her quotidian *podvig* (a Russian key-word, meaning feat, achievement, heroic exploit)[7] became the subject of a modern folk tale very Russian in form, mood, mechanisms, and details.

As Maria Kravchenko noted in her study *The World of the Russian Fairy Tale* (following Vladimir Propp), "In the *skazka* the action usually begins with the hero's (or heroine's) departure from home. The hero's journey represents, as it were, the axis of the narration, during the course of which he must overcome any number of difficulties, and survive a succession of trials or ordeals, usually with the aid of supernatural helpers. The tale ends with the hero's return home as soon as the last obstacle is removed and his goal is achieved" (1987: 80).[8]

---

couplet perfect for the moment or situation at hand. Such a skill (of memory and homology) is highly valued in most Russian discursive settings. A corresponding phenomenon is also greatly valued: collective delight often ensues when the occasion or the occurrence being discussed perfectly corresponds to the (pre-existing) cliché or proverb. This suggests a cultural appreciation of the integrity or continuity of social action/occurrence and discursive structures.

[7] In a breathless exhibition of Russian exceptionalism, Nikolai Roerich wrote in 1945 that "no other European language has a word even approximating [the meaning of *podvig*]." "The heroism that is proclaimed by fanfares cannot convey the immortal, all-conclusive thought contained in the Russian word *podvig*. And what a wonderful word it is" (cited in Likhachev 1981: 130). This word appears constantly in discourses about shopping and other forms of procurement. It is uttered both ironically and sincerely (often both tones combine as one). One late fall day I went with a friend to her dacha outside Moscow to carry home the apples that had just fallen and were threatened by frost. After traveling in crowded trains, taking a bus, walking some, gathering apples in the cold, packing them into backpacks, and bearing them home to Moscow on our backs, at the door to her apartment my friend said, "We completed a *podvig*," and her husband rewarded us with plates of delicious pan-fried potatoes. This story perhaps conveys some of the meaning of this word *podvig* in modern Russian usage. See also Tumarkin's (1990) elegy on the *podvigi* of Andrei Sakharov.
[8] Propp's *Morphology of the Folktale* (1968) is built around the key structuring element of the protagonist's journey. See also Wosien (1969) on the element of the journey in the Russian tale. Propp's *Morphology*, the first structuralist treatment of folktales, is still regarded as an

The *Babushka* story, set in the difficult era of shortages, clearly was structured around such a journey or quest. The narrative began with exactly that element Propp designates as the first (and invariable) action or "function" of the folktale: "One of the members of a family absents himself from home" (1968: 26). This act of leaving is connected with the lack of some substance (one of the second grouping of functions Propp identified in the folktale); the particular substance is unidentified in the story, but signified by the empty string bag (which is called *avos'ka* in Russian, meaning "on-the-off-chance-bag"). These details intrinsically evoked a common Russian folktale incantation, connected with a protagonist's departure: "I will go I know not where; I will bring back I know not what." In the way this story was told in the family, *Babushka*'s intention was at first left unstated—lending a mood of mystery and suspense compounded as her absence dragged on (although it was pretty clear she was on a quest, still she might have fallen into grave danger; this was an era of rampant rumors about the rise in violent crimes). The suspense was increased in the telling by the device of describing the family's concern and perplexity.

Finally, after her "sustained ordeal" (which is another of Propp's central functions) *Babushka* returned home triumphantly—and this is the way the tale always ends, although with variations on the details. The final mood was one of awe, veneration, and celebration.

Some elements of this everyday tale warrant additional comment. The tale at hand diverges from the folktale in that the central action takes place off-stage, as it were; the narrative frame remains in the apartment from which *Babushka* has departed instead of following her as it would typically follow the protagonist. But *Babushka*'s ordeal is familiar to all: the long line, the cold, the faith it takes to wait in the line, not knowing if supplies will run out just as you reach the front, the constant intrusions of "more important," more aggressive, and just plain sneaky persons into the front of the line, the precious ration card, and the valuable "reward" at the end—sugar for the family.

In Russian life, sugar is indeed a precious substance, having many material and symbolic implications. Necessary for preserving the fruits of the forest for the coming winter, sugar is also used for making *samogon*—home-brewed alcohol, which is an occupation endemic in the countryside

---

essential tool in folktale analysis, although it has been further elaborated (and condensed) by many other scholars (see especially Maranda and Kongas-Maranda 1971). Propp uses the term "functions" to mean key actions, which are functional in that each facilitates the development of the overall structure in a particular direction. "Functions of characters serve as stable, constant elements in a tale, independent of how and by whom they are fulfilled. They constitute the fundamental components of a tale. The number of functions known to the fairy tale is limited" (Propp 1968: 21).

where *samogon* always served as a universal equivalent of labor, more respected and trusted than prosaic and often useless cash.[9]

Sugar's other important use is for sweetening tea, along with vodka a ubiquitous beverage of familial and ritual gatherings. During the war there was a saying "to drink your tea with a glimpse (of sugar)," (*pit' chai v prigliadku*), which meant there was only enough sugar to look at and imagine tasting (Moskoff 1990: 225)—a sad image of a favorite Russian treat accessible in hard times only via fantasy, an image that sums up the parameters and poignancy of hunger and deprivation in the Russian context.[10]

This real-life story of *Babushka's* pursuit of sugar was so touching and resonant within *Babushka's* own family not so much because it neatly followed the immutable morphology of Russian folk stories as because folktales and the life tales are built around the same flexible structure—a morphology which is itself kept alive and fresh because it has long been in constant circulation in both Russian talk (especially life stories) and in aesthetic entertainments of all kinds and levels (fiction, poetry, movies, songs). Basically this is the same kind of structure that Ortner refers to as a "key scenario," which encapsulates in narrative form "clear-cut modes of action appropriate to correct and successful living in the culture" (1973: 1341). The question of how such a scenario could have survived despite persistent and profound social and political changes (revolution, modernization, urbanization) is a difficult one. I would argue that such scenarios have survived in part because they have penetrated those cataclysms through and through, from top to bottom: they make sense of those events and even help to make those events possible, by valorizing personal sacrifice and humility and highlighting the overcoming of innumerable obstacles as a *modus vivendi*.

This narrated event was also poignant because it partook of the basic sacred vocabulary of the Russian tale—an elemental lexicon that includes such day-to-day materials as sugar, bread, salt, tobacco, and tea and such

[9] One unintended consequence of Gorbachev's anti-alcohol campaign was the bulk purchase and hoarding of sugar for brewing alcohol. Soon after distribution of alcohol by the government was radically cut back, sugar disappeared from the stores. People then bemoaned the fact that they had no way to preserve fruits for the winter, thus no way to "ensure a supply of vitamins for their children." At a symbolic level, this conflict is a battle between male and female realms—the male realm of drinking, the female realm of nurturing, the male substance of vodka versus the female one of preserves. Interestingly, these two realms are mediated in the person of the *babushka*, the one who makes preserves for her family, but—as is common in villages especially—brews alcohol to sell for money.

[10] The saying is a take-off on the typical expression referring to the way Russians used to drink tea; by biting off a piece from a sugar cube, holding it in their mouths and sipping the tea through it: *pit' chai v prikusku*. It is very unusual in Russia to drink tea without sugar. "White like snow, in favor with everyone" goes the old riddle.

abstract but recurrent themes as danger, heroism, endurance, and hope. These are some of the key symbolic elements which construct Russian-ness, and each of these irreducible elements could inspire its own arche-ology of conventional reference.[11] Together, they supply the potential for infinite semiotic combination and application. The very fact of the rela-tive limitation—the small size—of this semiotic toolbag contributes to its meaningfulness. If wealth entails variety, in terms of objects, tools, diver-sions, foodstuffs, wardrobe, and so on, poverty entails a lack of variety. Russian narratives turn this lack of variety into a virtue of simplicity. The deployment of these key elements in narrative creates an embrace of familiarity, continuity, connectedness—and magic, a kind of magic that even the twentieth century has failed to disperse or repress. About the fairy tale, George Gibian writes that "the conventionality of a Russian fairy tale gives the aesthetic pleasure of recognition and familiarity; it may serve as a mnemonic device in oral narration; but above all, it raises the tale from the ordinary world to a realm where magic exists and anything is possible" (1956: 245).

But the reciprocal is true too: the conventionality of the Russian life tale and the constant circulation of its small range of elements raises life itself from the realm of the ordinary. *Babushka* herself was raised, in the tale of the sugar quest, from "mere" grandmotherliness to the level of the won-der tale where she could stand as a symbolic embodiment of the value of female dedication and faith.

Here is a second tale to consider with these narrative reciprocities in mind. This one was told me by my poet friend, Masha; it was woven into the fabric of one of many long talks we had, over tea and sweets. "One day last week," she said,

> I went to meet a woman, a stranger, in a subway station, to pick up a pack-age of *samizdat* [self-published, underground] poetry. Over the phone, I asked, "How will I know you?" and the woman told me, "I will be wearing a bright blue coat." Having waited on the platform a few minutes, sud-denly I saw a blue apparition walking toward me. Nancy, you cannot imagine. This woman wore blue, a sort of bright azure blue from head to toe: azure coat, with a perfectly matching wool hat, azure gloves, hand-bag, and even her boots: azure. Looking at her, so well coordinated, I felt such a deep sense, feeling. The image of that woman remains indelibly inscribed on my mind: it was the image of a woman, can you imagine this, Nancy, a woman who must have spent literally years assembling that bril-

[11] Judith L. Goldstein makes the same point about Iranian Jewish women's "magical narra-tives." She comments that "the symbolic vehicles of [their] stories are mortars and pestles, sugar cones, rugs and clothing . . . objects with which they are intimately associated in daily life" (1986: 147).

liant outfit, you know what it is like shopping for clothes here, you take what you can get and women work so hard to assemble a fashionable outfit or two, it was so poignant to see this woman; she told me she had found the purse in a store on her one trip to East Germany. Her grandmother somehow found some perfectly matching blue yarn and made the hat. That is our Russian woman.

Masha's story was mundane but also magical. It was a tale resonant with traditional forms and forces, a tale about the mystery of a woman's self-creation, about the magic symbolism of dress and color, about powerful helpers like *babushki* who can spin perfect hats out of found skeins of yarn. In the telling, it was also about the self-creation of the narrator: as Russian woman, as poet, as cultural witness, as articulate teller (and embroiderer?) of tales. As Sandra Stahl commented, "the successful teller of personal narratives engages the listener in an adventure—not simply the plot of a story, but rather the shared activity of exploring the teller's world, the teller's identity" (1989: x).

All the elements of these stories were significant, profiling the scapes of person and world in a system of symbolic details: the transmission of the manuscript (exchange of a powerful object); the setting in a location of mythical grandeur (the Moscow subway—a place where many strange "underground" transactions have occurred over the years); the astonishing blue lady—who seemed upon apprehension a magical being, but was upon reflection a regular Russian woman capable of enormous feats of ingenuity and determination—*podvigi*.

Among other things, both of these tales were about female identity and its fabrication. The two tales interestingly contrast with one another, suggesting the contrast of different stages of the life cycle or the different faces of Russian femaleness; the first was about female self-sacrifice, the second about female self-creation (or the impossibilities thereof). Both took place in the context of a world within which femaleness has been essentially related to suffering, endurance, and magic (Dunham 1960). In this light, the following text from the famed Russian poet, Yevgenii Yevtushenko, part of an article he published called "A Nation Begins with Its Women," has special import:

Nobody is saying, of course, that men do not suffer from the continuous shortages. But women obviously bear the brunt. It is they after all who are constantly searching and improvising to cope with the situation. Foreigners are surprised at how smart many Soviet women look these days. How much ingenuity is behind every detail of a Soviet woman's costume. Foreigners admire the hospitality and culinary talents of our women. They have no idea to what lengths they must go to find all those little tidbits (which incidentally would grace a royal banquet). A Russian woman shops for the home, for the children, for her husband, and only then for herself. Try getting a kilo of frankfurters, half a dozen boxes of detergent, a pack of disposable diapers, some razor blades and a pair of nice looking shoes that do not cost the earth—all in one round of shopping! (Yevtushenko 1990: 318)

The author's main point in this article was not, of course, that men should participate in "woman's work" but that women should be freed from outside work, appreciated and not taken for granted, to enable them to work only at their natural domestic tasks and be spared the double burden. This kind of text, of course, stems from and perpetuates the essentializing of gender and gender roles. But it also shows the subtle fetishizing of the magical "yeast" of female suffering and travail—a theme which runs through the old folktales.[12] Most of the ordeals of female heroines in the folktales were trials of faith, tests of the endurance of brides coercively married to animals or monsters or cruel tsars; these husbands become handsome, wealthy, kind, and human once the heroine has shown her faithfulness and ability to produce desired objects magically from impossibly meager materials; on this subject see Kravchenko (1987: 170–179).

Masha rendered another tale over tea one day, several months after the "Woman in Blue" story; with surprising precision (almost as if she had read it, though I doubt that she had), this story echoes Yevtushenko's seemingly sympathetic text about women, shopping, and self-sacrifice. Constructing herself as torn between her new opportunities and her allegiance to her circle of friends, this young but increasingly well-known Russian poet described for me her first sojourn abroad to read her work, a three-day trip to Hungary. She forged a mythic scene out of a moment's window-shopping. "I stood in front of a shop window and could not help weeping," she said.

They had given me enough Hungarian currency that I could have gone in and bought myself a pair, but then I thought of all the people here, all my friends, *bednenkie*, poor little things, and I knew that I could not buy boots for myself when everybody is so poor—so I used my money to buy small

---

[12] It permeates Russian literature as well. The conventional portrayal of "the Russian woman" by Russian men often seems to reflect both sympathy and thrill at the woman's difficult position, such as in Dostoevsky's story "The Meek One." The main elements of this portrayal are summed up in the following reflections of the main character: "In my eyes she was so conquered, so humiliated, so crushed, that sometimes I felt agonies of pity for her, although sometimes the thought of her humiliation was pleasing to me. The thought of our inequality pleased me" (1971: 315).

presents instead, just small change, pencils, soap, tea, and so on. But I wept because our Russian women will never have boots like those.

Each of the texts quoted above shows this mythic "genre" of the feminine *podvig* of tragic or at least poignant self-sacrifice and endurance running through narratives about shopping. In many ways, these tales were about the moral self-proving of women, so much like the recurrent trials of Russian fairy tales—where the heroine proves her spiritual purity by not choosing the object or path that would most benefit herself. There are myriad complications to this topic, however. What the Russian woman is giving up by not buying those craved boots is not simply nice new boots. Dressing, fashion, the cultivation of whatever charm, style, or beauty can be created from the materials at hand—this is the Moscow woman's artistry, her poetry, her communicative practice, which functions on many simultaneous planes of semiosis and which says volumes about the era, about shifts in politics or spirituality, about household economics and creative resistance to existential conditions.[13] In Russia, a winter culture, not to have the right boots is to be missing a crucial element, a building block for the rest of the story of "self." This emphasis on footwear has a long (and class-based) history: there is, for example, an old proverb that "the peasant wears bast (straw) shoes so the master can wear soft leather boots."

In other lights, shopping (and hoarding) seemed to be a favorite contemporary adventure—for women, men, and even children (despite the mythology as depicted by Yevtushenko, it is not only women who go shopping). I often heard shopping portrayed as a feat of perspicacity, patience, cunning, connection, and endurance, or characterized as sport. One man told me "We feel like *bogatyry* [legendary Russian warriors, usually much larger than life, depicted in Russian epic tales] when we go shopping. You go to buy bread and you feel yourself to be a mythical character, having many dragons to slay along the way—for instance, one store might be closed when it should be open. Shopping is like a mythical journey. Going home with a box of matches—you feel like a hero."[14] An-

[13] A striking comparison could be heard in media accounts of the women of Sarajevo, who say they were determined to keep themselves looking nice despite the seige and endless shelling of their city; in radio interviews I have heard them explicitly describe this attention to personal appearance as a form of resistance to the atrocity of the war. See Drakulić (1993) on this point.

[14] There were, it is crucial to stress, two distinct kinds of shopping: that of mothers (and often grandmothers) who were usually the ones most under pressure to procure something with which to feed their families, a pressure that enforced their endurance of daily, lengthy standing in lines; and that of "browsers" who for one reason or another (age, gender, marital status) were free to fail at their shopping attempts, or to wander freely, reaping the thrill of serendipity.

other Muscovite explained this feeling, saying she loved "the peacefulness of standing in line, and the thrill of maybe getting something at the end."

The absurdities of Soviet life and provisioning could provide the material for discursive journeys into the much-appreciated zone of irony. One feminist friend, Maya, graced with a keen sense of humor, could reel off intensely funny and involved sagas about trying to accomplish something in the difficult arenas of Moscow bureaucracy and business. On one occasion, as part of an epic story about her attempts to organize a feminist conference (the first ever in Moscow), she delivered a litany about female bureaucrats and their distinctive ways of hampering progress:

> She will suddenly take out her compact and begin adjusting her lipstick, right in front of you, without a word, and then stare at you as if you are crazy to be interrupting this. Or she will just stare at you; only women can really pull that off, the long, cold, unblinking, immovable stare. Men are bad, but women are the real totalitarians. It is they who maintain the status quo in our society.

After this she switched to a saga about how she managed to get her apartment painted.

> Men are easier to deal with. Sometimes you just need a bottle—or a series of bottles. Like how I got the apartment painted, begging and bribing, begging and bribing. It was so dirty before. I had to go round and round with the maintenance agency. But finally with a little "encouragement" they came, suddenly appeared one day with a dozen buckets of paint. It was not exactly the color we wanted, but you have to grab an opportunity when it arises. They had paint left over from somewhere else. So they painted the apartment. That is why it is the color you see here. It is absurd, I know, but that is our Soviet life, one absurdism after another, a life of absurdity! What would we do for entertainment without it?

Every wall in Maya's three-room apartment was painted the same color—a shiny and saturate saffron yellow. As we sat in her flourescent kitchen drinking coffee, Maya used her personal stories about the difficulty of life to illustrate her views of Russian absurdism; but she also thereby managed to distance herself in a certain way from other female speakers, since her litany was spoken with a tough, ironic tone and her stories focused on the humor in her ordeals rather than the pain. Perhaps the deliverance of such ironic stories was a way speakers had to advertise their ability to navigate the Soviet bureaucracy, with the help of cleverness, confidence, patience, and vodka.

In a related comment, a male informant described "the acute feeling of insult if you have not managed to get something despite all your perseverance." Sometimes this feeling of "acute insult" resulted in the disruption of the peacefulness of Russian lines. Competing in popularity with the stories of female patience, and those about the thrill of "getting something" was a third genre. Tales of shopping arguments, violence, and the horrors of standing in line were told with great glee.

One woman whom I interviewed, a prominent feminist writer, relayed a shopping tale of this kind in the course of a long litany about the hardships of her life and life for women in Russia in general. "Some things happen only to me," she said:

> I went to the meat store to try to get some scraps for my poor dog. You know how hard it is for dogs and cats these days, poor things. I stood in line for a long time, but then suddenly I spotted a pile of rotting entrails that nobody else would take, just sitting on a pan off to the side. So I went over and started to take some but an old lady saw me and thought I was taking something worthwhile and raised a ruckus and suddenly she punched me—right in the nose!

It seemed to me that shopping violence was a performative genre in and of itself. Once in a neighborhood department store I happened into what was nearly a small riot. Tiny battery-operated fans had suddenly appeared for sale. There were probably one hundred women all pushing towards the counter trying to get one. I stood in the rear of the store, amazed at the boisterous desire of these women for these fans and at their frustration when the salesclerk announced that they had sold the last one (it was not summertime). Clearly the women in the crowd did not believe them (salespeople routinely set aside a certain portion of their stock to sell to friends and family) and they were screaming at, insulting, scolding, and threatening the clerks, and each other, in extremely colorful and heated language (the very specific language of in-store altercations, a genre in its own right). The police were finally called, and their arrival calmed the women down, if only by giving them an authority to whom to complain.

On another occasion, I stood in line with a friend in the wine department of a huge store on Kalinin Prospect in central Moscow. We stood and stood, but the line hardly moved. Finally it became clear why: there was a constant flow of strong young men slipping in at the head of the line. Nobody cared to challenge them until an older man almost anonymously threw his hat at one of them. The young men came threateningly into the crowd looking for the culprit, and when they found him, a whole mêlée broke out, with bottles flying through the air, and people pushing and shoving and screaming. The clerk threw a plastic wine carton into his stock, and a whole case of bottles shattered; at that point many people fled what seemed like mounting danger.[15]

These common scenes of shopping violence stood opposed to the folk-loric tales of the patient shopping ordeal as greed and envy were to equitability and generosity; these contrasting stories thus highlighted a basic Russian value opposition. This opposition was further highlighted by a slightly different genre: "envy tales."

Many such stories surfaced in discussion of the cooperatives. Gorbachev had allowed coops to come into existence in 1988; Soviet law was amended to allow private formation of very small enterprises in certain trades (food-service, craft production, maintenance and repair, and the like). Within a short time, newly founded cooperatives became a visible part of the Moscow landscape and a hot topic of Moscow conversation. Most of this conversation was disapproving; cooperative owners were termed speculators, and their activities were defined as "schemes to get rich quick by cheating the people." The infamous exploits of a few cooperatives (such as ABV, which secretly tried to sell stolen Soviet tanks to a European buyer) stoked the telling of these stories and the general characterization of coops as sleazy, suspicious, mafia-run enterprises.[16]

But discourse of this type was nothing if not self-examining—as John Thompson (1990: 21) puts it, "a pre-interpreted domain." There were as many conversations about why Russians denigrated the coops as there were conversations denigrating the coops (and often both conversations were rolled into one). One of the most often-voiced social truisms of the perestroika years went like this: "the Russian *narod* would rather destroy the whole village than let someone get more than his or her share." This crucial bit of cultural gospel was pronounced far and wide, from pulpits

---

[15] The tales of Daniil Kharms, a writer who died in the 1930s, perfectly capture the peculiarly Russian style of appreciation of these kinds of violent mêlées. The behavior of people in sugar and vodka lines comes up often in his short-short stories. Zoshchenko's famous tales also capture this phenomenon vividly.

[16] Interestingly enough, cooperative owners quickly formed a caste-like self-definition as honest, liberal, forward-looking, hard-working business people. Once when I was trying to rent an apartment, the cooperator-acquaintance who was helping me said about a prospective landlord (apartment holder), "Oh, you can trust him, he's a cooperator." Within a very short time, he had assumed a professional identity and a concomitant affiliation with others of his ilk. Later, he absconded with large sums of money from his own partner, at which point I assume he developed a new story.

both private and public, as a joke and as a tragic truth, by people who despised this desire to level the social field and by people who promoted it, and most often by people who bemoaned it at the same time as they could not escape endorsing it and sympathizing with it themselves, at least in certain contexts or applications.[17]

During late perestroika, this uncontrollable passion for leveling was the preferred (native) explanation for the fact of Russian economic nondevelopment, which was said to be the result of people's envy for one who has even a little bit more than others, envy that tears apart anything that has been produced over and above the "normal," shared level of existence. "If someone gets rich, everyone else wants to kill him," said one informant:

> they want to make him as poor as they are, even if he has helped them in some way through his industriousness. This is what will happen to the cooperatives. Even if they make life better for people, providing much-needed services—they will be destroyed since Russians cannot stand somebody else getting rich. Russians will kill you for a space in traffic, they will slit your throat if you have a better place in line!

Through this kind of ironic exaggeration—which was very widespread (I heard the same phrase "Russians will kill for a place in line" on ten or twenty separate occasions), people illustrated their idea of the force and intensity of Russian envy. Paradoxically, even when they were decrying this envy, their anecdotes and tales contributed to it, by naturalizing and essentializing it as a part of Russianness, and thus promulgating an image of the national character which, although it seems very nasty, also comes across as trenchantly amusing, generating a sort of "pride in Russian cruelty and absurdity" which Russians observably enjoyed.[18] A favorite type of anecdote summarizes this well: A genie grants one wish each to an Englishman, a Frenchman, and a Russian; the Englishman asks for a coun-

[17] As Dundes argues: "One need not assume that all the folk ideas of a given culture are necessarily mutually reconcilable within a uniform, harmonius worldview matrix" (1972: 99). He invokes, for example, the way that Americans are socialized to value the "rugged individualist model" while being simultaneously indoctrinated to value a democratic principle of cooperation and majority rule.

[18] There is a Russian saying—"to cut off the branch on which you are sitting"—which at the time was often seen depicted in newspaper cartoons and other visual media, as a metaphor for some of the political and economic actions of the day. A popular tale by Gogol, "Friends Turned Enemies," also centers on these exchanges. Other anthropologists may appreciate the fact that there is a long tradition of sorcery and "spoiling" in the Russian village. See Ivanits (1989), Lewin (1990), and Sakharov (1991) for commentary. Taussig's (1987: 394) idea that envy tales explore "implicit social knowledge" is quite applicable here.

try manor and the Frenchman for the ability to attract the most beautiful women; the Russian asks for his neighbor's house to burn down (or his cow to die—this anecdote has innumerable variants).

One beautiful, clear day I was strolling with a friend when a spontaneous version of this joke occurred. "Isn't it beautiful today?" I asked. "Oh yes," he said. "All we need is for a few neighboring houses to burn down, for our neighbors' pets to croak, for there to be some trouble here and there, then it would be a really delightful day!"

Envy tales were related closely to the genre of tales which I call "spitting in the neighbor's soup." In traditional Russian folk tales, there is a significant sub-genre of stories about neighbors spying on each other, cheating each other, tricking each other, fighting, and taking revenge against each other for small offenses such as the intrusions of a goat. In contemporary Russian conversation, there was a similar genre of stories about how badly neighbors treat each other. These were told with great amusement; as if playing off and resisting the socialist-realist icon of mutual help, trust, and giving, these stories fixated on how much comrades and neighbors fought, eavesdropped, tattled, stole, coveted, jinxed, and otherwise made life miserable for each other. The paradigmatic story of this type has the coinhabitants of communal apartments avenging some slight perpetrated by their neighbor by putting hot pepper in, or spitting in, or in the vilest form of this story, urinating in the neighbor's pot of soup which is simmering in the collective kitchen. People found these stories funny because of their fabled idea that, for Russians, revenge is sweeter than reconciliation. I asked an informant to what extent he thought people actually experienced or participated in this nastiness. He answered that "everyone does! Look at communal apartments and offices—hotbeds of hatred!" [19]

Stories of this type were in wide circulation, in part, I think, as a way of throwing forth a vivid contrast to propagandistic illustrations of the goodness of the Soviet people and their indefatigable spirit of cooperation. The construct of mischief done to one's enemies presented a satisfying fantasy of selfishness as a contradiction to the utopian construct of communalism, which itself may have arisen as a contradiction to the peasant actuality of bickering and envy. Clearly these two visions (and forms of practice) have been in long-standing cultural orbit around one another.

---

[19] There are still many communal apartments in Moscow, although most of their inhabitants are elderly persons, divorced people who had to take rooms in communal apartments when splitting up with their spouses, alcoholics, and refugees. It is more and more becoming a marginal lifestyle, but for the wartime generation communal apartments were the norm. As far as offices go, I had many chances to observe or hear about the plotting, envy, and vengeance that goes on among coworkers.

Mischief, Power, and Gender Constructions

As Vera Abdullaeva noted, "the fool in Russian tales might not be smart, but he is wise and cunning. Fools are unencumbered by the romanticism that besets the bright ones. Down-to-earth creatures, fools are happy with what they have. It is the smart ones who turn out to be quite ordinary, even naive. Fools defy the norm, and not just because they are lazy. The smart ones lead boring lives, go to work, look for bargains, and are afraid of being taken advantage of. By contrast, fools are idle, carefree, and happy-go-lucky, and frequently break the rules. The fool is a contemplative, self-sufficient philosopher—the most intimate folk hero" (1996: 224–225).

Abdullaeva's remarks speak to a construction of male identity which appears in day-to-day life as much as it does in Russian folktales. If shopping tales were a predominant genre of stories told by and about Russian women (and used to define Russian women), mischief tales were the outstanding genre through which the identity and nature of the Russian male was exposed, explored, and enjoyed. A certain kind of modestly destructive mischievousness was a key emblem of Russian maleness in broad distribution in Russian talk. It was, similarly, a fiction, a one-dimensional representation of the reality of men, but one that seemed to be marked with value and transmitted widely through several genres. One joke that touched on this subject went:

> What is one Russian?—A fool.
> And two Russians?—A fight.
> And three Russians?—A vodka line.

The joke, of course, was about Russian men. The implication of the first line is dual; it refers both to the fabled (holy) foolishness of Russians and to the Russian idea that it is foolish to be alone. From this it follows that it is better to be with a friend, so as to enjoy a good fight, or best of all to be with two friends—to enjoy a bottle of vodka (three to a bottle is one vodka-drinking norm) and achieve the desired state of drunkenness (after perhaps enjoying another good fight). Thus was male identity, both individual and collective, rhetorically normalized: maleness entailed friendship, which entailed friendly drunken conflict.

Sometimes repressed, due to a sense of the impropriety of discussing certain subjects with women, tales of the drinking, brawling, and sexual wildness of Russian men were nevertheless a popular genre which emerged in certain contexts (at casual parties among close friends or acquaintances of the same age, or at parties where intoxicated or mischievous men might start to tell stories). At one gathering, a friend, Tolia, related the tale of a trip to a beer bar not long before. Beer bars are below-ground rooms where beer is served in huge mugs and consumed standing at high counters. They are like caves, crowded, noisy, dark, dirty, smoky, and reeking of beer. This man regaled our group with descriptions of the "action" in the bar he visited: how it seemed to him that the men were getting drunk just so they could have fights, how mugs were flying around, friends were as if ritually punching each other in the face, falling to the floor, getting up and drinking even more, each holding the other up, laughing, then fighting some more. It seemed that his description might be exaggerated, but the exaggeration made this narrative an epic, a myth, signaling that there was something culturally cherished in the telling. The whole company listened to this story with immense mirth, especially to the parts where Tolia imitated the fight: "*Rrrrrrraz po morde, baaaats, bukh*" (the Russian equivalent of "one straight to the kisser, bam, bop"), repeating these exclamations over and over and gesticulating energetically as the laughter grew more uncontrollable. Tolia offered to bring me to the bar to see the scene for myself, but I never took him up on this invitation. In any case, it was possible to see drunk men fighting on the streets (and, sometimes, drunk women fighting with drunk men). Crowds always gathered to watch (from a safe distance) these bits of street theater, women issuing horrified murmurs, men watching with amusement.[20]

Mêlées such as these were a popular feature of current films, which were full of such scenes (for example, Kira Muratova's "Asthenia Syndrome"). Also popular in 1989–90 were films focused almost entirely on drinking, casual sexual adventures, "anti-social" and marginal lifestyles ("Black Rose—the Emblem of Sorrow, Red Rose—the Emblem of Love" and "Taxi Blues" are just two out of many films in this perestroika-era genre).

At a birthday dinner I attended, Andrei, an eccentric writer, delivered an hour-long monologue about his own sexual mischief, going way overboard in his performance, partly for my benefit. Brazenly, he filled his sentences with quite vivid pornographic language and slang, unusual for someone essentially sober (he drinks little). He exhorted one older woman at the table to go out and have a sex life, to make herself happy (she was long-divorced). Throughout his monologue he used the coarsest Russian profanities possible. He managed to depict sexual life as both sacred and rudimentarily animal; one minute he was saying that the female womb is "the center of the universe" but the next he was describing intimate female

[20] There is a famous proverb which sums up one Russian attitude to such fights: "*Milye braniatsia tol'ko teshatsia*" which can be translated, "Sweethearts abuse one another only to amuse one another."

parts as tricky and disgusting, only good for pleasure. However, he went on to say that:

> Pure pleasure is, I think, the most important in the world. Fucking plays a major role in my life. Even in kindergarten the teachers scolded me for sneaking a look under girls' panties. I even looked under the teacher's panties, as I recall. It's cosmic there, vagina is the essence of creation, of being. I am a real *babnik*—a real fucker. I have to have *babas* [dames, broads]. By the way, I think Western *babas* must be better than our stupid Russian babas—they must know all the sexual tricks and positions; our *babas* are just boring in bed. *Babas* are goddesses, yes, but they are so filthy, so awful. Sex is filthy—I love it, but it is so profane. Drinking tea—that is a spiritual activity, we only do that with those we are close to, colleagues, friends. Sex, you can poke anyone, any *baba* will do.

Note the opposition he set up between profane sexual relations and sacred social intercourse (over tea); what he romanticized in this case was not chivalrous love but the passion of camaraderie.

At another party, I met Nikolai, a devout Christian who was a talented artist and a long-time active member of dissident circles. He was also an active seeker of sexual and alcoholic pleasures; from him and from his friends I heard numerous tales of wild parties, drinking orgies, partner swapping, seaside pick-ups,[21] some of which resulted in marriages, others in unwanted pregnancies, and still others in lovers fighting with angry husbands. My expressions of astonishment at the wildness of these stories (and my demonstration that I was not morally offended) encouraged their flow and embellishment; my informants took a particular thrill in sharing them with an American. His brother informed me, with bemusement, that Nikolai and his friends often went to their church after intense debauchery, confessed to their priest their great remorse over these activities, experienced forgiveness, and started all over again.[22] This image of the

---

[21] Sea-coast vacation resorts are a favorite site for stories of sexual adventures, pick-ups, drinking bouts with untoward results, fights, etc.

[22] In no way do I wish to imply that most Orthodox Christians were sexual mischief-makers. The majority of young believers whom I met followed the rather conservative norms of Soviet Russian society, pursuing something like a temperate bourgeois family ideal. And many devout believers seemed to be trying to personify the ascetic ideals of strict Orthodox Christianity. There is, however, a long tradition of stories about intense debauchery by priests, monks, and other true believers. This is reflected in contemporary literature as well as in many off-color Russian folk stories, proverbs, etc. The stories in *Russkie zavetnye skazki* (Intimate Russian stories), collected by Afanas'iev in the mid-nineteenth century and published in Russia for the first time in 1991, contains no less than a dozen stories concerning the sexual mischief of parish priests. Although these are stories and not histories, it is clear that they point to a complex of behaviors familiar to Russian peasants, and amusing to them as a way to point out the hypocrisies of those with power.

alternation—or the intimate relationship—between profane and sacred behavior is archetypal in Russia, as it is elsewhere (though each culture's representations take their own peculiar shapes).

In April 1990, at a time when stores were continually growing emptier and emptier, much talk went around about the kinds of alcohol to which people were resorting; Gorbachev's anti-alcohol campaign was still going and sales of alcohol were kept very low. At one evening party I attended, a round of stories started with tales of how people were using rubbing alcohol to make cocktails; another person added that he had heard people were using a certain kind of *eau de cologne*; another intensified the story by telling of someone she had heard of who made cocktails out of an oven-cleaning substance. The issue of whether these tales were literally true or not (they probably were) was less important than the mixture of horror, humor, and satisfaction at the Russian willingness to experiment in the quest for intoxication.

Tales (and recipes) like this have been around for a long time, and circulated widely especially during the war years and throughout the *gulag*. But they were distilled in the 1970s in the famous underground novel by Venedikt Erofeev, *Moskva–Petushki*. This widely circulated manuscript, the tale of an alcoholic's long and very drunken attempt to get from Moscow to the town of Petushki, two hours out of Moscow, was beloved among Russian readers of *samizdat* literature. At one point, the author reveals recipes for different kinds of cocktails involving various toxic substances. Since these were only slight exaggerations of real recipes, used by real alcoholics in the absence of other intoxicants, the effect of reading them is devastatingly sad and funny at the same time. A short passage conveys a bit of Erofeev's marvelously poignant irony:

> I present to you the cocktail "Bitches' Brew," a beverage which overshadows all others. This is more than a beverage—it is the music of the spheres. What is the finest thing in the world? The struggle for the liberation of humanity. But even finer is this (write it down):
>
> | Zhiguli Beer | 100 g. |
> | "Sadko" Shampoo | 30 g. |
> | Dandruff Treatment | 70 g. |
> | Athlete's Foot Remedy | 30 g. |
> | Small Bug Killer | 20 g. |
>
> The whole thing is steeped for a week in cigar tobacco and served at table.
> (Erofeev 1980: 70)

It has been suggested that Erofeev's besotted literary journey is structured around the stages of the cross; the protagonist-narrator is in constant communion with a host of angels (as well as a panoply of bottles). The author is clearly celebrating, in his very idiosyncratic way, the other-worldly logic so familiar to Russian speakers, a logic in which the beatific is found in the brutal, the lofty in the banal, the sacred in the profane. This text is about multiple transcendences: through his devout drinking and other forms of mischief Erofeev's protagonist transcends the strictures not only of day-to-day existence but indeed of all practicality and purpose-fulness—especially the utopian purposes of the state.

In May 1990, after years of drinking, struggling to survive as a laborer and translator while writing his own works, and trying to create some peace for himself, Venedikt Erofeev died of throat cancer; he was in his early fifties.[23] As befits an Orthodox believer, his body was laid out, and his soul was "sung out" at the Donskoi Monastery in Moscow. The church, the churchyard, and part of the street was packed with friends and devoted readers mourning his passing, standing all afternoon as the priests chanted and sang. Why did this tale of desperate, completely deranged, and disoriented drunkenness become for so many people a sacred text, its author labeled a "prophet" in the literary press—even though the work was officially published in Russia only in the very last years of Erofeev's life?

Sacred mischief-making, as a genre of both behavior and narrative, is one mode—a very popular and recognized mode—of mounting a challenge to the pragmatism and material concerns of everyday life while also mocking the (often absurd) rationalism of state projects and promotions. While alcoholism as a bio-medical/social phenomenon is a serious and tragic problem in Russian families and for the polity as a whole, alcoholism as a performative/narrative phenomenon offers endless possibilities for an elaboration of ironic resistance to the mundane, practical disciplines of family, community, and state. At the same time, however, fantastic state projects which defy the laws of nature may have some parallels with fantastic bouts or lifetimes of drinking which ensure their own surrealistic existence.

Although mischief might initially seem to be a particularly male form of resistance, it may also be seen as belonging to the entire population, which through exhibitions and tales of male mischief could celebrate the inability of authoritarian systems and practical utility in general fully to repress or shape life practices.[24] Erofeev's mischievous prose, which fol-

---

[23] For some interesting biographical details, see his letters to his sister, published in the journal *Teatr*, 1992 no. 9 (September).
[24] Female mischief was clearly implied by male mischief. Some women were open about their carousing, just as some women smoked openly on the street. But female steadfastness has long been of great symbolic and spiritual value in Russia, so female debauchery was

lowed in the lush Russian tradition of absurdist writing, challenged official representations of "Soviet Man" with a vivid picture of the beloved Russian sot-on-a-binge, trying to make his way home, that Russians could not help but sympathize with and be amused by, even though they may have been horrified at the same time. Erofeev himself symbolized challenge on three fronts: he was at once religious, mischievous, and defiant of official power with his "underground" creativity—which represented the secret, mischievous, and ultimately mystical Russian "soul."

In official Soviet representations (socialist realism) the serious, responsible male image dominated. It would be going too far to say that Soviet aesthetic dictatorship and censorship allowed nothing else, since around the edges of the normative representation of the iron-jawed, iron-willed man of socialist morality there always hovered other, more mischievous (and more interesting) archetypes. The effort and investment put into the development and propagation of the sober, serious male model was, however, extraordinary. Ironically, although I heard few stories about it, in actuality this type of self-representation/self-production seemed predominant; that is, most of the men I saw or spoke with expressed, through their anecdotal life histories or other narratives, sincere commitment to their work, their families, their society, and their own sobriety.

Mischief was, then, not so much a typical way of being for men as it was a symbolic tale of resistance, autonomy, and transcendence of the social order which many Russians enjoyed telling each other and occasionally acting out. The same philosopher who explained the concepts of *narod* and *dusha* (Chapter 1) described the whole realm of mischief—especially extramarital mischief—as "the zone of freedom."

> In some ways all of this was considered to be legitimate; it was a free area where anyone could basically do whatever he could, the only area where one could exercise initiative and smarts, wits, and so on. People were interested in it, even old women would laugh at jokes and tales about it . . . well, for instance, there is a joke where the husband comes home; the lover hides under the bed; the husband figures out that something is up and

---

always much more secret. In fictional representations it almost certainly required a tragic ending, which male debauchery can escape. A good example of this was the film *Interdevochka*, which was very popular in 1989–90. This film concerned a young "hard-currency prostitute" in St. Petersburg who met and married a Swedish customer, became a Swedish wife, suffered boredom and depression, and caused the death by sorrow of her own mother. The *interdevochka* died in a self-caused car accident on the way to the airport to attend her mother's funeral. Russian cultural logic dictated that this young woman suffer and die for her sexual and drinking transgressions, as well as for transgressing the borders of her motherland. As Marjorie Balzer pointed out (personal communication), Anna Karenina is surely the original *interdevochka*.

tosses some chocolate under the bed, and suddenly they hear chewing. . . .
This was always regarded as a free zone, even in pre-revolutionary Russia;
peasant humor is full of sexual adventures and deceptions. This was always the only place where people could be free, even for an hour, steal
some kind of fun which they were not supposed to have. This is how you
could get more from life than you are entitled to.

Although old women might laugh at some jokes about mischief, it was
also clear that mischief stood in symbolic and sometimes literal opposition
to the forms of control emblematized and exercised by the mature female
part of the population. Several very commonly encountered genres of Russian speaking were predominantly female genres that could be grouped
under the general rubric of "discourses about social order" and generally
focused on the maintenance of behavioral order ("good manners"), on the
one hand, and classificatory order (observation of traditional cultural distinctions), on the other. "Women are the implements of totalitarianism in
Russia," said one informant (a woman), "they are the tools of conformism.
By ruling in their families with an iron fist, they uphold the entire social
order." Russians widely maintained that through gossip, nagging, scolding, advising, and the other discursive mechanisms at their command, as
well as through their occupation of key posts of social control (as bureaucrats, teachers, doctors, etc.) women contained and controlled men, other
women, and, of course, children, and thus had an important shaping influence on society as a whole. In Moscow, I encountered examples of these
generic forms widely; a detailed discussion of all their styles and ramifications would require a separate study. Here I would like to comment on
only a couple of features of these discourses.

Many imprecations, reproaches, and instructions given by women were
constructed so as to point to (and thus recommend or demand) cultural
norms of behavior. In response to "bad" behavior, women often scolded
by saying, "What uncultured behavior!" The Russian terms *nekul'turnyi,
nevospitannyi*, and *nevyderzhannyi* (uncultured, uneducated, and unrestrained) were epithets commonly used to signal impropriety; one woman
scolded her little granddaughter for failing to thank me for taking her picture: "Who is an uneducated person?"[25] In public settings, linguistic offenses (using obscenities), bodily offenses (sitting improperly), offenses
against norms of politeness (such as not giving up one's seat on the Metro
to an elderly person or speaking loudly in public), and offenses against
gender norms (women smoking openly while walking along the street)

---

[25] A belief exists in Russia that if one says thank you after having a picture taken, the frame
will turn out blank; maybe the tiny girl knew more than her grandmother?

often provoked female scolding based around the terms mentioned. Hundreds of small and large mistakes could be made in public that would call forth these epithets from strangers, almost always older women (though older men also could scold quite well). Breaking into lines and other major public infractions resulted in even more active scolding, again with older women taking the lead; this genre of scolding could sometimes produce real marvels of oratory.

The oft-remarked brusqueness of Russian saleswomen was, in fact, a genre of this scolding variety. Foreigners encountering it for the first time usually interpreted it as pure rudeness stemming from the fact that there is no incentive to be polite in the absence of free market competition. In fact, the saleswomen's way of speaking to customers was a mark of social class and category, an expressive genre which in many ways was an essential part of the entire sport of shopping. Private scolding and instruction were also performed mainly by women, who were thus charged with and in discursive control of defining and reproducing the boundaries of proper, normal, Russian behavior.

The second feature of women's scolding and complaining is that it was often focused around the fetishized ideal of social order in general, as if women had an eye on society as a whole. Individual exhibitions of improper behavior frequently called forth exclamations about the decay of social order generally, about the decline of morals, principles, decency, and spirituality. I go into this in more detail in the section on women's litanies (Chapter 3); but here it is important to note that women's discourse often projected an icon of societal order (in Russian: *poriadok*), which embraced everything from domestic tidiness to an abstract but vaunted sphere of "spiritual values."

These female-owned discourses, although cast in a semi-religious idiom, tended to dovetail with Soviet propaganda about decency, morality, and good behavior (itself cast in a religious idiom and tone). The genres of mischievous behavior and talk (marked as male genres) were thus oppositionally related to these markedly "female," order-upholding, morality-proclaiming genres.

To what extent these female genres were expressions or signs of real power in (self-proclaimedly patriarchal) Russian society is hard to measure. Indeed, there was a bountiful repertoire of jokes, proverbs, and other discursive mechanisms that played on the paradoxes entailed by the co-existence of different forms or realms of social power. This power-sharing was often taken as an entertaining paradox in the face of an ancient tradition of absolutist patriarchal ideologies and ideologies about the absolutism of Russian patriarchy (two rather different things). A joke that I heard twice from men and once from a woman (the details each time were slightly different) satirizes this paradox and the cultural ideologies which circulated around and through it:

A wife, talking to a friend about her marriage, says, "I make all the trivial, unimportant decisions—where we will vacation, if we will move to a new apartment, if we will buy a car. . . . My husband makes the really important decisions in the family, you know: can we build Communism in one country? Should the two Germanies reunite?

This joke played with the question of what constitutes real power in both families and nations, at the same time that it mocked male demonstrations of powerfulness and satirized male and female representations of female subservience. A related category of speech, "tales women tell about husbands," also supported the paradoxes (and structures) of male–female relations. This was a genre told from a stance which managed to combine complaint, comedy, condescension, and indulgence. Masha, who married a musician towards the end of my stay in the field, described her life thus:

Aliosha likes his life very much; he wants nothing to change! In the morning his mother, who lives upstairs in our building, makes his kasha [porridge]. I go up in the elevator and get it and bring it down for him. His mother does his laundry; I do all the shopping and cook dinner for him. I go on errands for him all over town—he is too busy building his career in the theater. He has the psychology of a little boy: he looks at his life as if from the side, not really attached to it, almost a nonparticipant in his own existence. He is like a little boy.

This account was told to me cheerfully and even with pride, perhaps in her own just-discovered maternal abilities and capacities. Lara, a middle-aged woman, laughingly depicted her husband's ways about the house:

He has really excellent tricks; he has it all worked out so that in the end he does not do anything. One day he rages and scolds and yells if I ask him to do the slightest thing: go to the store, for instance; I end up doing it myself instead of facing that abuse. His more common technique is just not to do anything—he just waits and ignores everything, does not even feed himself, so that in the end I start in and do it because I cannot stand it. Another good trick he has—he starts doing something, peeling potatoes for example, but he does it so haphazardly, peels are flying around the kitchen, half the potato ends up being wasted . . . that I cannot stand it and end up taking over. He is so clever! He knows how to get everything exactly as he wants it, so that he is the tsar and I am his servant who does everything for him.

Olga, a professional woman in her early forties, offered this fable, which was both joking and complaining:

We were a progressive couple; it was in the 1970s and we lived together for about a year before we got married. He was generous; he did almost all the cooking, he kept the house immaculately clean, he was a real darling. Then we got married and the very next day he somehow completely forgot how to boil water or fry an egg—and to this day he has not remembered how.

Natalia's account came across more as pure complaint, although it was couched in a historical perspective:

You have to understand, you have to grasp the history here. The generation that is adult now, my generation, was raised by women who went through the war and lost lots of men. For them, men are utterly precious beings, whom they raised as little gods, investing all in them, spoiling them terrifically, appreciating their very presence on the earth. Now these same men are husbands, they demand the same from their wives that their mothers gave them. Even though he goes to work very early, and I work late at night, my husband demands that I get up at six in the morning to fix his morning coffee. If I refuse, if, for instance, I just sleep through, he will be mad at me the whole day, refuse to speak, go around pouting, and so on. We have discussed this a thousand times; I have explained that it is unfair, impractical. I have offered to organize everything the night before so that he can fix his own coffee easily himself. He refuses even to heed my argument.

A somewhat different historical take on these relations came from Tania, a social scientist in her late thirties:

Soviet life has made human beings absurd. Soviet life is absurd life, we have had seventy years of absurdity. Especially the men are not normal here; they are totally warped by the system—women, after all, have their domestic lives, a woman can take pride, create a sense of herself by taking care of the house, the family, her husband, but men cannot, and they cannot provide for their families either, as in any normal society in the world, because the system will not let them really accomplish anything. So they become just pathetic, pathetic creatures. Men feel domesticated, turned into domestic pets. They want a little drama; sometimes they get it by becoming little tyrants in their families. That is the only power they can enjoy.

All these stories reflected and reproduced a structure of relations between spouses defined less by patriarchal principles than by maternalism—to call this matriarchy would hardly do. These stories turned patriarchy upside down via mini-exposés of intrafamilial relations: in them the patriarch was merely a spoiled little boy (albeit one who could make life miserable) in domestic orbit around the all-controlling, all-managing, all-giving mother. These stories—be they cultural clichés, fairy-tales, or accurately descriptive—were extensively and constantly circulated, serving to help reproduce certain expectations regarding male and female behavior and relationships.[26] Even the mourning or mocking of this norm was a key to its reproduction in society over time; I have discussed this at greater length elsewhere (Ries 1994). The same narratives that, while lamenting these structures, strived to explain them via historical contextualization actually validated and even valorized them by constructing Russian men as victims of history in one or another form, with women as the eternal attendants and caretakers of sacrificial males.

The absence of men has been a prevailing theme in Russia, among all classes, for several hundred years. From the time of Peter the Great until the end of serfdom in 1861, peasant men could be forcibly conscripted from their home villages for army service (which might mean a term of up to twenty-five years, in effect for life, depending on the era). After that, peasants were conscripted for relatively shorter terms, but conscription nonetheless had a significant effect on the male population (see Bushnell 1985). During industrialization around the turn of the century, millions of peasant men went to work in factories in towns and cities, while their mothers, wives, and children remained in the villages;[27] major wars took even more away, as did rural collectivization (Fitzpatrick 1994: 218), exile, and labor camps. The paradigm of a society based on the steadfast presence of women and the habitual loss or absence of men, and the narratives and other communicative genres that accompanied this paradigm (marking it, decrying it, making it poignant, making it valuable), thus have a

[26] Sociological studies have shown the wide spread of such relations in Soviet/Russian society. See, for example, Lapidus (1978) and Porokhniuk and Shepeleva (1982). Natalia Baranskaia's novelette, "A Week Like Any Other" (1969) presents a poignant literary representation of male irresponsibility and the female double burden in the household. See also Dunham (1960) and Sariban (1984).

[27] In the post-emancipation period, many women and children also went to the cities, where they too worked in factories and sweatshops, and lived in factory-owned barracks and dormitories. See Glickman (1984).

long tradition; among Russian folk songs, a great number touch in some way on this theme of lost or absent men. Most of these songs, narrated from a woman's point of view, combine mourning and pining with promises of unwavering faithfulness. (Of course, there are also many anecdotes and folktales that undermine this image of faithfulness by depicting the wife running to her lover as soon as the husband leaves; no powerful social image can remain unsatirized). Many of the stories that Russians told, and the stances that Russian women and men adopted, derived from or in other ways related to this key scenario, which casts men as desired, important, perhaps wounded (or self-wounding) visitors in a symbolically female society—that is, a society built by, on, and through the labors, discourses, and demands of the female, or, as I have heard some Russian women say, on the bodies of women (one feminist commented to me that Russian women are "cannibalized").

Structurally, the symbolic female was the omnipresent horizontal field that supported the occasional, celebrated vertical rise of the symbolic male.[28] However, while the horizontal/female and vertical/male were complementary fields of power and activity, each requiring the other and defining itself in contentedly contrastive relation to the other, in another mode they were agonistic fields, battling it out in the realms of narrative. As I have argued above, male mischief was acted out and savored in popular telling as a social/discursive uprising against the domesticating efforts and oratories of the level and orderly female sphere. But as Tania's story suggested, mischief is what men had to make in the absence of dramatic political events and cataclysms like war and revolution.[29] In their tales about themselves, men "*guliali*"—stepped out, caroused—as a way to absent themselves and thus fulfill the paradigmatic cultural plot. Challenging the primacy of the tale of female sacrifice-by-endurance which surrounded them, men created a colorful drama of male extremism, male battles, and male absence via their shared construction of mischief.

[28] Resonances of this archetypal spatial symbolism can be found throughout Russian folk art—for example, in the most basic motif of traditional Russian embroidery, the diamond divided into four smaller diamonds, which is the main symbol of female, field, and fertile earth (male figures make extremely rare appearances in Russian embroidery—which is a horizontal female field); or, in the binary principle of Russian folk dances, where female dances are based on movement in fluid, horizontal lines across the space of the dance while male dances are composed of many kinds of dramatic leaps, emphasizing male occupation of vertical space. Hellberg (1986) comments on the role this spatial symbolism played in Soviet ritual.

[29] That mischief and male sacrifice in war are related is reinforced by the existence of military discourse, which stresses the importance of military service in the formation of men. In an interview, one general with whom I spoke discussed at great length the idea that military service is "the male university." This image was encountered widely in the media.

A slightly more intense version of the mischief tale was created through the popular reproduction of images of male dangerousness. Early in my stay in the field, one man with whom I was acquainted professionally insisted that I should be very careful about conducting interviews with men, because all Russian men are dangerous when alone with a woman. Another male friend, who later became my husband, tried on a number of occasions to talk me out of meeting men for interviews. Once he became very agitated upon learning that I was going to meet an artist and his wife. "There is no wife!" he insisted. "Artists are very dangerous sexually! He is bound to attack you!" When I insisted that there could be no danger, because I had spoken to the man's wife over the phone, he said "Go, if you want to; get what you deserve for not listening"—a true folktale line, in Propp's terms, an interdiction. (I often violated interdictions of this kind, with no untoward results). Several male informants, themselves strangers who I was interviewing alone, warned me to be careful about being alone with other men.

While I never doubted the potential dangerousness of some men, since male aggressive insistence was readily observable and sometimes experienced, the myth of male danger seemed more a form of self-creation than a description of reality. One acquaintance enjoyed talking about what a scary, potentially violent man he is, forceful and hot of temper where his interests are concerned. Although what I observed of his behavior suggested that he was actually rather shy, his stories about his own toughness depicted a heroic, threatening, avenging figure. (This mythology of the dangerous man also allowed many men to construct themselves as gentle, responsible exceptions—probably a very important ramification of all this talk).

An affiliated mythification occured around the image of Russia, which through one complex of images and tales was portrayed as being terrible, rapacious, violent, and ruthless. This "masculine" facet of Russian self-portrayal stood in contrast to the complex of "feminine" national self-representations.[30] Myths or fables about Russia's dangerous "masculine" countenance were widely traded and enjoyed, appearing in the press and on television in various (sometimes subtle) forms as well as in oral transmission. One set of representations concerned Russia's danger to

[30] These two complexes could also be viewed as representations of Russia as male and female. Both valences were actively acknowledged and employed; they were culturally complementary rather than contradictory. Thus, Russian has the two nearly (although not entirely) interchangeable words, *rodina*—motherland, homeland, native land; and *otechestvo*—fatherland, native land. *Rodina* certainly has a more sentimental, nostalgic, even tragic tenor, while *otechestvo* has a sterner, more political quality. The differences in the deployment of these two words is a fascinating subject; see Cherniavsky (1961).

the West; privately spun tales of this sort interestingly dovetailed with older, that is, pre-perestroika official stances, ideologies, and national self-representations. At one point during the rambling monologue that I quoted before, the writer Andrei declared that

> The West has everything: food, commodities, even excellent women—so it is of course, extremely frightened by the USSR. Having everything, and knowing that we can destroy everything the West possesses by the push of one button, the West is desperate to see signs here of humanitarian culture. So the CPSU dishes some out in the form of poetry, the arts, to reassure Western peoples. . . . But it is a hoax.

The inclusion of "excellent women" in his list of "what the West has" signaled the relationship of this speech about the state to a trope of sexual conquest (or annihilation); here, the threatening USSR and the threatened West. Andrei's explanation of current history was relayed with an ambiguous attitude, combining pride in the savage magnificence of this threat and genuine disdain for the anti-humanistic ruthlessness of the CPSU. Tales like these about the menacing USSR were fairly common, sometimes related very seriously; many Russians expressed their full support of Margaret Thatcher's and Ronald Reagan's hard-line policies toward the Soviet Union, and declared that such firm, even aggressive stances towards the USSR were necessary to prevent their own nation's inclination to international mischief. There is nothing more flattering and bolstering to one's self-image as dangerous than to be taken as dangerous by a powerful enemy; and Russian talk (both private and public) which acclaimed the courage and resolve of the West vis-à-vis the "Soviet threat" was a roundabout exercise of self-appreciation of Russian mischievousness and strength.

At other times this mocking–appreciative self-representation was created through sardonic humor about the threat that Russia (the USSR) presented to world order (which nonetheless reveals a certain pride in awfulness). There was, for instance, a whole genre of jokes about how terrible things would be when Communism took over in other places, such as "what would happen if Communists took the Sahara Desert? In a few years even the sand would be in short supply" (Zand 1982: 25). On one level, as political resistance, these jokes and tales served to contradict the perpetual flow of state propaganda about the Soviet Union's role as the architect of true world order and prosperity. But on another level they glorified and reproduced the image of the Russian male / Russian *narod* as a powerful, menacing, mischievous hooligan, wreaking havoc on the so-

cieties and economies he/it touches, contaminating and spoiling everything along the way.

Every tale and every corpus of tales encounters its contradiction, however; as Luthi (1976: 364) writes, "Proverbs call for their opposite or for a
parody on them." Contradicting tales of male mischief were stories and
other talk forms in which images of male self-control reigned. In the
course of his long and graphic soliloquy, Andrei told a tale that rather
contradicted his other ideas and self-representations. "No human ever
achieved anything without conscience," he said, and spun the following
legend:

> I happen to know a man who is a really good wrestler, a champion fighter,
> a giant of a man, both in body and in soul. One night he was at a club with
> his girlfriend, a beautiful woman with whom he was in love, and another
> friend, also a professional wrestler. Four drunks, looking to pick a fight,
> insulted his girlfriend right in front of him. But he refused to fight them,
> knowing that with one blow he would make life-long invalids of all four
> of them, that he could cripple them easily with no difficulty. In spite of the
> insult, he followed his conscience. His friend immediately started fighting
> them, and made cripples of them. After that the girlfriend was really mad,
> since he would not defend her honor, and she left him right away and
> went off with his friend. But he kept what was most important . . . his
> conscience. And with a drop of conscience, a person can achieve some-
> thing in life—in poetry, in sports, whatever.

This fable started with the possibility of mischief but moved from the
mischief tale into the genre of Russian epic, where giant men roam the
social landscape and exercise their noble souls. Ironically, this tale echoed
certain socialist realist plots, contradicting mischief, positing something
supposedly greater, higher, and nobler: masculine power restrained.

But a joke I heard turns this kind of tale on its head, subverting the
drama of the male *podvig*. It was told to me by an older man whom I interviewed, who included many droll anecdotes such as this one in his narratives about the Great Patriotic War (World War II). "Well, the subject
of heroism reminds me of a joke we used to tell each other all the time,"
he said.

> There's a barge. There's a woman on deck . . . but then suddenly she has
> fallen overboard. People shout: "Look, a woman is drowning!" There are
> lots of sympathetic exclamations and cries but nobody does anything.
> Then one man, diving overboard, saves the woman. Back on deck, every-

body praises him, practically lifting him up, surging with gratitude and high appreciation: "A hero, a hero, what heroism!," but the man finally gets a word in and says, "Wait a minute with your damned heroism and tell me: who the devil shoved me overboard?"

This anecdote was a reference to the wartime practice whereby Red Army officers would stand in the rear and shoot their own soldiers if these failed to advance under orders (sometimes clearly to their own deaths) and then praise the heroism of these same unwilling soldiers. At the same time, especially in its contemporary telling, it is a subversive reference to the whole corpus of discourse—official and private—about the value of self-sacrifice.[31]

Sacrifice vs. Mischief: Male vs. Female?

This brings us back to the beginning, to tales of feminine endurance and self-sacrifice. What general points can be made about the narratives encountered in this brief excursion?

First, it must be stressed that sagas like the one about the wrestler, valorizing male restraint, were encountered less often than male mischief tales, or tales and anecdotes that made fun of heroism. If the female envy tale is eclipsed by the endurance tale, the socialist-realist type of hero tale is well eclipsed by the mischief tale. Two clusters of social value emerge from all these stories and can be viewed in relation to each other thus:

Order	Endurance	Generosity	Heroism
Mischief	Resistance	Envy	Roguery

Initially it may seem that we could unambiguously call one of these sets of values socially constructive and the other destructive. But the Russian case calls for a more nuanced view of these attributes, one that takes into consideration the operations of power in the historical Russian/Soviet context. The first set of terms (above the line) corresponds exactly to some of the values glorified, advertised, propagandized, promulgated, sacrali-

---

[31] Thurston (1991) shows the extent to which such satirical anecdotes circulated throughout the Stalin era. As Emil Draitser pointed out (personal conversation), this anecdote hinges on the fact that it is a woman who has fallen overboard, and thus comments on (and contributes to) the devaluation of women by men. See Draitser (1982; 1989) for interesting discussions of Russian joking in general.

zed, and decreed by Soviet ideologues. The most widespread way of re-taining personal autonomy under Soviet rule was not through the political dissidence about which so much has been written but rather through the informal scorning of those values that were so cloyingly and ubiquitously touted by official cant, pedagogy, and sloganeering. So mischief, resis-tance, envy, and roguery have, in fact, been popularly treated if not as unambiguously positive values, then at least affectionately—as amusing, refreshing, spontaneous, and free. In terms of gender, what was positively marked (by frequency and emphasis) in tales about women was nega-tively marked (by infrequency and minimization) in tales about men:

Female endurance	Male mischief
Female mischief (envy)	Male endurance (restraint)

Narratives stressed the connection of women with the values of order, endurance, generosity, and heroism, and thus reinforced an association of female values and official values, which emphasized the same attributes. Male talk that put down official power (and there was no shortage of such talk) was, by metonymic association, also putting down female power, however paradoxical this seems. Of course, the reverse often obtained as well.

There are, arguably, several social consequences of the mischief com-plex (defined as two mutually penetrating and sustaining fields: behavior and talk). Aside from the immediate hazards of alcohol abuse in the work-place, mischief stories subtly consecrate the pilfering, monkey-wrenching, and lethargic nonchalance that have plagued (and continue to plague) Russian industry. On the one hand, these must be seen as creative forms both of survival and of resistance to the disciplinary modes of the state. On the other hand, they are, of course, quite problematic from a macro-economic point of view; and throughout Russian history, until pere-stroika, this problem always triggered totalitarian responses aimed at turning men into obedient and careful producers.

In 1989 and 1990, many voices were already raised against the celebra-tion of sex, drinking, and brawling that under perestroika became key performative symbols of freedom, and the August 1991 coup was, in part, an attempt to put all that back into the bottle of social control.

Fortunately, that effort failed, but instead of socio-economic rationali-zation and the internalization of Western-style discipline and produc-tivity that many people expected to materialize spontaneously, to a sig-nificant extent post-Soviet Russia has been characterized by the enshrinement of what I would call "deep mischief" in all its forms: drinking, gambling, sexual carousing, and the brutal—if entertaining—criminality of the mafia. In recent research in Russia (1994 and 1995), I have often wondered about the extent to which the pre-existing mischief complex provided the symbolic materials for the development of certain kinds of post-Soviet selves and practices. In the process of creating themselves as Russian women and Russian men, as responsible and mischievous characters in a fascinating chapter—the perestroika chapter—of "the Russia tale," were not people also continually pushing the story into the future, producing the raw materials of the next chapter as they occupied, interacted within, and even perhaps thrilled to the one going on around them?

CHAPTER THREE

Litanies and Laments:
The Discursive Art of Suffering

I think that the most basic, most rudimentary spiritual need of the Russian people is the need for suffering, ever-present and unquenchable, everywhere and in everything. It seems that the *narod* has been infected with this thirst for suffering since the beginning of time. This stream of suffering runs through all its history, not only summoned by external misfortune and poverty, but welling up like a spring from the very heart of the people. There is an indispensable measure of suffering even in the happiness of the Russian *narod*, for without it its happiness is incomplete. Never, even in the most festive moments of its history, does it bear a look of pride and celebration as much as one of being moved to torment. . . . It is almost as if the Russian *narod* delights in its own suffering.
— F. M. Dostoevsky, *Diary of a Writer*

Russians have always had in their hearts a special place for *victims*. You are right in saying the war was an incomparable catastrophe. But the victims of that catastrophe—the millions and millions of war dead, the countless orphans and widows—shall always, yes always merit our compassion, and our love.
— An elderly Moscow woman, cited in Tumarkin, *The Living and the Dead*

Of all the distinctive Russian speech genres, I would argue that the genre I have termed "litany" (Ries 1991) had a special significance during perestroika. Litanies encapsulated several dominant perspectives on the social transformations which were occurring and provided a crucial frame and set of semiotic codes through which people could process the tumultuous events of the day. At the same time, litanies effected paradoxical value transformations through which suffering engendered distinction, sacrifice created status, and loss produced gain. This chapter focuses on the litany as a speech genre that may have helped to sustain relative powerlessness and alienation from the political process at the same time as it lamented them.

Litanies were the building blocks of many of the conversations, both casual and formal, in which I took part or which I overheard during my fieldwork. The fact of overhearing was important because it tested the extent to which my presence—as foreigner, American, ethnographer, and stranger—affected the discourses I heard. Of course, my presence did affect the conversations in which I took part. In many cases, it was clear that people were litanizing, or doing so in particularly intense ways, precisely because they had an interested American listener. I was paying attention to people's stories of their life struggles; in a context where so many were suffering the same hardships, getting attention for one's own tales of hardship was often impossible. Furthermore, the litany encoded a subtle form of supplication, an implicit petition for assistance, and because of our relatively abundant power and resources, Americans were a logical object of entreaty. For these reasons, my presence surely stimulated the outpouring of litanies from my interlocutors. But the genre existed quite independently, echoing throughout Moscow at the time.

I heard litanies in subway cars, buses, and trains; on the street; during evening gatherings and holiday meals; in meetings of many different kinds of groups, committees, and panels; on television and radio discussion programs; in plays, films, and documentaries;[1] and in rehearsed or spontaneous declamations at political rallies. I also encountered them in all sorts of written texts. Many letters to the editors of the journal *Ogonek* and other Russian magazines took the form of litanies (for examples in English, see Riordan and Bridger 1992; Korotich 1990).

The Genre of Litanies

Litanies were those passages in conversation in which a speaker would enunciate a series of complaints, grievances, or worries about problems, troubles, afflictions, tribulations, or losses, and then often comment on these enumerations with a poignant rhetorical question ("Why is everything so bad with us?"), a sweeping, fatalistic lament about the hopelessness of the situation, or an expressive Russian sigh of disappointment and resignation.

---

[1] To give just a few examples of these publically performed litanies: On January 26, 1990, the liberal television news/variety program *Vzgliad* featured a segment showing the mothers of Russian reservists surrounding the Military Headquarters in Stavropol, demanding their sons' return; those mothers interviewed spoke in litanies and laments. Liudmila Petrushevskaia's play *Moscow Chorus* (*Moskovskii Khor*), which had its first officially sanctioned performances during perestroika, was composed of one litany after another, though Petrushevskaia is a genius at taking these to absurd lengths. The film documentaries of Sviatislav Govorukhin, such as *The Russia . . . That We Lost* (*Rossiia . . . kotoruiu my poteriali*) are litanies in their entirety. As an aside I should mention that many of Chekhov's plays (which I attended regularly while in Moscow) are full of litanies—a point which illustrates the temporal continuity of this speech genre.

One day I visited Natalia Viktorovna, a well-known and honored historian in her late fifties, for an interview in her book-filled apartment. She insisted on feeding me something while we talked, and we went into her small kitchen, where she made some toast with melted cheese and several small salads. I sat at her kitchen table as she chopped vegetables and spoke. For about half an hour she enumerated the various difficulties facing Russia; she mentioned shortages, official corruption, the spread of crime, the inefficiency of Russian workers, then went back to the topic of shortages. At this point she stopped cutting cabbage for a moment, and wielding her knife dramatically, she lamented,

> Such a life we have, a real theater, theater of the absurd. The things that happen here could never happen anywhere else, they could never happen in a civilized country like America. Do you understand what it means for the people that there is no aspirin, no insulin? The last meat I saw was nearly rotten, and so overpriced at that, who can afford it? This motherland of ours is so unfortunate, so unfortunate.

From this point, she went back to the beginning, offering additional, vivid examples of Soviet corruption and inefficiency, the difficulty of living with the breakdown in social services wrought by perestroika, and the decay in values she saw in contemporary Moscow. Her litany ceased only as I was leaving, when she kindly invited me to come back any time, saying, "I can't offer you more than a modest supper, living on my pension as I do, but it's nice to have someone to talk with. You are an unusual foreigner; you understand what our Russian life is like, how we live."

The litanies I heard could be elongated and detailed, as was Natalia's, each segment composed of a story illustrating the theme at hand. The segments could be as short as one word, however, as when one war veteran, an engineer in his sixties, speaking of how he was generally an optimistic person, prone to expect progress and change for the better, became momentarily pensive, and said, "However, sometimes, when I look around, and see all the vandalism, barbarity, drunkenness, degradation, criminality . . . Well, it is difficult not to lose hope." He pronounced the five key words in the typical musical intonation that marked the elevation of a commentary to the level of litany.

The different elements in a litany were usually related to each other through syntactical parallelism[2] or through thematic affinity. Sometimes

---

[2] On the structuring role of parallelism in Russian oral poetry, songs, epics, and laments, see Jakobson (1966). It is hardly coincidental that more spontaneous, day-to-day discourse forms like the litanies I describe here relied on this concatenating mechanism as much as do the formal genres discussed in Jakobson's analysis.

entire litanies were voiced by a single speaker, but they also appeared dialogically, with each speaker in a group adding her or his own element to the series. Russian litanies could be voiced with irony (or even self-parody), and they could be used to enumerate more positive elements of the social landscape, but the genre was usually marked by its very straightforwardly lamenting quality. Conversational litanies were intonationally similar to three more formal genres of Russian speech, the traditional lament (a strictly female genre), Orthodox church litanies, and the declamatory style of Russian poetry reading. Like these genres, litanies often involved a bitonal recitative style, poetic cadences, rhyme, and an overall circularity.

Conversational litanies shared many of these features. They often displayed an entreating attitude, although, significantly, in late perestroika the object of those entreaties was not at all clear; this lack of a distinct savior was itself one of the focal and tragic topics of litanies. Though there seem to be connections between religious, poetic, and lamenting genres and vernacular litanies, I would suggest that these be regarded less as one of derivation than of mutual ideological, structural, and stylistic reinforcement.

Conversational litanies were marked throughout by the style and tone of lament, and many litanies were capped by the rhetorical questions that are a hallmark of laments. The overtly lamenting portion of litanies was where the speaker turned reflective, commenting on her own litany and the testimony it offered to paradox or tragedy and posing key existential questions: How can this be, why are we so burdened, why is our life so full of suffering, why are we such victims, where is our salvation? This rise into high lament did not necessarily end the litany; often it would bring the litany to a climax, from which point it would start again with additional enumerations of grievance.

Speaking in litanies seemed to be a sort of sacral act, one that shifted the discursive context, elevating any conversation to the epic plane of the universal Russia tale and encapsulating the moment of its telling in a cocoon of poignancy and drama.[3] Even litany sequences of one-word elements

---

[3] A certain kind of nostalgia I often feel for Moscow centers on the aesthetic or emotional experience I had listening to litanies of suffering. Although it was painful to listen to them, they frequently provided me with a piercing, quite visceral sense of the intense, immediate, and real tragedies and absurdities of Russian life. This was, in fact, a sensation that Russians themselves acknowledged when listening to narratives of suffering. Indeed, the benefit of access to this cluster of sensations was a part of the multifaceted Russian ideology of suffering, as Dostoevsky characterized so well. The editor of *Ogonek* referred to the sad letters—litanies of suffering—received by his magazine as revealing "the art of pain" (Cerf and Albee 1990: 14; full quote is reproduced in Chapter 5). See Daniel Rancour-Laferriere's (1995: 247) intriguing comments on the exhilaration Russian discourses of suffering produce.

heightened or focused a conversation or monologue. For example, during part of a life story which referred to a wartime experience, one man intensified what he was describing by a brief use of litany: "cold, winter, hunger," which had the added effect of rhyme in the original: "*kholod, zima, golod*."[4] Perhaps it would be most accurate to say that litanies ritualized Russian speech, and their frequent appearance caused a constant oscillation between regular conversational or narrative planes and these ritual elevations (see Lavie 1990 on similar ritualizing allegories in the speech of Bedouins of the South Sinai).

Litanies established, even if only for a few moments, the kind of ritual liminality Victor Turner describes as "a moment in and out of time, and in and out of secular social structure, which reveals, however fleetingly, some recognition (in symbol if not always in language) of a generalized social bond that has ceased to be and has simultaneously yet to be fragmented into a multiplicity of structural ties" (1977: 96).

This "generalized social bond," at the same time both archaic and imminent, was the fantasized bond of connection to and belonging in some kind of moral community—a community of shared suffering. As ritual recitations, litanies invoked and created access to that belonging. One detail which demonstrates this is a particular way that litanies were often structured: having begun in the first person singular with a story about personal travail, difficulty, or loss, the speaker would switch without warning into the first person plural, into a lament about "our" general difficulty, the "our" implying Russian, Soviet, intelligentsia, *narodnyi*, or some other field of identification.[5]

Speakers could invoke identification with a variety of groups or social categories. Among the fields of identification discerned in litanies were those of class ("we working people," "we intellectuals"), profession ("we scientists," "we coal miners," "we schoolteachers"), gender ("we women," though rarely, "we men"), age group ("we pensioners" or "we young people"), life experience ("we veterans," "we victims of Chernobyl," or "we who suffered in the train wreck at Sverdlovsk"). Such cate-

---

[4] The ethnographer Bruce Grant mentioned a similar litany he heard on the Far Eastern evening news while on Sakhalin Island at around the same time: the anchor intoned about the national condition of "cold, hunger, and devastation (*kholod, golod, i razrukha*)" (1995: 29).

[5] In a recent paper discussing the discourse of political actors in post-Communist Russia, Michael Urban finds the same tendency to slip between the personal and the general; he terms this phenomenon "oscillation of number" and discusses the power of its application in political rhetoric: "Oscillation of number in the first person pronouns 'I' and the (inclusive) 'we' (*narod*) enables speakers to construct themselves as vessels from which flows an alleged popular will, thus enveloping their own solutions to problems in the urgency of national purpose (strong representations) while substituting slogans and catch phrases for persuasive argument" (Urban 1994: 747).

gories often merged together and cut across each other, so that, for example, "we veterans of the Great Patriotic War" identified the speaker with both an age group and a life-experience group. Every such identification also conveyed a host of other meanings. When pronounced with a certain familiar intonation, "we women," for instance, automatically conveyed the many predicaments of Russian femaleness: lack of status, standing in lines, struggling with husbands, making do with meager materials, worrying about sick children, and so on.

Through this habitual employment of synecdoche, a discursive operation so conventional as to escape most people's notice (Dundes 1972; Bourdieu 1977: 167), private travails were incorporated within a collective saga; the synechdoche worked in the other direction as well, so that discussion of the travails of a group also implied those of the individual. This one discursive operation thus served simultaneously to define personal identity, collective identity, and national identity, and the relations between those levels. By invoking these groups so ritualistically, people were, of course, creating them in a certain sense, or at least reifying them.

Litanies and Cultural Stance

Litanies helped to constitute a recognizable (and easily stereotyped or parodied) Russian stance, disposition (Bourdieu 1977: 214), or mood (Geertz 1973: 94–95). Stance is posture, in the sense of both the physical and the emotional postures that express particular perspectives, values, desires, or expectations. The stance expressed through litanies was usually that of a victim, a sufferer both private and collective, both immediate and eternal. The agent of this victimization could be a powerful individual (in 1989, Stalin and Gorbachev were popular villains), a social group other than the speaker's, or even the universe itself—or, to put this latter in a more Russian vernacular, the victim of fate, of life, of the ineluctable Russian condition. This stance relied on and was related to the ideological construction of Russia as an inescapable realm of tyranny, absurdity, suffering, privation, and loss.

Though I have come to consider the stance of the victim to be a primary one in Russian discourse (and other performative posturings), it was by far not the only one, but instead entered into dialogue with other key Russian stances, each of which asserted different forms of situational identity: uncontrolled, irrational exuberance (the "holy fool" stance), immovable indifference (the bureaucratic stance), stoic endurance (the *babushka* stance), and so on. In the scheme of Russian discourse forms, the antipode of the litany may be cant, that pious, self-satisfied, promotional genre which epitomized much official Communist propaganda and many other realms of public speech (such as the particular discourse of Soviet-era tour guides). A few key features characterize the dialectical opposition of these two genres:

Litany/Lament	*Cant*
other/fate blaming	self/nation/Russia praising
fatalistic, stress on hopelessness	utopian, stress on powerfulness
theme: loss/lack	theme: gain/talents
feminine or female-dominated	masculine or male-dominated
past-oriented	future-centered
sorrowful	enthusiastic
pessimistic	optimistic

If cant is, in many ways, a genre of power discourse, expressing a stance of association or identification with the institutions of authority, litanies are a genre that asserts the innocence of the relatively powerless (which is, paradoxically, a form of *moral* power—a point to which I shall return). Not confrontational except in extraordinary circumstances, but not exactly passive, either, the litany expresses a collective complaint about a subservient social position and a contradiction of the "official story" (Scott 1990).

In 1989 and 1990 there was thus, not surprisingly, a notable absence of litanies in the talk of people occupying positions of relative power. Being in Moscow before the breakup of the Soviet Union, I had many opportunities to interview representatives of Soviet officialdom—government bureaucrats, military authorities, political spokespersons, and party functionaries. These interviews were devoid of litanies. There were occasional moments of poignant sentimentalism, as, for instance, when one war veteran described the stirring arrival of American jeeps, chocolate, and tinned meat to help with the war effort. There were mentions of personal loss and national loss in the war, discussions about the effects of the repression of religion in Soviet Russia, and so on—the types of conversations certain in other circumstances to arouse litanies and laments—but these were communicated without relying on this genre. In private conversations, persons of official rank might resort to litanies, although many times I observed at dinner parties, for example, that those present who had some kind of assured status in their careers stood apart from the general litanizing. Those, however, who had gradually slipped from status, such as retired men, might litanize, often about the state of degradation in the nation's morals brought about by perestroika. This is another tendency that shows that the litany/lament is associated overall with a relative (or situational) lack or loss of formal status or power.

Gender was marked in litanies in particular ways. The litanies I heard from men were usually more ironically inclined than those of women; I would suggest that this reflects the traditional divisions of discursive labor which allocated lamenting to women and joking to men.[6] Moreover, the details which colored male and female litanies came from the respective professional and symbolic male and female domains. While men might spin off litanies about politics, the military, or the economy in general, women usually focused on shortages, the unmet needs of children, or their problems with unruly husbands.

Litanies: Theme and Cultural Stances

In general, litanies were focused around the human losses of the past, the momentous social upheavals of the present, and the uncertainty of the future (or the certainty of struggle and privation in the future). Despite the enormity of these subjects, because of the broad commonalities of Soviet existence and the conventional nature of speech, a fairly narrow range of specific themes and details constituted the building blocks of this genre. When focused on the past, litanies mourned Russian losses during the revolution, the Stalin era, and/or the Great Patriotic War, and lamented the huge sacrifices made by the Soviet people—sacrifices that perestroika seemed to invalidate. Often they deplored the way human lives were distorted to suit the absurdities of Communist projects and ideologies. Litanies centering on problems of the present focused on the great difficulties and the new absurdities of day-to-day survival, or on the "moral decay" of society (criminality, delinquency, violence, apathy, etc.). Litanies about the future bemoaned the apparent dead end, the sense that there was no clear path towards a better life in a more civilized society; in the extreme, these litanies predicted total social or even global apocalypse. In real conversation, many litanies traveled through past, present, and future, circling backwards and forwards in time, relating practices and events of the past to the contemporary and future state of people and society. Especially apparent in litanies was the complex range of possible stances to-

[6] In pre-revolutionary Russian society there were many formal and lexical discursive gender divisions; laments, for example, were strictly a female affair, produced by women themselves or by professional lamenters during rites of passage (for example, wedding laments; see Balashov 1985), times of personal loss (funeral laments), and times of community loss such as war; see Bazanov (1975). On the topic of gender-specific Russian peasant discourses see Anikin (1975: 33) and Howe (1991: 49–65). Though by no means universal, in many cultures lament is specifically a female discursive genre; see, for example, Alexiou (1974), Caraveli-Chaves (1980), Seremetakis (1991), and Holst-Warshaft (1992) on Greek women's laments; Briggs (1992) on women's "ritual wailing" among the Warao of the Orinoco Delta of Venezuela, and Grima (1992) on lament among Paxtun women living in Pakistan. Lamentation is clearly associated with relative or situational powerlessness; thus it is not surprising that it is so often a female form of discourse.

ward Soviet history and degrees or modes of identification with the socialist project; a great diversity of attitudes toward the changes occuring during perestroika were clear as well.

As is true with any talk, every litany was a multifaceted articulation of the speaker's identity and world outlook. The often mundane details which people incorporated into their litanies signaled or stood for much larger social issues and stances toward those issues. So, for example, when Natalia Viktorovna lamented the shortages of aspirin and insulin, she was signaling the vast range and degree of privations suffered by the people during perestroika; she was also relating current hardships to the historical predicament of her people as a whole and assuming a very female stance of commiseration with the long-suffering community she had discursively constructed. It should be noted that, though she lived a simple and dignified life and was known to be a person of the highest integrity, Natalia Viktorovna was a fairly elite member of the intelligentsia, someone who had access and privileges unavailable to many others. But at least in the space of this litany, she identified herself with the moral community created through shared suffering and difficulty, thus effacing the boundaries between her social group and the Russian people as a whole. Through its smallest details, then, each litany conveyed a panoply of meanings and signaled a complex blend of political, social, and moral positions and outlooks.

Social Identification and Blame through Litanies

It is possible to delineate four predominant lines of social identification that litanies marked and affirmed. This categorization is highly schematic, and thus effaces the constant (and often contradictory) movement from one stance to another which took place in actual talk; it also obscures the many possible subfields of identification (by gender, locale, profession, etc.) which could occur during a litany. Nevertheless, it does characterize certain general patterns of social affiliation which this genre conveyed and reproduced. The four different types of litanies I discuss here are designated as "anti-Soviet litanies," "pro-Soviet litanies," "populist litanies," and "Russophile litanies." Since identifications are inherently slippery, multiple, and overlapping, these designations are only intended to organize litanies in an approximate way.

Anti-Soviet Litanies

Many of the litanies I collected were essentially humanist and somewhat Western-looking in their sentiments; they were the most common litanies heard among the liberal intelligentsia. They often centered on the themes of the absurdism and tragedy of Soviet life. Logic, common sense and human rights were the abstract victims of these litanies; the people as a whole could be invoked as a more concrete victim, though often it was the creative intelligentsia whose victimization was highlighted.

The abstract "villain" of these litanies was the Communist project itself, but this was often personified by Stalin, the KGB, the police, the *apparatchiki*, and all the individuals who supported totalitarianism in various ways; Lenin himself could also figure here, though there was much disagreement about the extent to which he was responsible for the tragedies of Soviet history.

Though such litanies had long circulated, especially among the intelligentsia, their explosion in private conversation was triggered by the policy of glasnost, which had allowed, for the very first time since Krushchev's brief thaw in the 1960s, the publication of works that revealed and explored the harsh realities of Soviet history, and especially of Stalinism. After a slow beginning in 1987 with a few key pieces of historical revision (and critiques of Soviet historiography), by 1988 revelatory works of history, autobiography, and fiction were erupting throughout the media (see Nove 1989 for a detailed treatment of this process). The impassioned discussion of previously taboo topics—Stalinist repressions, collectivization, the *gulag*, Communist corruption, the poor state of the economy—began to fill the most prominent literary journals (*Novyi mir, Znamia, Druzhba narodov*, and others, all with circulation in the millions) and several magazines and newspapers (especially *Ogonek, Moskovskie novosti*, and *Literaturnaia gazeta*); attention to these issues in the electronic media escalated similarly. Many of these media revelations took the form of litanies— some subdued, some fervent and emotional. It is difficult to convey the intensity with which the population, and especially the Moscow intelligentsia, devoured and discussed this outpouring of "truth," and to depict the intensity with which they responded to the general exposure of pain and suffering with litanies about their own experiences. Here I offer just a few examples.

After viewing a very graphic theatrical version of Solzhenitsyn's *One Day in the Life of Ivan Denisovich* with a friend, I asked him how he was struck by it.

> Well, it seems to me to be an accurate portrayal of our everyday lives. Of course, we saw exaggerated conditions, extreme conditions, but basically it shows our day-to-day existence quite well. The humiliations, the arbitrary uses of power, the absurdity, the cruelty which can hit you at any time. This is what I have experienced my whole life: in school, in the mili-

tary, at work, everywhere. All our social relations are like that, in fact. We have been conditioned to accept this sadistic world as being normal and natural. That play was a perfect metaphor for our society in general.

Though pronounced fairly calmly (unlike most litanies, which were much more emotional), this short text shows how speakers connected their own experiences to a larger social or historical frame of reference; by so doing, my friend located himself within a metaphoric *gulag*, suggesting that he was in some ways as much a victim of totalitarian practice as was, for instance, Ivan Denisovich (or Solzhenitsyn).

Much more dramatic (partly because of her gender) were my poet friend Masha's litanies. Every time I spoke with her, at a certain point she would sigh portentously and lament about some recent struggle in her life; she too always managed to connect this to a larger frame. Though these usually evolved spontaneously within her long and colorful mono-logues, sometimes I stimulated these outpourings with a question or com-ment. One afternoon, I asked her what she thought about a certain poem by Akhmatova which I had just read.

Akhmatova? Akhmatova? You think just because she is the greatest poet of the twentieth century that I have read all of her poems? What I have read has been passed around in typescript. I have typed out copies for myself, of whatever I could get. You don't understand, Nancy. This is an absurd country. This is a country where poets aren't allowed to read real poetry, where artists can't see real art, where musicians don't hear contem-porary music, where nothing is as it should be. You can't imagine my life. I try to write something good, something that will contribute just a little beauty to my people. But how can I do that? Can I know what beauty is when it has been kept from me my whole life, when all I see around me is ugly, deformed, dishonest? Our revolution was a disaster. Solzhenitsyn was right, it was the triumph of evil in the world. Our revolution—all it did was make it possible for the most evil people to have the most power.

Naively, I tried to argue with her, claiming that there was some good in the ideals of socialism if not in the practice of it. She answered me fervently:

How can you say that, when we have the *gulag*, when we persecute our most brilliant people, like Solzhenitsyn? When in fact all our people are just slaves, we are all just slaves, mindless, without souls, without any sense of beauty, truth, kindness, human goodness? The revolution de-stroyed Russia. And now I spend my whole time trying to find a doctor who can heal me. There is something wrong with me. I don't know what it is, it is vague, and I have been to all kinds of doctors; they give me this homeopathic remedy and that, but nothing works. I think perhaps it is my soul that is sick. How can you cure a soul? How can you cure the soul of a whole people?

Her lament went on for quite a long time beyond this; circling round and round the same themes, often coming back to the common metaphor of the illness of the body politic and the need for healing the very souls of the Russian people. As was typical with these litanies, she never prescribed a possible medicine, usually declaring that it was a hopeless situation, a "fatal illness." It is interesting here to note how her field of identification shifted: at first it was herself, then the creative intelligentsia that suffered, then she broadened it to encompass "a whole people." Her occasional use of the passive voice made her identification of the "villain" slippery as well.

The elderly daughter of a well-known Russian writer was much more consistent in identifying the intelligentsia (or intelligence) as the victim, though she imputes responsibility to both the Soviet system and to the Russian mentality. In an attempt to characterize and explain the exceptional nature of Russian life to me, Elizaveta Mikhailovna declared:

It is impossible for you Westerners to understand our lives. The Western media gets it entirely wrong, trying to understand us rationally. Russian reality is based on absurdisms—economic, social, even scientific [ekonom-icheskie, obshchestvennye, nauchnye . . . the vowels in these words were elongated in the typical litany mode]. All of our life is based on absurdity, impossibility. Russian daily life is simply absurd and preposterous. And in science! Soviet scientists were forced to follow mythical scientific heroes, in direct opposition to Western scientific discoveries. For many years, for example, the work of Linus Pauling was disallowed, and the same thing happened in biology, genetics, and every other field. Truth was simply ignored! We invented our own truth! Which is bad enough in life, but when you do that in science . . .? How does this happen? It happens because Russians have always cultivated and taken pride in their own ignorance, their ignorance of the most basic things. Russians have a special ability to believe lies, propaganda, baloney [chush']. People here are deeply ignorant, of their own history in the first place. And now . . . I look around, I get many letters, and it is clear that the younger generation is totally nihilistic; they just value nothing, they value nothing at all. I think we are heading for civil war, for complete disintegration. It is a nightmare.

Elizaveta Mikhailovna wove together past, present, and future, blaming Soviet absurdism on what she saw as the Russian "ability to believe lies, propaganda, baloney"; although Russian herself, she thereby marked her belonging in the elite community of the dissident intelligentsia, for whom the courage to seek out the truth beyond the absurdism of Soviet reality was the highest value. Although clearly democratic in her values, she also mourned the social decay that seemed to accompany liberalization; she expressed a loss of hope in the power of knowledge and truth, seeing around her only the nihilism of youth and its potential to contribute to "complete disintegration."

One of my friends, a Russian speaker of Armenian descent in her late thirties, produced a long litany about totalitarian social practices, in which she invoked, in parallel structures, the regimentation of Soviet schools, summer camps, and youth organizations. She meticulously depicted the strict military order, the totalitarian leadership, the rules and regulations which made a children's camp "like a slave labor camp." "We are hopelessly conditioned by all these experiences. We are poisoned, tainted, ruined by the bad ways we treat children in this country. We are all warped by our totalitarian conditioning, and we pass it on to our children, even now, even despite ourselves."

Her speech segued from this litany about the "ruined Russian people" into one of hopelessness, and finished with a litany that employed the trope of a dead end street (*tupik*) to describe her country's predicament. Yet in her next breath she began another story, this time a tale about the horrors suffered by her friends in Baku during the pogroms against Armenians and Russians, and she ended this story with a cry of commitment to fight against "fascists" and "fools."

Although she had started with a litany about the hopelessness of undoing totalitarian character patterns, she managed to end with a proclamation of the need for self-empowerment. In a way, I think she was caught between two views of herself, one as "hopelessly conditioned" and thus powerless and innocent, the other as having some inkling of a more active way of being. One thing I learned from such productions was that litanies are not like logical discourses; like religious or poetic texts, the litany is not necessarily consistent. A litany is a declaration of a complex identity and cultural location; its truth emerges in a poetic idiom rather than a logically congruous one (see Lavie 1990 for examples of the similar, seemingly contradictory "poetics" of Bedouin speech).

Many litanies were much less political, dwelling without such a broad perspective on the topic of "Russian degradation." Often they marked a professional affiliation, and they frequently lamented the situation in the stores. One night, two acquaintances drove me home from a concert in their car, and on the way, regaled me with a litany of their professional difficulties. They were both musicians, and they lamented about the ways their creativity was affected by the lack of inspiration and decent venues available under the "degrading" conditions of perestroika. This they followed with a litany about the difficulty of emigrating; this particular litany was certainly shaped by my being an American, but it also had a lot to do with their need to justify their quest to emigrate—to separate themselves from their community. The woman turned to me and said, portentously, "Do you know how humiliated we are?"

> Imagine, a musician, an artist spends his time thinking about where to get some new sheet music, or some boots, or thinking, "Now, where am I going to get a chicken to throw in the pot for some soup on Sunday?" What kind of life is that for anyone, much less an artist? Thinking all the time about some scrawny chicken. That is not real life and it is impossible to be an artist under such conditions. This is why we want to leave.

This litany was, in a way, a commentary on other litanies, specifically those about the travails of shopping; part of what it lamented was the psychological degradation brought about by the constant buzz of litanies of material difficulty. One thing that is striking here is that the same social reality could produce quite different responses and valuations; compare this litany about the degradation Soviet shopping produces to Masha's magical tale of the azure woman. In that story, the condition of material deficits was the context that allowed the narrator to produce a moving image of proud feminine self-creation. In that telling, the azure woman was surely not "degraded."

Sometimes a conflict of self-identification could emerge in litanies about shopping voiced by younger, more liberally inclined people. Moving between images of himself and his friends as alternately degraded and triumphant, Yura, a cooperative worker already making a lot of money, delivered an internally contradictory litany. At first he lamented what he called "the lowered consciousness" of people who were fixated on getting something, "a new jacket, some shoes, a chicken" (chicken, and meat in general, were common symbols in shopping litanies). Yura said he and his friends spent all their spare time going around the city trying to get good "stuff"—meat, Reebok shoes, Western jeans, "something that business people in the West never have to worry about! You can just go to any store and buy whatever you like. How are we supposed to get anywhere when we have to spend so much time shopping?" In the next sentence his tone shifted, however, as he added proudly that his Levi jeans were his most prized possession, that because of how much effort they had taken to acquire, they were for him "like gold." This kind of discursive shift, from litanizing about the difficulty of Soviet life and its degrading effect on the psyche to celebrating a valued pair of jeans, shows that the same predicament could be presented in very different ways—even by the same person, even within a single conversation. Blue jeans were transmuted into "gold" only through the quest-like process of their acquisition. The situation of deficits could, thus, be marked either positively or negatively, depending on which aspect of personal identity was being highlighted.

After that brief mention of his beloved blue jeans, however, Yura went on to lament the difficult position in which cooperative workers and owners found themselves:

> Although we are providing services that everybody needs, and they are thrilled to be able to hire us to do things for them, efficiently, quickly, without the hassle they would face—not to mention waiting ten years!—to get something done the Soviet way. . . . Despite the fact that they need us, and we are single-handedly rebuilding this country, people hate us; they say we are crooks, thieves. And they want to destroy us. They feel they are doing justice when they cheat us, they don't pay us for the work we do, they spit in our faces, they lie about us to the authorities. How are we supposed to accomplish anything in this situation? This is an impossible place to do honest work. Communism has destroyed people's ability to work. They don't even value hard work when it benefits them. Cooperators—we are the only honest, hard-working people in the entire country.

Paradoxically, a few months after I spoke with him, Yura stole several thousand dollars from the co-owner of his cooperative (also an acquaintance of mine) and disappeared.

Pro-Soviet/Anti-Perestroika Litanies

A certain kind of litany was often heard from patriotic older people, especially those who had lived through the war. These litanies bemoaned the changes wrought by perestroika, especially decisions to introduce a market economy and invite Western investors (who, it was said, would steal the USSR's resources and provide nothing in return), the "evil" of cooperatives and others who supposedly wanted to "get rich quick at the expense of the people." The victims in such litanies were sometimes the Communist faithful, but usually it was the *narod* in general, the innocent, honest people who had sacrificed all their lives in order to build a good future, a future that was, so the logic went, being mindlessly demolished by Gorbachev and his ilk.

Pro-Soviet litanies also often lamented the explosion of self-blame which glasnost had brought forth. "That [the Civil War, Stalinist repressions] was all in the past. We should let it lie," I heard one man say. "Stalin did what he had to do considering all the enemies the Soviet Union had at the time; we shouldn't judge him from the vantage point of today." The villains blamed in pro-Soviet litanies were Gorbachev, the nationalist leaders of the Baltics and other breakaway republics, and, as the Berlin Wall came down and the East European satellites pulled out of Moscow's orbit, "our ungrateful brothers in East Europe for whom the Soviet people have sacrificed so much." Lenin appeared as a kind of savior in some of these litanies, showing the way to socialism if only people would continue to follow his lead rather than ridiculing him and the cult that grew up around him.[7] Since in the perestroika period there were few hard-line Communist leaders with any acknowledged charisma, there were no specific contemporary saviors, though the Party could be invoked as a possible source of relief from the changes of the day. The politics of pro-Soviet litanies ranged widely along a continuum from fiercely Communist (even pro-Stalin) to more moderate socialist. The more moderate the litany, the less likely was the villain (Gorbachev, for instance) to be excoriated and condemned in ferocious, even threatening terms.

"Complete disintegration" was one of the most frequently encountered phrases in these litanies. The ritual enumeration of disintegration centered on images of the self-destruction of the body politic, the spirit of collectivity, the Soviet economy, national talent, and socialist creativity, morality, courage, and order. On any number of occasions I listened to litanies (with one or more tellers) that touched on each one of these supposedly disintegrating elements of the social fabric. Sometimes the elements would be enumerated in the abstract, and sometimes they employed specific examples.

A litany on this topic was performed one afternoon at a meeting I attended of a group of "student diplomats." After a long discussion of the problems posed by the world's nuclear arsenal, the teacher who organized

[7] Arguably the major "religion" of the Soviet period, the cult of Lenin is thoroughly discussed in Tumarkin (1983); see also Lane (1981). Throughout the Soviet period parodies of the Lenin cult circulated widely, especially in the form of jokes, but also in parodic songs, underground literature, and art. Many of these parodies surfaced and were published during glasnost. It is important to distinguish, however, between parodies of the cult of Lenin and parodies of Lenin himself, which were much less frequent. For believers, of course, there was no difference between ridiculing the cult and mocking the man.

"Lamenting at a Communist Rally" (Photo by John Einarsen and Robert Kowalczyk)

the meeting presented a skit, complete with props, costumes, and student actors, concerning the problems of crime in the Soviet Union in 1990. The skit was entitled "The Battle against Criminality" and was structured entirely around a sequence of pedantic litanies delivered by the teacher herself. In lamenting tones, she gave statistics on crime's increase in the USSR, which she followed with a litany about the degradation brought about by new social freedoms (her deliberate parallelism meant to suggest, of course, the relation of these two realms); briefly, she switched into a didactic mode for an exhortation about preventing crime, declaring that it is within every child's power to prevent crime (by not throwing rocks through windows); after this she asked children to bear witness as to how crime had affected their lives. Several students added their own examples and comments to the general litany, which the teacher then closed with a prototypical litany about how terrible the current crime, drunkenness, and lack of discipline were, what a nightmare people were enduring, and how unless preventive measures were taken all young people would be completely corrupted. The spectacle climaxed with a musical skit visually suggesting a comparison between the "dissolute, capitalist" NEP-men of the 1920s and the cooperative owners of perestroika, implying that foreign businessmen were somehow connected to all the corrupt and corrupting goings on.

Ideologically, this litany was an only slightly veiled protest against liberalization, which presumably induced disintegration and jeopardized social order. It seemed to accuse Gorbachev, cooperatives, and Western influences simultaneously. Such litanies were by no means rare at the time, and they were good indicators of a relatively conservative stance, that of people who preferred order and control over the wild excesses of "freedom." Such people were clearly much more likely to have identified with the intense social controls of the Soviet era and to have internalized Soviet propaganda about the moral depravity of the West.

Reflecting these orientations in a short but ferocious litany, one older man, a recently retired historian, declared: "We've gone and imported greed, aggressiveness, and jealousy from the West! That's what underlies the terrible situation you see here now. Cooperative owners are speculators, thieves, just like all your Western businessmen." Echoing his sentiments, a younger woman in the room said "Yes. They are all out to get rich quick, before the crackdown."

"Populist" Litanies

"Populist" litanies focused on the general category of the *narod* as victim, and emphasized how the people had always suffered at the hands of the elites. The relationship between the people and the powerful was characterized as being inherently immutable and unjust; but, as with anti-Soviet litanies, there was often some implication that there was something about Russian culture or mentality that generated this social predicament. Significantly, there was no real savior to be discerned in this picture; these litanies often ended with lamentations of the hopelessness of the social situation, invoking the common trope of the "dead end."

Such litanies were most often heard from women, and they very often began with accounts of the dire situation in the stores and the profound difficulty that women were facing in taking care of their families. One afternoon, during tea with my friends at the Institute, a woman recounted her futile search for a particular medicine needed by her son. After a chorus of sympathy, and promises to keep an eye out for this drug on their own circuits of the city's pharmacies, one woman mentioned an article that had just appeared in the newspaper *Izvestia* explaining that the disappearance of drugs had occured because factories had been summarily shut down for polluting the local environments. This brought on a round of collective lamentation.

"There you have it," said one woman: "It is our general stupidity, in this country. It's hopeless. Whenever we solve one problem, we create another, and this will go on forever and ever. It's always like this in Russia. There is no logic to anything. And who suffers? The people suffer, especially women and children. But those at the top get *their* medicines from abroad, so they don't care."

"Yes," said another woman. "It's terrifying, it's a nightmare. What are we to do? We get our freedom to speak but we also get free from everything else: food, medicine."

"It will always be like this in Russia," said a third woman. "It's hopeless, absolutely hopeless. There is no way out. And everything will get worse and worse."

"No!" declared a more optimistic woman, "we must take part in demonstrations, instead of passively sitting home waiting for change!"

"What good will that do?" said the first woman. "Nobody will pay any attention. It's hopeless."

Sitting with me on a park bench one day, a middle-aged male writer vividly pronounced a long litany about Russian cruelty and absurdism:

Look at our history. It's all tragic, from the very beginning. The Tatar Yoke, Ivan the Terrible, Peter the Great, you know how many poor Russians died so he could build Petersburg? The *narod* is meaningless in all these projects, just meaningless, like specks of dust. Russians have always been nothing but slaves. Maybe we even like our slavery; it absolves us of any responsibility. Then, the horror of the revolution, the civil war, one Russian against another: terrible. Only in this country. Only here. Only Russians could do that to each other. Stalin, the *gulag*, the war—how many millions perished because of our stupidity, our absolute lack of concern for human life? Our leaders just threw the bodies of Russians down at the front by the millions, a human barricade, just ground into the mud. No strategy, no attempt to protect lives. And now! More of the same; Gorbachev's absurd perestroika. What's it for? To see if we can survive again without food, without the basic things that people need to live even a simple life. Give us a thousand years, it will all be the same. It's in our genes. Russia will never be a civilized country.

This was a kind of oration I heard dozens of times from people of many different ages and occupations. The details were basically the same, whenever this litany was recited, although it could resound with either a lamenting or a bitterly ironic tone; the difference in stance was usually related to gender. One friend in his late thirties loved to regale me with accounts of the ordeals he had suffered in his life at the hands of "sadists"—army officers, bureaucrats, and other officials whom he called "hooligans." After telling these stories with some glee, he often turned bitter and recited a refrain about Russia in general, using rather sharp language: "This country, this is an accursed, foolish, fucking, terrible country. A thousand years of this fucking absurdism . . . and it will never change."[8]

Russophile Litanies

Russophile litanies stood in sharp contrast to those I have just presented. Whether overtly or implicitly, they treated Russia, ("the motherland") as the long-suffering victim of outside oppressors. Very different strings of culturally charged adjectives, also with rhyming feminine endings, were used to characterize the motherland-as-victim: unhappy, unlucky, poor, exhausted, much-suffering, deceived, defenseless, all-forgiving (*grustnaia, neschastnaia, bednaia, izmuchennaia, mnogostradal'naia, obmanutaia, bezzashchitnaia, vseproshchaiushchaia*). The Russian *narod* appeared as the corollary victim in Russophile litanies and could be described using the same terms. But there were other victims as well: the Russian Orthodox tradi-

---

[8] The string of adjectives in his refrain always rhymed, and sounded much more intense in Russian: *prokliataia, duratskaia, ebenaia, uzhasnaia.*

tion, the Russian tsar and his innocent family, the Russian earth, Russian peasants, the Russian gene-pool and the sacred values of the Russian past all were present in the Russophile pool of sacrifice and suffering.

The motherland's tormenters were equally many and various. Communism/Communists led the parade of villains, followed by the godless West and non-Russian (especially Caucasian) peoples of the Soviet Union; special vituperation was reserved for Jews and Zionists. The most visible contemporary hero-savior of the Russophile litanies was Solzhenitsyn, although other writers, artists and public figures were invoked. (See Kathleen Parthé's intriguing work [1997] on the revitalization of Russophile identities in late Communist Russia.)

I noticed one example of this type of litany rendered in a ritualized form on a television variety show one evening. A tall male singer, of what Russians regard as classical Russian appearance, dressed in a prerevolutionary military officer's uniform (the uniform of the Whites in the civil war), stood with his feet set firmly apart, arms behind his back as if chained, staring fixedly upwards, and sang a song called "Rossiia," a long litany enumerating the main events in Russia's tragic history, ending with the lament: "While reading the diary of a martyred White general, I am trying to understand, how could you give yourself for execution to the vandals?"

Such lamentation was one of the key mechanisms through which a nationalistic Russian identity, repressed in certain ways though not altogether during the Soviet era, was reintroduced into public circulation; the martyred White general was a synechdoche for Russia itself. Images like this one, which lament the self-relinquishing of "Mother Russia" to various "ravishers" (Bolsheviks, Jews, and recently, Western capitalists), have been significant in the development of contemporary nationalist discourse (cf. Zhirinovskii 1994).

I found it difficult to listen to these nationalist litanies—and there were many—which blamed Jews, Zionists, the Jewish–CIA conspiracy, and so on for all the torments of Soviet history, or, alternatively, for the destruction of the Soviet Union under perestroika. I now regret that, due in large part to the repulsion I felt hearing them, I did not make it a point to collect and study these litanies in detail; an entire study could (and should) be devoted to the analysis of nationalistic, and particularly anti-Jewish discourse. In fieldwork in Yaroslavl in 1994 and 1995, I paid much more attention to these litanies, in part because they were a very frequent theme of people's talk, even among the generally liberal intelligentsia.

There was an entire range of less vicious though also nationalistic litanies which could be heard. One day, I went to a Moscow school during the visit of a group of teachers and their teenage students from the Baltics. We left the students and went to the lounge for tea, which was served quite ceremoniously. After a while the Baltic teachers left, and I was co-erced into staying for another cup of tea. At this point, a collective litany (addressed to me) began, about how the teachers from the Baltic repub-lics, which were just then asserting their independence, no longer needed their Moscow compatriots. "After all we have done to help them," said one young teacher sadly. It was unclear who she meant to say had been helped—was she speaking of her friends, the teachers, in particular, or of the Baltic Republics as a whole? This blurring of groups was common in litanies like this. Another teacher picked up this theme and intensified it (Luthi 1976), referring first to the situation in the Baltic Republics, then to the question of East Europe (this was a few months after the Berlin wall had come down and East European countries had declared their indepen-dence from Soviet power): "We Russians must be compensated for all our investments. So much help we gave . . . so many years . . . so many of our sons, 150,000 or so, we gave defending the Czechs alone . . . and now they call us occupiers. So much we gave to free them and now they turn and call us occupiers."

Similar litanies about Soviet (Russian) relations with other countries and who had sacrificed more in the relationship were frequently heard in the media. One segment on *Vzgliad* showed Vietnamese citizens flying out of Moscow's Sheremetevo Airport laden with Soviet goods: toy guns, pharmaceutical supplies, and others. They were being interviewed by a Russian reporter, and, clearly defensive, one man said, "We want to sell this stuff at home. Why should we be made to feel guilty for this?" The voice-over announcer enumerated (in litany tone) the kinds of goods the Vietnamese were "exporting" and closed with the declaration: "Their big brothers are suffering now, too, and need to keep their precious goods to themselves." This one statement is referentially rich and complex. It ac-knowledges a common (even metaphorically familial) heritage of "suffer-ing" but then draws a line, differentiating the "younger" victimized Viet-namese from the "older" victimized Soviet people. (It also illustrates the hoarding mentality not too surprisingly found in the context of chronic shortages.)

As can be seen from the examples presented above, litanies played a key role in the expression and negotiation of collective identities and po-sitions in the social world, issues that were crucially important in the revo-lutionary time of perestroika. At once both personal and political, litanies positioned individuals, collectives, and even nations relative to others, and whether explicitly or subtly, they asserted that the speaker's group was the long-suffering victim of some other party, or of some metaphysi-cal force, such as fate or national character.

One interesting aspect of litanies was that they often inspired a sort of competition among speakers to assert themselves or their groups as the supreme victims in a hierarchy of victims. In the next section I offer a few examples of the ways in which this competitive litanizing might manifest itself.

Hierarchies of Victimization: Competitive Litanizing

The tension in urban–rural relations is a very old and bitter theme in Russian discourse, and during perestroika it surfaced in the form of a competition to see which party suffered the most. A rather drunk old man in an early morning milk line complained long and hard about how bad Moscow was. "Moscow is nothing but ministries, ministries, ministries. Ministry of this, ministry of that. And everybody working in a ministry, all they do is hoard things, steal things, take things, get things for themselves. That is why it is so good here, and why we have it so bad everywhere else in the country." Such litanies, in which the rest of the country was seen as victimized by the large urban centers (especially Moscow) were commonly heard among non-Muscovites; the letters to the editor of *Ogonek* and other publications often featured such litanies. Many Muscovites, in contrast, lamented the depletion of goods in the stores as being the fault of the "outsiders" who always came in droves to shop. "I know they have it hard out there," said one acquaintance, "but we are struggling now, with ration cards for everything. And the provinces are keeping all the goods they used to send to take care of Moscow. It is easier out there! They have the farms, they can feed themselves. Why do they have to come here?"

At a formal meeting in Moscow's newly opened feminist research center, a dialogical series of competing litanies touched on several of the main themes of sacrifice, and demonstrated the various ways spheres of identification were discursively deployed.

One female journalist said: "Women produce everything in this country: children, socialization . . . the child is the result of female labor. Then women give the fruit of their labor away to be killed or warped in the army. You—women—must guard the fruit of your labor. You are producing soldiers."

A woman responded: "But you are producing. . . . We consider the labor of producing children labor for oneself. Thus this labor *must* be unpaid."

"The government takes our children away!" the journalist answered.
"You are saying that until the age of eighteen they are ours and then after
that they belong to the government?"

The other woman replied: "And what if he goes off to another family,
gets married?"

"That is his choice," remarked the journalist.

Impatiently and angrily, a male journalist who was attending the meeting cried: "Aren't you Muscovites ashamed before your sisters of other
towns, other cities? Your position is a Moscow one. Most of the heavy labor done in the rest of the country is done by women. Eighty percent of
the children in the rest of the country are ill. Most families in other cities
live in slums built by Stalin before the war."

At this point the male journalist was interrupted by a barrage of disagreement. One contextual aspect of litanies was that people did not seem
to like being on the accused side of things, even if that meant being a Muscovite in relation to other parts of the Soviet Union. As people do everywhere, Russian speakers had many deflective maneuvers for interrupting,
ignoring, or overriding blame directed at them.

In this exchange, several fields of identification came into play. Initially,
the female journalist invoked the category of women in the third person, as if she were an external representative of women's concerns, then
she shifted to the second person, as if she were an advocate addressing
women directly; when challenged, she immediately shifted to the first person, and attached herself to the category of all-sacrificing mothers. Her
speech was delivered in a litanizing tone from the beginning; her cry, "the
government is taking our children away," was open lamentation.

In his turn, the male journalist tried to negate the sacrifice of Moscow
women by summoning an image of more victimized women outside of
Moscow. He did not succeed in this, since the women present insisted on
the primacy of their own status as sacrificial victims of the state.

One of the strangest litany competitions that I heard took place over
dinner one night at a new acquaintance's. A woman in her sixties, Varvara Andreevna was a life-long Communist, an intellectual, a teacher of
Marxism-Leninism, and a veteran of the war. Each of these fields of identity provided her with grounds for various litanies through the evening.
Also at dinner with us were two graduate students, Oleg and Tania, who
worked with Varvara Andreevna and who were also firm believers in the
Party. Once the topic turned to the subject of national losses, it scarcely
strayed from it (it was rather hard, in some groups, to leave the litany
mode for something lighter; male irony had a certain leverage, but in this
case there was no irony available). Varvara Andreevna opened the litany.

So much has been lost to this country because of the depletion of our intelligentsia. So many left, before the revolution, during it, after it, and before the war. Then many intellectuals were killed fighting the war. You cannot possibly imagine what a loss this has been, and continues to be, for our country. You know, when I finished my war service and went to school, to the university . . . instead of a professor, there was a boy, a mere boy. All the older male professors were gone. The boy stood in front of the class and opened a book of philosophy, and he read to us, he just read to us. He was no professor, he was just a boy, reading to us from a book. That was no way to learn. But there was no one left, they had all been killed in the war. . . . They had all left, volunteered, and gone off and died. Or they went to camps.

Here Oleg broke in and added, "Yes, you know, I am thirty-five years old and I am part of a lost generation. We are all, those people of my age, a lost generation. There was nobody to teach us, to pass on the wisdom of the past. Our teachers did the best they could, but so much was lost, that when it came to us, we suffered under a real lack."

His litany went on for a while, detailing the many ways the loss of an older generation has affected current society. In this litany the speaker appropriated the sacrifices of others—the faculty members lost to war or camps—as his own loss; the same operation was present in Varvara Andreevna's litany, although in hers it was more subtle. After Oleg, Tania pitched in, and switched the conversation to a slightly different direction: "Well, this is all true. And then we have today. Everything is being dismantled, changed, devalued. Everything we know. I go to my school, to teach Marxist theory, and I have no idea what to say. And nobody can tell me, what I should say. I am a teacher without a subject."

From here the conversation turned to the topic of Stalinist labor camps and all the human losses among the intelligentsia. I brought up the subject of Jews killed in Nazi camps as a point of comparison, but Varvara Andreevna abruptly interrupted me:

No, it is completely different. Our camps were much, much worse. The Nazis, you see, were killing other people, others [*chuzhie*]. They were killing Jews and Gypsies. We, here, in the Soviet *gulag*—we were killing *our own*. And it is much worse to kill your own people than to kill another. It is a violation of every human logic. Our camps were a much worse phenomenon.

In this passage, two groups of victims were compared, and the Soviet intelligentsia, with whom the speaker identified, was positioned as a more legitimate victim than the other. Another woman of the same age group, who had also served in the war, had a similar perspective in her litany about the war: "In Germany so much repentance has been directed at the Jews and so little towards those who really suffered from the Nazis, for instance, the Russians. The world has paid no attention to our suffering."

The implication here is the same as in the previous litany: attention paid to one set of victims is somehow taken from (or unavailable to) another. And it was not merely attention that was desired, but a kind of distinction: the distinction that would come from being the ultimate victim in a hierarchy of victims.[9]

One day I went to visit a woman who had endured particularly difficult and painful life experiences. A mutual acquaintance had arranged our meeting almost by chance, thinking I could perhaps help this woman in some way (which I tried to do, getting her medicines and other things she needed). When I first arrived at her two-room Moscow apartment she was somewhat distrustful, but because I listened intently to her stories and laments, her misgivings gradually fell away. At the end of our visit she embraced me and repeated several times that she considered me a "good girl" and hoped to see me again.

In her early seventies when I visited her, Mariia Fedorovna had been intensely affected by the events of Soviet history. After what she described as a happy childhood, her life had become a sequence of tragedies. Her husband had been arrested just after the Great Patriotic War for participating in an informal political discussion group. When he was given a long sentence, Mariia Fedorovna followed him into exile. She struggled to survive the extreme hardships of life in a Siberian village for nine years while her husband served out his sentence; one or two days every week she stood in line to deliver bundles of food, books, letters, and clothing to the prison gates in the hope that they would reach him. After his release the couple made their way, eventually and with great difficulty, back to Moscow, where her husband began to gain fame as a philosopher and to attract unwanted attention from the authorities. Harassed for many years, in complete frustration he finally left the Soviet Union, leaving Mariia Fedorovna behind. Although she expected that he would summon her even-

[9] A fruitful comparison can be made between the competitive litanizing I have described, and the grief-sharing events of Paxtun women depicted by Benedicte Grima. She writes: "I conducted my research among both Afghan refugee women and Pakistani women, all of them Paxtuns. The rivalry between the two groups manifested itself in competition for who had the most *gham* [grief, worry, loss]. . . . Once, when I spoke about my research on suffering to a group of Afghani women in Peshawar, their major comment was, 'If you think the Pakistanis have some sad tales to tell, you ought to come hear ours. Our women will make you cry until you don't want to hear any more. What do the Pakistani women know about pain and suffering?'" (1992: 32).

tually, it became increasingly clearer, as years passed, that she had been abandoned. After this realization struck her, Mariia Fedorovna had a breakdown, alienated most of her friends, and lived as a recluse for many years. Her husband never contacted her. Only with the coming of glasnost, and the freedom to release her story, did she gain a feeling of composure and serenity. She had written several articles about her life, these had been published, and she had begun to feel, as she put it, vindicated. At the present time, however, Mariia Fedorovna was trying to make ends meet on her small pension, while suffering from a painful, chronic disease that limited her mobility.

These were the bare bones of her life history, which were laid out for me over the course of seven hours. Mariia Fedorovna's childhood friend, Elizaveta Dmitrevna, who was visiting for a few days from Kiev, sat me down in the kitchen and fed me, and the two women told one story of suffering after another. They relied on each other for commentary, embellishment, and reminders of subsidiary stories of suffering and loss. They relied on me to provide a constant stream of sighs and sympathetic interjections like *"Koshmar!"* ("what a nightmare"), *"Uzhasno!"* ("how awful"), *"Strashno!"* ("how terrifying"), and the simple *"Oi."* This mode of participation, which I had picked up mimetically through months of communicative experience, was necessary to the flow of litanies.

Through all of her stories, Mariia Fedorovna emphasized her position as a singular victim, but she frequently invoked the suffering of others as well. In her litanies about her days in Siberian exile with her husband, Mariia Fedorovna included him in the frame of victimization, with the Stalinist system, labor camp authorities, and faithless friends as the villains. However, most of her litanies concerned what she said was a double victimization: the fact that her husband left her even after all she had sacrificed and suffered for him; she often commented, apropos of this, on the general victimization of women in Soviet experience. Often this litany flowed dialogically between Mariia Fedorovna and Elizaveta Dmitrevna, who recalled certain key poignant details to add to the enumeration of grievance.

The tale of suffering and injury that they thus poured out for me in these litanies was multi-directional, multi-layered, and multi-resonant, with old and new and old upon new. What was amazing for me was to hear how poignantly Mariia Fedorovna held on to ancient suffering, and transformed it into a vital narrative of the present: a narrative of all the ramifications of a life's suffering, suffering upon suffering within suffering. "You see what a life it is," she said a number of times, "a life like a novel."

Indeed her life was like a novel (a very Russian novel), in several senses. In the telling, her life was as if capsulized, in the frame of the litany. Her life was handed to me in brief chapters, not in chronological but in poetic order, circling and spiraling from one terrible incident of loss, sacrifice, or humiliation to another. It was like a novel also in the sense that it was a transactable object (cf. Grima 1992; Abu-Lughod 1986); along with the newspaper clippings and photographs and books with which she illustrated it, her story was Mariia Fedorovna's most valuable possession, something that was all her own, and it was one that accrued value and depth in the telling. As with so many of my Russian informants, the losses, miseries, and privations of her life had become all Mariia Fedorovna really owned and the only thing she had with which to transact in the world. Her husband's fame had added qualitatively and quantitatively to her suffering and loss, but this magnification of her travails had also become her greatest claim to an archetypal Russian identity. As glasnost developed, she went from being a *persona non grata* to being a person with a story to tell, a litany of suffering to share. Journalists and writers had contacted her for her story; she proudly showed me a scrapbook of clippings about her life which had appeared in print during the late 1980s. In the hierarchy of victims, Mariia Fedorovna had achieved a certain moral status, and she seemed reluctant to grant other people a similar status. When I mentioned the name of another woman whom I had interviewed, a woman with a similar, exceptionally hard life history, Mariia Fedorovna disparaged the other woman and minimized what she had endured. Mariia Fedorovna was clearly protective of her own position in the hierarchy of victims; the moral status this position conferred was perhaps the only real comfort she could take from her grievously difficult life.

The Social Logic of Litanies

On the immediate level, litanies were a vehicle through which people could convey their vital, though varied, social concerns and political perspectives. Litanies were culturally patterned expressions of fear, anxiety, disappointment, frustration, and the other strong emotions which the turmoil of perestroika had engendered. On another level, litanies communicated a range of subtle—and sometimes contradictory—messages about identity and worldview, personal aspirations and social expectations. Litanies, however, were not merely a way of speaking about the world but also a way of *acting* in the world; in other words, like all forms of talk, they were as instrumental as they were expressive (Austin 1962). Ultimately, litanies reaffirmed and reproduced certain fundamental dispositions or stances and key structures of cultural logic. There are four general aspects of litanies that need to be considered as part of an overall interpretation of their social functions and cultural significance.

The first thing to recognize is that power was the key theme in this genre. The relationship between powerful forces (personified or not) and the powerless objects of those forces (characterized individually or collectively) was the focus of perestroika litanies. In effect, litanies divided Russian society into these two essential categories—victim and villain (good and evil)—and provided a moral commentary on the many dynamics of the relationship between them.

One underlying implication of litanies was that the speaker's group was morally superior to other groups, as marked by degrees of suffering or victimization. Even if not explicitly so, litanies were thus always competitive, for to establish that your group was the most victimized of all was to achieve a specific kind of social virtue: the virtue of powerlessness in a context in which power was characterized as immoral or evil.

The subtle discursive operations of the litany thus performed a kind of social accounting; every utterance of a litany was a calculation of social and moral situation, one that not only made *sense* out of particular life experiences and losses (as many anthropological arguments would construe it; see, for instance, Evans-Pritchard 1937 and Geertz 1973: 100–104), but indeed made *value*, or even some kind of symbolic privilege out of them as well.

The litany held up personal or collective experiences of suffering or loss as the criteria by which a degree of deservingness or entitlement might be established. The peasant logic of "limited good" (Foster 1965), of course, pertains here, and underlies the litany's competitiveness.[10] There is only so much recompense for suffering available, by far not enough to go around, in a context where so many have suffered so much.

The second operation that litanies performed was to demonstrate the power of the speaker, and the speaker's group as a whole, to endure whatever hardships their society could deliver. In this sense, litanies were closely related to the tales of heroic shopping and female endurance described in the previous chapter. Through litanies, people could demonstrate not only their moral status but also their culturally valued powers of character: stamina and strength both psychological and physical. If they were still alive, functioning, and even successful in their attempts to accomplish something despite all the cruelty and foolishness, then

[10] As the narrator of Solzhenitsyn's famous story "Matryona's Home" (1970: 44) declares: "I observed that the keening was not merely an expression of grief but contained an element of 'politics.'" In this story, through their lamenting at her funeral, various family members asserted their innocence in the death of Matryona, the story's protagonist, and their concomitant right to inherit her belongings. The psychological functionalism inherent in Geertz's argument in his famous essay "Religion as a Cultural System" (1973) I think greatly oversimplifies the multiple—and, as Solzhenitsyn puts it, quite *political*—operations that discourses about suffering can perform in a society.

they must be people of extraordinary constitution, cleverness, and determination.

A third way of viewing litanies is as a mode of entreaty. At the same time that they asserted the sacred or moral virtue of individuals or social groups, litanies were ritualistic appeals for overall deliverance: from the cyclical upheavals of Russian life, from authoritarian repression, from empty shelves, from poverty, from needless suffering, from absurdism. The litany was thus a kind of supplication (quite like Orthodox litanies and ritual laments), an almost prayer-like recitation of suffering and loss, directed toward some vague source or possibility of social redemption. Litanies bespoke a longing for some kind of relief or redemptive transformation. However overtly people expressed their pessimistic despair, the very utterance of their complaints implied some hope, albeit muted, of the possibility of relief. I shall return to this issue later in the chapter.

A fourth way of interpreting litanies was suggested to me by several Russian friends and colleagues. This perspective on litanies may seem to challenge the others offered here, but if we keep in mind that litanies address an underlying concern with power and innocence (in all their guises), it should be clear that it complements rather than contradicts the other two.

One phenomenon I observed several times was that people who seemed to be getting along quite well in their lives might resort to litanies, decrying in general terms how terrible things were, how hopeless the situation, and so on. As Olga quipped, when I expressed confusion over the gap between a mutual friend's lamentations and her seeming prosperity, "She doesn't want us to know how well she's doing! She doesn't want to stir up our envy, or have us ask her for help."

I hesitate to view such concealing of good fortune as deliberate manipulation; rather, it seemed to me that people work on their own self-construction through litanies, trying to perceive and promote themselves as "good people," living the life of relative poverty which has for so long been ideologically construed as connoting honesty and morality—and perhaps, at the same time, as Vladimir, a literary critic suggested in 1994, trying not to make someone else feel badly:

Concerning your favorite theme, laments: It stems from the famous lament of Yaroslavna [from the epic poem *The Lay of Igor's Campaign*, c. 1165] which has a great cultural content and has influenced many things, many theatrical monologues as well as the style of elementary day-to-day complaints: "Oh, how badly I live, there is no money, no this, no that." The lament is like an SOS: "Oh help me, people!" But the lament also fulfills a veiling function, it has a camouflaging side, because if, living among people, you have managed to pile up three dollars more than someone else, you can't disclose the fact that you live better, not because the Russian person is sly, but because someone else will be ashamed, if he knows you have more than he.

This practice of masking the positive may also rest on traditional beliefs about "unclean forces" (*nechistye sily*), which stand ready to foil anyone's plans or destroy their happiness.[11] Russians often avoid circulating good news to prevent the cataclysms that these vague forces might cause. For several months, one friend had tickets for her first trip to the United States, but she did not inform her colleagues until just before she was to leave. When I questioned her about it, she said simply, "You never know. There are *forces*." I asked a number of people about this, and all—even scientists—agreed that she had to keep such good news a secret, and that there were forces that made telling too much a dangerous thing to do. Following Sangren (1991), I think "unclean forces" can be seen, at least in part, as an alienated representation of the very real powers within Soviet society that conspired against the fulfillment of individual dreams and plans.

Litanies could thus perform any number of cultural operations simultaneously. Litanies could: create multiple fields of identification and belonging; declare the moral sanctity, integrity, and innocence of particular collectives or individual selves; assert the power of the powerless to endure and navigate the most treacherous difficulties; offer a vague entreaty for deliverance from those same difficulties; and distract or mislead "evil spirits" or the spirit of social envy. In the process, however, litanies expounded and reproduced significant ideological paradigms and modes of social orientation.

Like any potent cultural practice, speaking in litanies had unintended consequences that ran contrary to many of the expressed or implied desires of the individuals pronouncing them. Whatever their immediate social or cultural benefits, I would argue that this genre of speech may have helped to perpetuate some of the very social conditions that it decried.

The Unintended Consequences of Speaking in Litanies

In a recent essay, Michael Urban discussed the problems posed by what he calls "the politics of identity" in post-Communist Russia. Analyzing the conflicts that led up to the storming of the Russian White House in the

---

[11] On these forces and other magical beliefs in modern Russia, see Conrad (1989: 435) and Parkhomov (1984).

fall of 1993, he argues that much of the political process in contemporary Russia has been typified by the flinging of labels of opprobrium against "the other" (party, politician), labels that demonize the other as "Communist," "corrupt," or "criminal" and blame them for all the troubles of Russia, past and present. This powerful semiotic coding was accompanied by the deployment of various legalistic weapons in attempts to prove the other group's criminality and annihilate them politically. These discourses effectively "disabled those instrumental–strategic activities ostensibly aimed at negotiation, compromise and consensus" (1994: 739). Urban notes that "pragmatic orientations are overwhelmed by mythic notions retrieved from the past and the possibilities for political dialogue become lost in antipathetic claims pitched around competing ideas of national identity" (737).

The discursive logic of these political practices is fundamentally the same logic that structures litanies and which litanies reproduce. It is based on the symbolic construction of victims and villains, innocent and guilty—a logic or "story" that admits no real possibility of mediation.

Urban hints at the existence of a larger cultural field—that made up of everyday discourses—in the context of which this highly charged political rhetoric occurs. I would suggest that litanies (and related discourses) constitute that field, that they are a diffuse but very powerful reproductive agent of the politically destructive ideological paradigm that characterizes much of contemporary Russian politics. Although, as Urban points out, Russian speakers "frequently resort to tropes such as 'political theater of the absurd' or 'political zoo'" (745) when describing these impasses at the top, their day-to-day litanies may subtly reaffirm the deep logic of this construction, the conviction that there is an unbridgeable chasm between good selves and evil others, or, in Russian vernacular, "ours" and "alien" (svoi–chuzhoi).

This kind of ideology effectively reduces the ability to perceive social groups as interdependent and may impede mediating processes at many levels of a society, even the most immediate or local. Although the litanies of the perestroika era regularly lamented the civil violence of the past and prayed that the country's various factions would be able to avoid civil war, they also commonly cited that as a terrifying possibility. As Elizaveta Mikhailovna declared at the end of her litany about the intellectual absurdisms of Soviet culture, "I think we are heading for civil war, for complete disintegration. It is a nightmare."

The paradox here is that at the same time discourses like litanies decry violence, they reinforce the belief that there are unbridgeable social or political dichotomies. This in turn can lead to or justify the kind of violence that occurred in Yeltsin's war with Khasbulatov and the Russian parliament. In no way do I mean to suggest that day-to-day talk leads directly to such cataclysms, that speakers are responsible for the social turmoil that has existed in Russia in the past few years; the causes of this are many and enormously complicated. However, the widespread and perpetual reproduction and valorization of ideological paradigms such as the "victim–villain" complex certainly do little to defuse the potential for violence and social disintegration.

Litanies may also entrench the deep cynicism and despair that separates citizens from political processes. By constantly affirming the profound powerlessness of the self and of the associated collectivity, litanies reinforce a sense of hopelessness and futility and undermine attempts to imagine or invent even small-scale solutions to local problems.

As I have pointed out earlier, until I began to understand litanizing as a genre of speech with all of its concomitant powers to reproduce thought-paradigms, I was constantly challenging them with my own American speech form of optimistic (and perhaps naive) "cheerleading," but finding myself vehemently contradicted. People would sometimes ignore me, or they might answer me by saying something to the effect that "that is a fine way to think in a democratic/civilized society, but *here, in Russia*—it's an impossibility." In any number of conversations with my female friends and acquaintances, I responded to lamentations of the terrible situation of women in Russia by suggesting that feminist perspectives and methods of protest might offer women some social leverage. The answer was almost invariably that "you live in a wealthy country, where women have a much easier time providing for their families. We don't have the *luxury* of thinking about some glorious ideal of women's liberation. That is a privilege of women in bourgeois societies." While I remained convinced (by evidence of the accomplishments of social movements among impoverished women in many societies) that this is untrue, it was often impossible for my contradictions to get past the ideological walls put up by *discourses* of futility. Often, I was accused of promoting utopian solutions; but as one woman put it, "we are tired to death of utopia, of revolutions. We just want to get by quietly down here and be left alone to live our lives in peace"—a remark to which I could formulate no response, because it rang with such poignant validity.

Mystical "Salvation" from Social Crises

Despite their disparagement of utopian solutions to social problems, people occasionally proposed magical resolutions to the traumas of the time. A third category sometimes figured in litanies, and I term this category "the savior" in keeping with my other archetypal designations (victim and villain). The "savior"—whether a human being or some more vague entity—acted as an equalizing force, negating contradictions, effacing distinctions, restoring a mystical social unity, and undoing hierarchy. Occultism was quite popular at the time (in part because it was finally allowable as a genre of entertainment). Several times during fieldwork, I heard myths about the possibility of supernatural intervention. One evening, a young woman told me that she had read that the ecological crisis in Russia was affecting those who live parallel lives in the fourth dimension, and that soon these beings would get in contact with us to help us do something about it. On the occasion of their first open staging of an Orthodox Christmas dinner, one of my friends excitedly informed those at the table that Western astrologers were learning Russian, since they believed that in 1993 a messiah would be born in the vicinity of Perm (a city in the Urals)—a messiah who would save the world. One woman, the daughter of a former minister of trade, had also heard this and believed it as the first woman did; the rest of us expressed some doubt. Of course such magical stories circulate in most societies at times of or in situations of extreme hardship, where it is hard to imagine the effectiveness of more concrete modes of salvation.

A rather unique type of salvation was offered at the time by a man named Kashpirovskii, a hypnotist who appeared on television to hypnotize the viewing audience, as well as the country as a whole, into good health (I discuss this in more detail in chapter 5).

Kashpirovskii began to lose his veneer after a few months (though he regained it within two years, when he was elected to the parliament as a people's deputy), but faith in another savior, the dissident physicist Andrei Sakharov, only grew until his death in December 1989, when he was elevated to the status of martyr, and people talked of him as if he had been their only possible savior. In this vein, one newspaper editor told me during an interview, "Only Sakharov spoke out when we attacked Afghanistan." A feminist informant mourned that "only Sakharov took the feminist movement seriously." All around, people could be heard saying "only Sakharov cared about . . ." or "only Sakharov understood . . ."—the plight of the poor, the disabled, the elderly, those suffering in the aftermath of Chernobyl. It was commonly said that Sakharov was the only person who could have accomplished the necessary socio-political changes; he was viewed as singular because of the combination of his high scientific achievements, high moral courage, and high level of suffering. On the day of Sakharov's funeral, tens of thousands of people valorized Sakharov, his suffering, themselves and their own suffering by standing in line for hours in bitter, bone-chilling, wet and slushy cold. At the ceremony Sergei Kovalev, a long-time dissident activist, emphasized the rarity of saviors:

"Andrei Dmitrievich always said what he thought and acted in accordance with what he said. He never had a choice to be silent—that was the kind of man he was, the way he was made. He never had a choice, and this was the characteristic of his gift. Every country has a saint."

What all such doxologies about Sakharov were saying was that integrity, conscience, and wisdom are innate—not learnable—and that only someone with such an extraordinary degree of those qualities could redeem the society. Kovalev's statement that Sakharov never had a choice, that he was made to act in the way he did, that his character was a gift—all these asserted the essential nature of stance and identity. I would argue that statements such as this one reflexively naturalized the powerless stance of the victim-*narod*. By reifying the singularity of people like Sakharov, by sanctifying the idea of the rarity of saints, they validated the idea that society is composed of two essential fields—power and powerlessness—with extraordinary mediators appearing very occasionally in between. Ironically, this is hardly what Sakharov himself spoke of imagining for his country; his own political message was from the beginning about democratization, not the sacralization of more charismatic saints.

Anderson, Chervyakov, and Parshin (1995) argue that democratization requires changes in the language of political leaders, a shift from the obfuscating, didactic modes that characterize authoritarian rhetoric to ones more in line with popular vernacular, which thus facilitate communication between leaders and citizens, discursively bridging vertical cleavages in the power structure. Authoritarian rhetoric, they argue, has a disenfranchising effect; because it is inherently content-free (and even nonsensical), it promotes the cynical dissociation of populations from the political sphere. In recent years, these authors have detected a positive change in Russian political rhetoric as politicians recognize the necessity of connecting with voters, and their experimental findings indicate this has had a similarly positive effect on voter affiliation.

It seems clear that an important parallel process must occur in the speech of people outside government officialdom as well. In dialogue with transformations at the top, citizens (and citizen activists) of democratizing societies need to move away from the kind of language Kovalev used, language that in subtle ways symbolically reaffirms the distance between rulers and ruled.

Russian Identity, Suffering, and Escape

I found it significant that when a Russian translation of Norman Vincent Peale's *The Power of Positive Thinking* began appearing in kiosks around Moscow, people clamored to buy it and read it. Acquaintances said they found it compelling, but their comments were punctuated either by jokes or by sighs, which conceded the difficulty of adopting positive thinking in their cultural milieu. They thus tacitly cited the power that negative thinking has had in their lives: with their jokes and sighs they let it be known that they thought negative thinking was powerful enough to encompass and absorb any instruction in positive thinking that could be offered. This does not mean that many Muscovites were not working very hard at reformulating their discourses and worldviews.[12] Classes and workshops were beginning to be offered all over Moscow at this time, many of them styled after Western self-help and self-improvement programs and focused on developing confidence and optimism. I heard a number of almost prideful laments of disappointment with such classes, however. The magical self-transformations that were expected did not materialize, and many people were left more disheartened, and with another layer of material for litanies, than before.

In April 1990, I spent some time with an extremely bright and energetic young woman, Vera. She was actively pursuing two occupations simultaneously: one was a fairly high-status management position in a ministry and the other, a cooperative venture. Despite these engaging careers, however, she spoke with great cynicism about her country's predicaments:

> I think the best thing knowledgeable consultants could do would be to tell Western companies not to waste their time here. I've seen how slow and futile it all is. I was very dedicated at first, but now I think, what's the use? I think I should just do some black market trades and then sit around all year . . . sleeping. The only thing to do in the USSR right now is sleep. I know that's a depressed reaction. But the other side—McDonald's for instance—is a disgrace: it gives people a glimpse of something they can never really have; it rubs their poverty in their faces. The only hope is for people to be allowed to visit the West for a while, two or three years each, so they can really see how it might be, get an inspiration that they might bring back with them. But anyone who has such an opportunity, why should he come back? He should just *leave*.

The inherent form of the litany was one key to its socially reproductive power. It was circular rather than linear, a mythical rather than a pragmatic discourse. Litanies went around and around without straying from the well-worn trenches of their own sorrowful fetishes, except when they

---

[12] It is fascinating and chilling to note in this regard that when McDonald's opened in Moscow they trained their young workers in "cheerfulness"; this training included a segment on "how to smile"—one of the stranger practices of capitalist colonization.

leaped drastically (by means of the savior category) into the realm of transcendence or utopia. While it was easy to go from litany into utopian dreaming (as in Vera's idea that people should have a chance to experience life in the West for a few years), it was not so easy to go from litanies into discourses that portrayed life (or politics or economics) as a "problem to be solved." Litanies could be parodied, but it was hard to contradict them or challenge them with different ways of looking at Soviet/Russian society or with visions of gradual social improvement. In effect, the litany ideologically determined and structurally contained the range of possibilities open to the imagination. It reinforced and reproduced a view of Russian society as constituted by immutable sets of "villains" and "victims," where progress could occur only through vengeance or transcendence.

This circle of discourse was one of the social conundra from which my Russian friends were trying to extricate themselves during the perestroika years. It was the "dead end," reproduced partly through their litanies of the dead end. A certain lamenting question sounded through Moscow like a chant: "How can we escape?" "Where is the exit?" "Who will lead us to the exit?" The answer resonated just as widely. "There is no exit." "We are in a dead end." The conservative writer and newspaper editor Aleksandr Prokhanov, interviewed by Bruce Grant after the putsch in 1991, answered a question about ways out by declaring: "Way out? What way out? I just told you—it's as if you find yourself in the middle of an avalanche on a mountain slope. The first fall of snow overcomes you, then the second, then the third. There is no way out. . . . It is like a volcano, a volcano, and how on earth do you stop it? You can't. . . ." (Grant 1993: 35).

This trope of imprisonment was a prevalent one during perestroika. Equally widespread, however, were the refrains: "We must become different people!" "Russians must become different people." "We must rebuild [*perestroit'*] our very selves."

The difficulty of cultural transformation in the time of perestroika was thus locally characterized not as a matter of simply "breaking down the iron curtain and enjoying freedom," as many in the West imagined, but as one of getting people to transform their minds, bodies, characters, values and "souls" just as they were trying to escape from the epic, mythical land of Soviet absurdism. Discourse made it seem that there were few ways out of that land, that epic; at the same time, few people seemed interested in trying to imagine an alternative social world. After all, the land they were trying to escape was constructed around one totalizing utopian project, so how could they possibly invest in another? Because of the particularities of Russian/Soviet history, it is quite understandable that hopeful projections of a better society would be met only with cynical dismissal. Litanies, however, certainly played a role in reproducing the very conditions that they decried, if only by reinforcing a sense of the inevitability of powerlessness and suffering.

To put it bluntly, this national story of victims, villains, and saviors, performed through litanies, has been a discursive mechanism that facilitated authoritarian social relations. It did this by essentializing these categories and their interrelations. By making the hierarchy of social categories "natural" and inevitable, and by asserting that they are undone only through the magical intercession of persons like Sakharov, litanies reaffirmed hierarchy, exploitation, and structural violence. By essentializing powerlessness, the iteration of litanies had the reflexive, unintended consequence of reproducing powerlessness. The fatalistic stance of powerlessness left a power vacuum, readily filled by those who spoke the language of power and could deploy their own power stances.[13] This is another way in which litanies helped to reproduce the very situations and structures that they bemoaned.

By attributing power to certain social groups, the litany in effect renewed the possession of power by those groups; this discursive or symbolic transfer of power was clearly discernible in situations where litanies were spoken in the presence of, or were addressed to, those powerful persons who were its implicit "villains." Meetings of various kinds were an important element of perestroika, and many of them, especially those featured on television, featured litanizing supplications. On one televised occasion, a deputy in the Supreme Soviet, litanizing about the "complete disintegration" of Soviet society, the growth of crime and human degradation, finished by asking Gorbachev, "Please, increase the level of morality and culture in our country." Another deputy, in a litany about growing interethnic violence, declared that Gorbachev should "create friendship between different peoples." Whether or not such requests could ever be filled, they effectively asserted the magic of power and the location of power in one man. Frustrated with this kind of assertion and all its social consequences, Gorbachev—who was, clearly, no Stalin, however much he enjoyed his position—complained in a televised speech one day (May 25, 1990) that "people always want simple solutions, a magic tablecloth [a popular Russian fairy-tale device] which will take care of us without effort."[14]

[13] In these chapters I have addressed the genres of Russian power discourse only peripherally. Since, however, they are complementary to the stories and stances of powerlessness I describe here, recording and analysis of such talk is an important project for future work.
[14] See Ken Jowitt on the tendency in Leninist regimes for the public, which has been conditioned to perceive the Party as all-controlling, to expect all social events to be in the realm of this control. "Events do not occur, decisions are not made, and facts are often not recognized as facts until they are allowed to occur or to be recognized" (1992: 72).

Another common line cried out at meetings (and in private conversations) was the idea that power had to be somehow "given over" or "transferred" to the people, as if it were an exchangeable, movable object rather than a complex system of political practices; this metaphor of power as object is one of what Jowitt refers to as forms of "(pre)political speech" (1992: 289). Of course, there is always some accuracy to this metaphor, whenever and wherever it is employed, in that there are tangible attributes of power, such as capital equipment, access to natural resources, buildings, institutions, and so on, the transference of which marks a transfer of power. But in 1989 and 1990 few people were addressing those attributes when they called for the transfer of power.

Incidents like these showed Russian society to be in a contradictory, transitional moment, a moment when both leader and people—powerful and powerless—wanted a reform of social relations, but when, because of a lack of democratic experience, a concomitant narrowing of political imagination, and an inability to put aside reliable genres of discourse, they could imagine only magical means to effect that transformation.

Existential Predicaments and Discursive Practices

Discourses do not exist in a void. The kinds of speech genres and discourses about suffering and victimization that I have discussed in this chapter clearly do not produce and reproduce themselves outside of or disconnected from the social structures in which they occur and to which they refer. They also do not emerge spontaneously, outside the realm of existing cultural forms and patterns. In this section I explore the historical context of Russian power relations with reference to certain discourse genres of the past that may have influenced their evolution.

Much recent scholarship has been focused on the social and psychological consequences of powerlessness and domination. Whether these stem from authoritarian rule, colonization, serfdom, enslavement, or incarceration, or from more diffuse sources such as structures of caste, class, and gender, certain modes of response—practical as well as discursive or symbolic—frequently appear, as James Scott has shown (1985; 1990).[15]

The long history of authoritarian rule and class hierarchy in Russia—including the enserfment of the peasantry, which endured almost until the twentieth century—generated various forms of resistant discourse. Some of this discourse was legalistic: peasant or worker petitions and supplica-

---

[15] Curiously, in his grand tour of discourses of resistance, Scott pays almost no attention to lamenting genres, even though these have been extensively documented and studied by other scholars.

tions to local and regional officials, and to the tsar himself, asking for relief from the often overwhelming extractions of landowners, were one of the most direct (and best-documented) modes of this resistance. Haruki Wada gives a typical and quite poignant example of such a petition, this one dating from 1905:

> SIRE, We the workers and inhabitants of Peterburg . . . come to thee O SIRE, to seek *pravda* [justice] and protection. We are impoverished; we are oppressed, overburdened with excessive work, contemptuously treated. We are not even recognized as human beings, but are treated like slaves who must suffer their fate in silence and without complaint. And we have suffered, but even here are being further and further pushed into the slough of poverty, arbitrariness and ignorance. We are suffocating in despotism and lawlessness. SIRE, we have no strength left, and our endurance is at an end (Wada 1979: 86).

Lacking much recourse to more immediate, direct, or pragmatic ways of improving their situation, peasants and workers signaled their last remaining hope through these sorts of petitions: they appealed to the mercy of the "just" tsar, who, it was fantasized, had the best interests of the *narod* at heart, but had no knowledge of its predicament.

In a fascinating and theoretically nuanced recent essay (1996), Sheila Fitzpatrick has categorized and analyzed a selection of the letters that Soviet citizens wrote to public authorities—including Stalin himself—in the 1930s; their genre is basically the same as those of the prerevolutionary period. Writers often cite their powerlessness, vulnerability, and victimization in relation to local bosses or authorities; they cite specific problems of day-to-day survival; and they elaborate on the misery and sense of despair in their lives.

The resemblance of both pre- and post-revolutionary petitions to the missives of the glasnost era sent to publications such as *Ogonek* is striking, but so is their resemblance to the spoken litanies and laments that echoed in Moscow in 1989 and 1990. All four types of discursive texts share the same idiom, utilize similar metaphors and tropes (the victim–villain complex), and seek justice from either a vague or a relatively distant (and thus rather mystical) authority.

Two other archaic Russian discourse genres are closely related to the social structures and practices of their time. Both of these exhibit the idiom of victimization, one in which "villains" are sometimes personified and sometimes as vague as fate or life itself. Both of these genres also signal and reproduce a general sense of powerlessness and futility.

The first is lament (*prichitanie* or *plach*). Laments were once performed on three ritual occasions: as part of marriage ceremonies, at funerals, and at the departure from the village of conscripted soldiers. Metaphorically dense, these laments were structured like litanies and focused on the many dimensions of loss entailed by departures and changes. A typical lament repeatedly described the impending separation and usually revolved around the question "Why?" In the case of weddings, for instance, the most poignant laments were those sung, or rather wailed, by the bride to her parents: "Why are you, mother who bore me and rocked me in my cradle, making me go off with a stranger into a family of strangers who will mistreat me and make me their slave?" The victim in wedding laments was the young bride, and by extension all young women facing the loss of girlhood and the painful departure from the parental home for the husband's father's household. The villains were alternately the parents who were giving the girl up, the man and his family who were stealing her away and robbing her of her independent, happy girlhood, and cruel fate, which ensures young brides' unhappiness (of course, this last could be seen as a mystification of patriarchal gender and marriage systems).[16]

In funeral laments the categories of villain and victim were more ambiguous, for the lamenter alternated between blaming herself for letting the deceased go and blaming the deceased for leaving. Laments for departing soldiers cast blame on the world outside to the village which was taking the young man away (for his twenty-five-year term of service); by association, these laments also blamed (although mildly) the tsar in whose name wars were waged and soldiers conscripted. World War II laments (for dead or departing soldiers) collected by V. G. Bazanov (1975) show the fascist armies clearly in the villain's role. They also show that at least in certain parts of northern Russia these genres survived well into the Soviet era.

Closely related to and supportive of these ritual lament cycles are the hundreds of folk songs that re-created and rehearsed the sadness of loss and separation. These addressed many typical circumstances: the departure of soldiers, the daughter leaving her parents for marriage, the agony of separation at death. The most poignant and most popular of such songs were focused on the separation of lovers (especially through war, death, or marriage to other people). Many of these songs were traditionally sung in an acute lamenting style, so much so that the nineteenth-century poet Nekrasov commented that "wailing is called singing in this country."

Another extensive complex of traditional Russian texts existed alongside lamentations and shared their idiom and ideology of futility. This

[16] D. M. Balashov's (1985) study of the ritual complex of Russian weddings in the Vologda region presents a rich selection of laments.

is the complex of songs, folktales, and epics about "misery" (*gore*) or "Misery-Misfortune" (*gore-zloschastie*).[17] Of these, the songs about grief, which were "women's songs," represent the earliest appearances of this theme, probably dating to pre-Christian Russia (Likhachev 1984: 102). Many versions of such songs are extant (see Rzhiga 1931). Besides sharing a basic form (structural parallelism) and idiomatic features, they are narrated from the first-person point of view (sometimes explicitly female, sometimes deliberately ungendered) and focused on a single conceit: that of being pursued by a personified Misery through either space or time. The song lyric below succinctly relates the basic formula of the *Gore* complex.

MISERY

Okh, young girl, beautiful young girl!
Wherever you ran to escape misery,
You never got away from misery!
I run away from misery into the empty field,
And misery runs after me like a rabbit.
I run away from misery into the dark forest,
And misery follows me with an axe;
I run away from misery into marriage,
And misery follows me with little children,
I run from misery into the grey earth,
And misery comes after me with a shovel.[18]

In the *Gore* songs, the ability of grief to follow a person wherever she goes is abetted by its talent for changing forms, adopting the faculties of animals, birds, and fish, acquiring whatever tools are necessary to maintain the chase, and entering through any of the openings presented by life-cycle transitions (birth, marriage, death).

In folktales, this Misery developed even more personified characteristics (many of them bordering on humorous, as is appropriate to the folktale genre). Its most significant behavior is its way of attaching itself to a person; it especially likes finding men in taverns upon which to fix itself permanently.[19] Indeed, there are many masculine versions of the *Gore*

---

[17] I have chosen to translate *gore* (pronounced gor-ye) as misery, though it also glosses as grief, sorrow, woe, trouble, and misfortune.

[18] From Likhachev and Vaneeva (1985: 70). The first three lines here are like an introduction, employing the device common in songs and laments of referring to oneself from the third-person point of view. The line about children refers to all the troubles and tragedies that having children invites and is reminiscent of the proverbs, "Little children, little troubles. Big children, big troubles" and "To be without children is grief. With children it's double."

[19] See the *Gore* tale in Afanas'ev (1985, 2: 341). A version in English can be found under the title "Misery" in Afanas'ev (1973: 20).

songs, generally concerned with the misery brought on by drunkenness and disregard for parental authority. In the folktales, which partook of an irony not found in any of the songs, the protagonists often managed to trick misery into jumping into a hole which was then sealed up.

The degree to which the conception of a partly personified Misery-Misfortune (*gore-zloschastie*) still exists in Russia is striking. Although it may not be given that (or any) specific name, something much like Misery-Misfortune is nonetheless warded off in various contemporary social contexts via numerous common gestures and utterances, such as the self-protection against unclean forces mentioned above. Whenever someone says something optimistic about their lives or their future, their statement is almost invariably followed by making a spitting sound ("t'fu, t'fu, t'fu") three times over the left shoulder "in order not to spoil it."

There is a complex continuity among traditional Russian laments, the Misery–Misfortune complex, and the contemporary litanies heard in perestroika times. Archaic Russian ways of communicating about the world are based around conceptual models of the world that bear striking resemblance to current Russian discourses. The same affect—lamentation—appears to have been as much a defining Russian stance one hundred years ago as it was in perestroika times, and the same value oppositions provided key dramatic tension.

The formal traditional lament and the contemporary litany of suffering thus share the same idiom, the same way of conceptualizing and talking about the problems and misfortunes of existence. Whether it was mystified as some natural force, specified in some political agency, or personified in an individual leader, the "heartless actions" of the powerful have been a principal (even fetishized) element in laments, the Misery–Misfortune complex, and in contemporary litanies. The corresponding minutiae of victimization, elaborated with fervor, have been very important in all of these discourses. Like their cultural predecessors, perestroika-era litanies were inherently about the structures of power in which both victim and villain seemed to be eternally enmeshed.

CHAPTER FOUR

Mystical Poverty and
the Rewards of Loss

Lacking hope for change, improvement, without a future, they had devised a counterworld, inventing their own version of what made "the good life."
—Barbara Myerhoff, *Number Our Days*

They were satisfied, these penniless people! They were all satisfied, these naked, barefoot, dear people of integrity!
—Inna Varlamova, "A Threesome"

Fairy tales teach us that wealth is perilous and poverty profitable. This solves the dilemma—"to have or have not." . . . In the Russian fairy tale, as in life, it is the poor who are oppressed, but it is the poor, the meek and the weak, who defeat the mighty (like the rooster who fools the fox).
—Zara Abdullaeva, "Popular Culture"

Throughout these pages I have alluded to the moral status that suffering and loss can produce. Suffering, enhanced through discourse, can socially exonerate those who suffer and even sacralize them. In Russia, in particular, spiritual merit has been associated with hardship and poverty, and this attribution has worked in subtle ways against people's explicitly stated images of the lives they wanted their society to provide.

I have suggested that one reason Russians have had such a hard time transforming their country in accord with their own idealistic social visions is that they have been "stuck" between two moral worlds, one a place of basically pragmatic values and practices (expressed through a Russian idiom, of course), the other an upside-down world where reverse logic rules, where suffering is blessed and loss is gainful. Although my informants complained about this "other" world (their "anti-Disneyland"), it had a great deal of value in their lives, especially in their construction of personal, collective, and national identities.

Here I provide more evidence concerning the existence and importance of this alternative world. To do this, I first examine some fairly straightforward proclamations of this inverted logic; then I explore the way that various life histories characterized transcendence as arising through suffering and sacrifice.

The Inverted World

Cultural value—especially sacred value—is difficult to measure or certify. Outside the spheres of propaganda, people do not usually come forth and say "we value this above all" or "we value this more than that." In fact, it often happens that the things people say are valued are actually secondary or parallel to other things that they never mention, or mention only in passing, or mention only offhandedly through personal narratives.

As an ethnographer in the field, my first clue about the value of hardship was simply that the people I met were always talking about it. Since the immense struggles of their lives were so apparent, people's stories about these struggles seemed, at first glance, merely descriptive commentaries on their experiences. However, these tales were relayed in poetic, heightened language (almost ritual language) and embroidered with poignant details, which I found to be folkloric in the regularity of their appearance and their simplicity; one could almost compile a lexicon of these iconic objects, the building blocks of many a story: bread, sausage, potatoes, boots, apples, sugar, tea, matches, salt, cigarettes. It seemed that there was a theater of the mind, where these objects took on vast proportions and were used as the vital, almost animate props in an ongoing performance.[1]

These magical stories, which often unfolded as segments of litanies, contained a certain formula, which struck me because, while it, not surprisingly, inverted Soviet official values, at the same time it almost defiantly inverted utilitarian values as a whole. This formula was expressed in very routine ways, in small but significant asides and jokes. Inverting what she perceived to be a rather universal admiration for Western order, a historian, describing to me a trip she had taken in the United States, declared: "Oh, yes, you in the West have beautiful cities, gleaming and clean, skyscrapers, gold, silver, so much wealth, so organized and orderly you are! But after two days I tell you, I long for Moscow, I long for our crooked streets, our irregular buildings, haphazard, but full of life, full of spirit in a way that your cities will never be."

[1] One point Anna Wierzbicka makes in her semantic analysis of the Russian key term "soul" is that the soul is "viewed as an internal spiritual theater, a place where events happen of a kind that could never happen in the world of inanimate things" (1989: 51). This suggests that "the soul" is culturally constructed as the location where the kinds of inversions I am describing occur.

This same topic could be used reflexively to illustrate a kind of crook-edness imputed to the Russian character. When I mentioned the eccentricity of urban orientations—the way Moscow streets seemed to run in every direction, one friend said, with a poignant yet ironic intonation, "Well, Russians . . . what do you want?" (*nu, russkie . . . chto ty khochesh'?*). In the same vein, once I asked Nadezhda, an elderly but incredibly droll woman, what she thought of the ubiquity of construction debris in Russian cities. "Ah, that's easy!" she said, simultaneously parodying both Soviet work patterns and Communist slogans: "It's a sign of our *anti-bourgeoisnost'*! Neatness, order, that's just a sign of counter revolutionary, petit-bourgeois mentality!"

On another evening, waiting for a train in the metro with a friend, talking about the situation in the stores, I asked jokingly whether people would suffer if there were ever a shortage of shortages. My friend answered, "Well, it was easier in earlier times, under Brezhnev, when you could go into a store and know you would get something, but this time is certainly more interesting. What would we do without our catastrophes?" Another man caught me in a joke: "You know why the United States has a much higher suicide rate than Russia? Because it's so *boring* over there! There, you wake up in the morning, and you know what's going to happen to you. Here, it's much more interesting: you catch a tram for the twenty-minute ride to work, and you get there two hours late! You go to buy sausage, but they are selling only videotapes!"

Sometimes, this playfully deliberate inversion of logic asserted itself more aggressively. There was a male conversational genre consisting of jokes about the loss of millions of lives in labor camps and during the war. At one dinner party, having heard some of these mordant anecdotes pass around, I asked the man sitting next to me to explain the motivation for such jokes. "We are proud of it!" he declared, smirking. "The more the better," he added, facetiously and yet seriously, too. "We are proud of our losses, and especially proud of the degree to which we manage to destroy ourselves. The more people who died, the greater our pride." By this he emphasized the phenomenon whereby pride-in-loss emerges from chronicles of Russian annihilation, self-destruction, deprivation, and economic cataclysm. Litanies, which emphasized these things, aided in that construction of Russia as a special kind of kingdom with a special kind of folk. This mythologizing—even through irony—of these bouts of seemingly absurd self-destruction is a kind of Russian cultural "deep play" in which the more that is lost, the more the "meaningfulness of it all" (Geertz 1973: 434) increases. As Dale Pesmen writes about the culture of suffering in Omsk, "As deterioration and loss are assumed to be constant, yet there is always more to lose, any paradox, anything problematic, any minor reference to badness seems to imply depth, infinity" (n.d.: 4).

These self-reflections of a cultural potential for both cruelty and suffering surely were not celebrating the real, the very devastating immediate qualities of poverty, loss, war, or authoritarian violence. It did not seem to me that in their daily practices Russians were ever deliberately attempting to maximize their problems and minimize their comfort: quite the contrary, many were striving to improve their material situations. They did this, however, within the shadow of an established set of discourses which dictated that more is less and less is more: that material wealth means spiritual poverty, while material poverty indicates spiritual wealth. It was always, therefore, possible for them to present their different life conditions as a sign of moral virtue. There are, of course, clear echoes of Russian Orthodoxy in this construction.

Alan Dundes proposes the term "folk ideas" to describe those widely held formulae which he calls "building blocks of worldview" (Dundes 1972: 96). While one might take issue with the "construction" metaphor he uses, Dundes's examples belie the concreteness of that metaphor and instead suggest the subtle ways in which such "folk ideas" feed into and reproduce what are ultimately extremely powerful ideologies and the social practices concomitantly legitimated and even sacralized through them. One of his examples is quite relevant to the discussion of "mystical poverty." He talks about the folk idea of "the principle of unlimited good" in American culture (explicitly contrasting the "principle of limited good" which George Foster (1965) found operant in peasant societies), an idea expressed in myriad small ways in day-to-day talk. Dundes argues that sayings such as "where there's a will, there's a way," or "the sky's the limit" represent a widely shared logic which has structured a particular kind of American worldview, one oriented towards optimism and the notion that everyone can succeed if they work hard enough. It seems preferable to think of these as ideologies, with all the potential for the mystification of social realities and power relations that term implies. The commonplace inversions of much Russian speech suggest the ubiquity of a quite different kind of ideology, one in which material striving subtly indicates immorality, loss of sacredness, and disconnection from ones' peers.

Material Life and Cultural Identity

An account which was part of a three-hour-long life history I recorded set forth these inversions explicitly. The narrator, Semion Arkadevich, was a man who had spent his youth in orphanages in the 1930s, served as a boy soldier in the war in order to eat, then "sat" for six years in a far Eastern Siberian labor camp, from which he was freed only after Stalin's death. He told his tale from the safe harbor of the kitchen of his hard-won Moscow apartment. I had asked him to share his war and camp stories with me, and to give me his general impressions about wartime and his country. One story followed another, and they were all mainly about *food*. (In almost all the Russian war stories I heard, as with litanies and conversation in general, food was a constant point of focus.) After several tales, one about selling a jacket for a piece of sausage, another about finding a single "tiny, tiny little carrot" and sharing it ecstatically with a friend, he paused, reflectively, and then went on:

> In my opinion, about the war . . . the thing I noticed. Kindness and humaneness always exist in inverse proportion to the extent of culturedness. . . . The higher the culture, the greater the wealth . . ., the less, the less. . . . The higher the culture, and I know this from experience, the higher the culture, the less humane, humane in the sense of sharing a crust of bread, providing shelter . . . to a stranger for instance. During the war, while I was wandering, I would approach any house. . . . I came to a house. It was very warm inside. . . . I found a destitute, destitute old woman in this tiny hut [*bednaia, bednaia starushka, v malen'koi izbushke*]—but she had a potato, her last potato, and she took her last potato and cut it in half and shared it with me.

This tale of the generous old woman, which may have been exaggerated and mythologized in the process of its telling, reinforced the link between sacredness and poverty, reiterated the seemingly paradoxical idea of the generosity of the poor, and vivified the cultural logic that a poverty of means is accompanied by a wealth of spiritual goodness.[2] This man even put it in modern, mathematical-sounding terms when he declared that kindness exists in "inverse proportion" to wealth.

After this story, he elaborated his theory by talking about the other side of the equation:

> When a person has a lot, he doesn't give anything away, but on the contrary, he wants more and more for himself. Strange. If you are dealing with

[2] In a discussion of Russian peasant morality and reciprocity, Jovan Howe refers to the tradition of collective aid described by the nineteenth-century *narodnik* ethnographer Englehardt, which echoes perfectly with my own informant's story: " 'Today they have eaten the last loaf of bread, from which they yesterday cut 'morsels' for those who knocked at their door.' Hence, the saying: 'the tiniest bit for oneself, and a piece of it for someone else, who has nothing to put in his mouth' " (Howe 1990: 47).

millionaires, what millionaire will give you half of what he has as any poor person will? Not even less than half! Will some billionaire give you a thousandth part of his wealth? No. I have noticed this wherever I have been, whatever situation. Big bosses, for instance, have no idea, they cannot remember what it is like to struggle by, like some lowly engineer. The engineer still knows, he helps his friends. . . . Or in the military, some guys have parents, who send them things, support them. But it is the poor fellow, without anything, any help—he's the one who will share his tobacco with you, he's the one who will give you one of his last cigarettes.

This idea was widespread in Moscow. Abundant were both long stories and quick philosophical remarks affirming the conviction that while people are poor, they are generous, but that as soon as they move up the economic ladder and gain materially, they lose spiritually. Speaking about provincial people, a common remark was that, "They are poorer out there, but they are kinder" (*oni bednee, no dobree*).

There were particular constructions of this logic among the creative intelligentsia; as one writer told me, "Money is so boring. My friends and I, whenever we have it, we try to give it away. We're always passing it back and forth among ourselves to get rid of it." More seriously, a female friend who spent her time among musicians said, "Whatever we have, we share openly. What is mine is theirs and vice versa. Even if we only have a little." One of her musician friends told me that this woman was both stingy and greedy—a contradiction which points out the conflicts between cultural identity and social practice.

The perestroika years saw commodity culture and the concomitant creation of social distinctions (Bourdieu 1984) emerge into the open. Many people, however, found this somewhat problematic, and the acting out and discussing of value conflicts connected with the commodification of life was thus a symbolic practice of perestroika.[3] This problem was very much on the ideological agenda in 1989–90, since cooperatives had been opening up and the question whether people should be allowed to get rich was being very hotly debated.

[3] This was by no means a new cultural conflict; a social debate about materialism existed throughout the Soviet period. See Stites (1989) on the semiotics of the egalitarian aesthetic in the revolution and its demise in the postrevolutionary era. In the 1920s NEP (Lenin's New Economic Policy) revitalized a demand for consumer self-differentiation. The 1930s brought a revalidation of certain forms of consumption and the beginning of rather modern expressions of commodity fetishism. Dunham (1990) and Boym (1994) both explore the development and encouragement of middle-class values under Stalin and elaborately detail the semiotics of Soviet bourgeois domesticity and consumption. Matthews (1978), Zemtsov (1985), and Willis (1985) give interesting insights into the developments and deployments of *klass* in various Russian (Soviet) contexts.

Two contradictory discourses concerning housing made their way into Russian conversations during perestroika. The one celebrated the free market, with a special fixation on a utopian image of America, where presumably everyone had access to a decent bungalow existence, while those who could do better for themselves were free to do so. The other discourse was fixated on the evil of class in Russia; its sad heroes were workers, collective farmers, and war veterans who had played by all the rules yet still lived in dismal communal apartments or apartments with no running water; its villains were the elites who appropriated good apartments for themselves at the expense of the less powerful. The paradox was that while, on the one hand, glasnost exposed the hidden Soviet class structure, on the other hand it allowed the first open valorization of the freedom of the market and the legitimacy of open class differentiation. These contradictory visions were mythically united in a utopian fantasy of democratic social justice which would see everyone minimally situated in a two-room apartment.

At an immediate level, such discourses suggested the resonance of a zero-sum mentality often ascribed to peasants (Foster 1965; Howe 1990): the idea that goods are limited and that anyone who strives for more is necessarily reducing the amount available to others.

One basis of indignation over social differentiation was the idea that people who wanted more were threatening collective identity and practice: they were, by their very activity, announcing that the typical Soviet lifestyle was not good enough for them, that they deserved more. This threw into question that lifestyle itself, which many people had managed not only to enjoy but to valorize as being simple but satisfying; not fancy but familiar. It threatened the linkage of poverty and sacredness on which certain forms of identity (and pride) had grown to depend.

Persons trying to differentiate themselves socially and economically were presented as challenging the continuity of *narod* identity, which, among other things, was defined by its massive sameness, by the sharing of common experiences—the experience of simple human pleasures, a customary aesthetic and set of life practices. When expensive foreign shops first began to open in Moscow during 1989 and 1990, these elicited a mix of curiosity, horror, envy, and indifference among Muscovites who felt they could never afford their wares (and who resented the fact that, until this was outlawed, all such stores required hard currency). "Such stores are not for us, not for the *narod*," as one friend said, with noticeable but perhaps injured pride, in the same phrase decrying that these stores were so inaccessible and asserting identification with a group that can do without such luxuries.

Partial or total self-reliance was another often-encountered mark of identification with the *narod* and its poverty aesthetic and ideal (and also a means of providing for a family). Dachas were central in this construction. In Russian dacha did not signify a place of summer "recreation"—at least for adults—so much as it did the headquarters of a family's self-provisioning efforts, as well as the place for an indispensable annual recuperation of mind, body, and soul from the effects of the city.[4]

The passionate cultivation, nearly scientific foraging, and intense food preserving—canning, curing, drying, pickling, and salting—which many Muscovites practiced at their dachas (often less than an hour's drive from the city) had, of course, several quite functional dimensions, especially in a time of increasing shortages. Like dedicated gardeners in any industrial society, however, Russians engaged in these practices simultaneously asserted their symbolic association with the ideals of resourcefulness, skill, discipline, and patience. Such practices also symbolized a connection (partly fantasized) with a simpler, more integral, and more independent peasant past. This was made clear to me when I visited one family at their dacha. The father (a computer scientist by profession) took me around their small plot to show me the family's gardens but also pointed out for me the dozens of objects he had made by hand, using traditional carving methods and scavenged materials. The yard was filled with homemade tools, benches, tables, and toys; he had built an old-fashioned well with a handmade bucket and crank; and the property was surrounded by fencing he had crafted himself. What was this if not symbolic association with traditional rural ideals and expression of the ability to make a whole world from scratch?

Different families followed different dacha regimes, reflecting their different facilities, ideas, and ideals. But most dedicated a lot of time to growing their own vegetables—cucumbers, tomatoes, squash, onions, carrots, beets, herbs, and potatoes. Fruits were also cultivated, especially apples and a variety of berries which were gathered and put up for the winter in great quantities. All such practices of a "natural economy" increased in importance during and especially after perestroika, when growing shortages and poverty seemed to threaten so many. But the pride with which people displayed their gardens, their colorful anthropomorphizing of the

---

[4] As I have argued elsewhere (Ries 1994: 246–249), the Soviet state relied as much on the collective effects of people's unofficial provisioning strategies for its survival as families relied on these for their survival. That is, without the massive efforts of citizens to carve their own support systems out of the margins and interstices of Soviet official systems, the state itself could not have continued to function as long as it did. Dacha activities played a central role in this.

"Selling Dried Mushrooms" (Photo by John Einarsen and Robert Kowalczyk)

fruits of their labors, and their dedication to this lifestyle signaled the symbolic value and identity they derived from these practices as well. As one woman said, "Up there in their fancy parliament, they can do whatever they want. The *narod* will get by down here, as always."

The ritualized (whether necessary or not) habit of standing in line was another fundamental way in which people solidified their belonging to the *narod* at the same time as they dealt with material necessity; classes or categories of people in the status hierarchy always had special access which kept them out of lines, and this fact of not having to deal with lines was one detail that demarcated them as non-*narod*. Especially in hard times like the perestroika years, the experience of being forced by need to stand in lines beyond endurance served as a daily demonstration of how much people could stand and nourished collective identification. A few years ago (March 17, 1991), *The New York Times* reported that some people had stood in line for a wanted commodity even under a spray of tear gas meant to disperse them; it is possible to imagine how a story like this might have circulated locally, illustrating, on the one hand, how dire the food situation was, but, on the other, how all-enduring and even powerful the people were in the face of obstacles. Of course, this image could be regarded both earnestly and ironically. Explaining my reliance on calendars, maps, and other ordering devices, to a quizzical acquaintance, I joked that maybe we Westerners do that for spiritual peace. "But what do Russians do for spiritual peace?" I inquired, and she answered without pause: "We stand in lines! We stand in lines, share our worries and health problems, and become a collective then and there, inseparable."

Whether through telling familiar stories or reciting popular jokes about lines the stance of patient endurance reflexively instilled in people the poignant value of poverty and powerlessness. In times of economic crisis, every deprivation and new degree of difficulty tolerated with the patient stance of the *narod* could be worked into stories to elaborate constructions of self and of the imagined community. The woes and indignities suffered might enhance access to the mythical social stage, a theatrical landscape of frustration, worry, hardship, and petty humiliation, which provided a passageway to the the fulfillment of class identity and augmented an ancient image of venerable Russianness. Much perestroika-era discourse positioned the *narod* as the main protagonists on this stage; the antagonists were "everybody else," everyone differentiated by status, access, power, family, connections, and wealth. Depending on many factors, including their opportunities and ambitions at a given moment, my informants might identify themselves with this mythical *narod* or risk distinguishing themselves from it.

Bread and Narrative in the Experience of Poverty

> Bread isn't subservient to decrees and ministerial directives—in the end it is above them all.
> "The Red Book of Karavai," *Ogonek* (July 27, 1991)

In the elaboration of the mystical poverty paradigm, bread was a substance that starkly marked a path of access into the realm of sacred identification. The key substance linking the entire *narod*, physically and metaphorically, bread, as represented in talk, permitted an inversion of social values, symbolically placing the *narod* "above" powerful others.

When I arrived in Moscow in early September 1989, there were already many shortages, but the basic foodstuffs of the Russian diet (bread, butter, sausage, cheese, tea, sugar, certain fruits and vegetables, grains, and cereals) were still available in state stores. By the time I left at the end of May 1990, even the most basic foodstuffs had become scarce in those stores in Moscow (and the situation was worse in other cities and towns). Nine months before, fresh fish and meat had been difficult to find, but there was cheese, and even sugar. In January 1990, cheese had vanished and supplies of sugar had dwindled, even with rationing. Noodles and infant cereal and boxes of salt filled supermarket shelves then, in quantities that far exceeded demand. But in March and April even these disappeared, and people began to talk of what they called the "absurd" need to ask their friends and acquaintances to bring macaroni home from trips abroad, instead of souvenirs (it should, however, be noted that most people had hoarded closets full of macaroni and other dried goods by then).

It seemed that there must always be bread, however, faithful bread, "to all people dear" as an old proverb goes: the basic staple of daily life, on which everyone could survive if necessary. As foodstuffs went, bread was in a category of its own; in hard times, everything else was extraneous.

But in early April 1990, for the first time the bread stores were empty of loaves by mid-morning. People talked about bread's disappearance all day long. They vituperated against the grain producers, who they said were holding back on production in anticipation of price increases. A couple of my older acquaintances told me they were starting to hoard bread, drying it and storing it in large plastic bags, in case there were none at all. The last time Russians had dried bread in this manner was during the war, but a certain comment had remained in circulation, used when trouble seemed imminent: "It's time to dry some bread" (*pora sukhari sushit'*). In perestroika times, this remark signified that things had become dire, that they had reached the point at which the real cultural theater began. Discussion of the disappearance of bread was both ironic and momentous, and it suggested that along with a very real level of material trouble, a level of symbolic intensity was being reached as well, connecting the present situation with all the earlier cataclysms of Russian history.

The cover of one issue of *Ogonek* magazine (July 27, 1991—the bread crisis only began in 1990; it lasted for a long time) summarized the material and symbolic significance of bread in one image: in a black and white photograph, an old man sat, gazing worriedly out of a window, his chin resting on his hand. In front of him, on a table, spread open as a tablecloth lay a newspaper, visibly entitled *Our Life (Nasha zhizn')*. On the newspaper rested two quarter-loaves of bread. The top of the photograph was superimposed with the title *NADEZHDY NA KHLEB* which could be translated as "hope in bread" or "hope for bread." The image of the old man captured the emblematic mood of the *narod* (anxious but quiet), as well as its worthiness and its suffering-filled history. The newspaper title, *Our Life*, tied the *narod's* survival and even its identity to these small chunks of bread.

The following story exemplifies the centrality of bread in the epic of the Russian *narod*. It is part of the life history of Semion Arkadevich from which I quoted earlier. I include the lengthy first part to provide context.

When the war started, our orphanages were evacuated, and I was evacuated aboard the barge *Ossetia*. Almost at once I ran off. . . . This was in 1941. By the time the Germans were getting close to Moscow I was already on the run. Sometimes I traveled standing on the steps of a railroad car. I didn't think at all *what* I would eat, or *what* I would drink. I just wanted to eat and I had to get to the front quickly. Not because I had to shoot or kill somebody there. I knew . . . just as any animal is drawn to find some salt somewhere and lick it, just like that a hungry person is drawn to get some food somewhere. And so I was drawn to the front, because surely I would eat somewhere there. I was all tattered, all emaciated and it was only owing to my good genes that I survived despite the hunger and cold. I first got to the front near Orel. I remember absolutely clearly how I got acquainted with one cook, some Uncle Pasha, and for the time I lived there, those soldiers gave me shelter and I lived right on the front line together with the soldiers. And I remember how Uncle Pasha was cooking a caldron of kasha and a caldron of soup and he had to feed . . . I mean he was cooking for three hundred people, perhaps, or maybe for two hundred, anyway it was a big caldron. But not more than twenty or twenty five people came to eat from it. It was cooked with canned meat, you know, such soup. I was eating and eating and I couldn't eat enough. I thought I would never stop. He was feeding me and feeding and feeding me. I spent several days there, they fed me I don't know how much. It happened like that. . . .

But I would like to tell you one thing, the most important thing to me during all this time. Right before the war I was walking one day and saw that a piece of bread was sitting on a road. It was from a loaf of wheat bread, not rye, it was a white piece of bread. That was during one of my flights from the orphanage. I wasn't hungry; I felt like it was embarrassing to take it but something stopped me. How can it be that a loaf of bread is just sitting there on the road? And then the war began. And for all those years to come when I was hungry, that loaf was always on my mind; you know just always was in my head, I don't know why. And so there, at the front when I was seeing all those battles, all the time that piece of bread was in my head.[5]

The folkloric resonance of this tale makes it clear that bread was the edge, the symbolic margin between the physical and metaphysical worlds. Bread was Semion Arkadevich's emblem of his own hunger, the thing he recalled for so many years, that he kept with him even in the present as his way of remembering what he had endured. To dream hungrily of bread was to be beyond hunger, to have passed into that realm where survival is miraculous, a sign of some hidden—and perhaps sacred—power.

The war was a constant referent in conversations during perestroika, marking the last time the *narod* as a whole felt so much on the edge. The loaf of bread on the road was a sign of the world-to-come, the world of loss but also of the elevation of the *narod's* collective power of endurance. In popular memory, the Great Patriotic War was often held up as a time of real collectivism and common purpose, a time of social unity arising spontaneously out of shared hunger and crisis without terror and exhortation from above (cf. Tumarkin 1991: 289).

A crucial point, however, is that the perestroika period was negatively compared to the time of the war. One afternoon on the outskirts of Moscow I hailed a cab, which I shared with a talkative man who, having no idea I was not a local person, prattled on and on to the driver, looking at me for signs of agreement (I quietly nodded my head). My fellow passenger expressed, summarily, an idea I had often heard: "Moscow has become so bad in the last years. . . . During the war it was so much better. Everybody pulled together. There was enthusiasm, excitement, energy, spirit. . . . Now all people think about is how to get rich. Life is no longer even interesting. Moscow has lost something that made her great."

Whatever their specific metaphysical coordinates, whatever the domain

---

[5] It may be relevant to note that items discovered lying on a road were always suspected of being ensorceled or "spoiled" (Ivanits 1989: 103). I bring this up to suggest the ways that Semion Arkadievich's story echoed traditional Russian tales.

of their significant details, all these stories and anecdotes suggested the existence of a Russian ideology in which the reduction of the safe, material world provided both an opening to and an elaboration of the sacred one; an ideology in which a crust of dried bread could be turned into a whole universe. In this regard, I am reminded of a passage from Elaine Scarry: "A privileged group of people . . . would probably never overtly justify its privileges on the greater pain, hunger, or frustration of the lower classes but rather on the mediating fact that the latter have less world (property, knowledge, ambition, talent, style, professionalism, and so forth). It is in many cases, of course, their pain and hunger that dissolves their world-extension, and their lack of world-extension that obscures their pain and hunger" (1985: 331).

Elite perceptions do, of course, mask the material and ideological realities of the impoverished, but Scarry's own construction elides something important, too: the *symbolic* world of the impoverished may very well be built around the experience of hunger; Russian *narod* identity seemed in many ways to be constructed through narratives of suffering and starvation. Surely, this elaboration of identity takes place not concurrently with the experience of hunger, but after its at least partial abatement; it was not the immediate experience of suffering that was expressed in Russian stories, but the remembrance or imagination of it from a remove. Still, it was elaborated, turned into an entire alternative world, a world impregnated with historical and spiritual property to the same degree it was deprived of material security.

This is the mystical poverty (or the mystification of poverty, depending on one's view) that anthropologists have found so often in peasant cultures. Like ideologies about the powerful healing magic created out of the social scars of colonial savagery that Michael Taussig (1987) described, this is a mythic idea about the magic of plenitude that appears when material plenty diminishes and even more so when it diminishes to nothing. This point of shared destitution, the point of total material deficiency, was a Russian cultural doorway leading past mere poetry and representation into the realm of a powerful mysticism, into a world of metaphysical belonging.

Through their particular mode of *bricolage* (Lévi-Strauss 1966: 16–36), many speakers learned to fashion an intricate and aesthetic something out of the little they had, whether under Stalinism, during the war, or in the chaos and empty shelves of perestroika. They proclaimed their pride in knowing how to make cultural substance and material out of nothing, like the magic tablecloth of Russian folk tales, which produced rich banquets for the poorest serfs right out of thin air. A certain form of Russian *narod* identity was thus constructed around veneration of this ability to produce rich worlds of meaning out of meager materials, or, more accurately, out of a range of materials that "They"—be they the elites, or Westerners, or any group with access to more conventional "stuff"—would consider meager.

The most important of these materials was language, since what could not be inverted in the material world could be overturned in the telling. In light of this, the comment cited in Chapter 1, "We may be poor compared to you in the West, but our Russian language is richer than rich," might be reexamined. I argued that discourses that construe language as wealth disguise or mystify the centrality of language in the construction and reproduction of ethnic or cultural identity. In addition, however, the metaphor of language as wealth offers great potential for resistance; it proclaims that language, that free and luxurious resource, is the most valuable of properties, more valuable than the tangible assets—limousines, dachas, social position—possessed by others. By iterating this idea, people can resist acknowledging the relative poverty and powerlessness which are their social conditions. This conventional notion of language as wealth allows people to imagine themselves as powerful possessors of the most important social resource and means of production. Through language, narrative, and stories Russian speakers could create themselves as valuable in a society which, despite seventy years of Communist discourse about the sacred value of "workers" and the *narod*, had never provided the material comforts or political status that were supposed to reward and acknowledge that value.

In effect, of course, this form of resistance mystified and disguised the objective power relations of Soviet society, thereby deferring native critique of those relations. As comforting as this ideology of the egalitarian value of language may be, it helps to reproduce the *logic* of hierarchy which is one of the very sources of its existence.

Saints' Lives: The Perfection of the Art of Pain

> Everyday life finds its continuation in the Saint's Life, as the Saint's Life finds its continuation in everyday life.
> —Valery Petrochenkov, "Christian Patterns in Soviet Prose"

Alongside the paradigm that aligned material difficulty and moral sanctity was the metonymic paradigm whereby suffering produced sacredness, whereby the more one suffered, the better a person, and Russian, one became. Geoffrey Hosking reported a conversation illustrating this idea: "Last year I talked to two writers in their fifties, men of real culture and human insight, who nevertheless assured me that today's young people, not having lived through serious deprivation and difficulty, were spiritually empty, and their literary attempts therefore insipid and lightweight" (1991: 69).

This valorization of identity through deprivation had its iconic representatives, persons (and even groups of persons) both mythical and real, who so dramatically or poignantly embodied the spirit of suffering and loss that they came to stand for the whole paradigm, indeed, for the whole "Russian tale." Talismans of Russian virtue, they reflected the people's own sacredness and moral status in the world. These iconic representations occurred in many forms: as characters in movies and books; through depictions of the Soviet socialist realist hero; and in the official war hero model, which dovetailed with the more spontaneous *narod* version. During perestroika such images appeared often in paintings and photographs of, for example, older women, faces marked by suffering and experience, but brightened by some inner transcendence. There were also paintings of *zeks* (prisoners in the *gulag*) depicted with haloes or in Christ-like positions.

Iconic representation of these sacred and *narod*-sacralizing persons occurred through narrative as well. Such narratives were one of the main genres of fiction published in the glasnost years; the tradition itself is one of the core traditions in Russian literature.[6] Hardly confined to the printed page, however, these narratives were one of the key genres of Russian talk. With no disrespect intended, I term these narratives "saints' lives," because their combination of mythic and sacred qualities were very much in the vein of the medieval Russian saint's life.

Contemporary saints' lives were stories—usually life histories—in which suffering and self-sacrifice figured centrally, as they did in litanies. However, although these two genres were equally focused on suffering and sacrifice, the subject of the saint's life shook off the shadow of this victimization, and, by so doing, achieved the status of a third category: savior or saint.

The saint provided a crux, or fulcrum, allowing symbolic inversions to take place. Like the icons in Orthodox worship, the saint's life was both the reflection of and the source of sacredness. It was a central point of transference into that other, inverted world to which I have been alluding. The saint's life concentrated the themes of litanies into a sharp focus at the same time as it reflected the spirit of popular virtue.

---

[6] See, for example, Dostoevsky's poor folk, Gorky's stories and novels, and Shalamov, Solzhenitsyn, and Sinyavsky on the camp world. Solzhenitsyn's "Matryona's Home" and *One Day in the Life of Ivan Denisovich* give marvelous examples of this construction of the saintly virtue of the poor, all-suffering, simple members of the *narod*.

Since the saint's life has been one of the core motifs in Russian literature, I open this discussion with a glance at Anna Akhmatova, who in this century has been one of Russia's most elevated saintly figures, personally suffering all the ravages of Soviet history and bearing witness to them.

Akhmatova and The Art of Loss

It is not incidental or surprising that Anna Akhmatova is one of the highest emblems of female suffering of the Russian twentieth century. Her iconic image, made visual by the famous photographs and paintings of her face in profile, has endured as a representation of the apex of suffering, witnessing, and remembering that her people endured but which she indelibly captured in her poetry. In her poem cycle *Requiem,* published for the first time in the Soviet Union during glasnost, Akhmatova cast the iconic image of herself as a contemporary saint into the cultural waters. *Requiem* begins with the following epigram:

> No, not under some foreign sky,
> nor under the protection of some other's wings,
> Then, I was with my *narod,*
> There, where my *narod,* most unfortunately, was.

After this statement of communal identification, *Requiem* continues with the following prefatory remarks:

In the terrible years of the Yezhovshchina, I spent seventeen months in lines outside the prison in Leningrad.[7] One day someone pointed me out. Then, standing behind me, a woman with blue lips, who had never even heard my name, stirred out of the numbness common to us all and asked me in a whisper (we all whispered there):
—And can you describe this?
And I said:
—I can.
Then something resembling a smile crept over what had once been her face.

At the end of her multisegmented requiem, the poet asks that, if ever a monument to her is built, it should be erected not near the sea, or in a

---

[7] The purges of the late 1930s bear the name of Nikolai Yezhov, who was Stalin's commissar of internal affairs at the time, charged with carrying out the program of mass interrogation and arrest. The relatives of prisoners stood in line outside Soviet prisons, waiting for news of their loved ones or to pass letters or bundles of food. All translations of Akhmatova here are mine.

garden, but on that spot, outside the prison, where she stood in line with her *narod* for seventeen months. Because, she writes,

> even in blessed death I am afraid
> to forget the rumble of the black Marias,
> to forget the hideous clang of the gates
> and the old woman wailing like a wounded beast.

The images and attitudes with which *Requiem* begins and ends capture the constellation of ideas and stances of the Russian mode of suffering in its most venerated aspect. The suffering Akhmatova depicts was endured collectively, and the poet (knowing herself to be one of Russia's greatest poets) thus insisted that her memorial be in the place that marks the center of her connection to the general suffering of the people.

The sufferer in Akhmatova's poetry is female: the poet herself, the woman with blue lips and effaced identity, the old woman wailing her lament. In contemporary Russian narratives, women have been that country's repositories of anguish, charged with keeping the whole spirit of suffering and sacrifice alive. Writing about Osip Mandelstam, one of the best poets of twentieth-century Russia, who was arrested and disappeared in the camps in the late 1930s, and whose poems were memorized and thus saved by his wife, Nadezhda, Charles Isenberg writes: "The roles are universalized: men perish in struggle, and women interpret their struggle, commemorate them—and, as other lyrics of this and later periods suggest, resurrect them" (1987: 171).

In Russian culture (as well as many others), the genres connected with suffering, sacrifice, and loss have been markedly gendered; from the ancient lamenting practices to this century's litanies, women mourn the loss of men. So prevalent has this pattern been, both as historical fact and as a mythic formula, that the mere image of an old woman sitting alone on a bench, a scarf covering her hair, her hands in her lap, motionless and quiet, conveys the spirit of loss, the silent message: "I saw it. I endured it. I was there."

In spoken form, in contrast to the perestroika era litany, which had a distraught quality, saints' lives were composed in solemn, almost serene tones. Where the litany stirred the air with its direness, the saint's life stilled the air with its acceptance. In Akhmatova's poem, this stillness was epitomized in the image of a statue, a bronzed figure from which, however, silent tears could flow.

Public texts such as Akhmatova's were, to use Geertz's term, both "models of" the experience of endurance and "models for" enduring. This duality raises a question about the political effect of such texts. Were they more protests of victimization or paradigms for the endurance of it, endurance that could lead to sacralization? Ronald Hingley has commented on this question in discussing the lives and work of Russia's four great (and long-suffering) poets of the twentieth century: Akhmatova, Mandelstam, Pasternak, and Tsvetaeva. With regard to this whole paradigm of suffering and loss, he writes, citing John Berryman,

> Perhaps any artist is "extremely lucky who is presented with the worst possible ordeal which will not actually kill him." If so, Russian poets have been particularly fortunate—except of course for those presented with ordeals that actually *have* killed them, in some instances after they have enjoyed for many years the full benefits that misery, privation, and terror can bestow. These blessings were showered on them so freely that Akhmatova sometimes spoke of Russian émigrés as "envying the sufferings" (how Russian a formulation!) of those who had stayed at home. Reporting this comment, Mandelstam's widow has dismissed it as grossly imperceptive. There was, says she, nothing in the least elevating about her own and her husband's sufferings: there was only terror and pain. (Hingley 1981: xiii)

Hingley's remarks capture some of the complexity of this whole issue as it has been battled out by Russians—and by Russian "saints" like Anna Akhmatova and Nadezhda Mandelstam. Though there are clearly many different Russian perspectives on suffering and self-sacrifice, nonetheless a complex ideology about these topics has been influential in Russian constructions of and presentations of self and nation.

"The Country's Dire Needs"

Andrei, a divorced writer in his late forties, told me he had deliberately chosen a life of voluntary poverty. He lived in a communal apartment in an ancient Moscow building, located so close to the absolute center of Moscow that he did not open his one window for fear of the noise and pollution from the steady flow of vehicles along his street. The entrance to Andrei's building was through an almost invisible doorway in one of Moscow's eighteenth-century courtyards—a yard created by the space between several crumbling two-story buildings. There seemed to be an interminable number of intermediary doors to unlock and go through before arriving in Andrei's hallway, half of which was actually a grimy, improvised kitchen area where the communal phone was situated; nearby were the doors to the bathroom and toilet which he shared with several other families.

Andrei's one square room was a fascinating, decrepit place, with ceilings almost as high as the room was wide. From bottom to top, the walls were covered with paper: black-and-white photos of Andrei and his musician friends, photos of famous people (especially musicians and poets) clipped from newspapers and magazines, original drawings on various media (napkins, envelopes, and other scraps, especially), texts of poems, slogans, posters, maps, menus, ribbons, and the like. Along the walls, a motley variety of homemade shelves bore up somehow under the weight of hundreds of books, record albums, tapes, boxes, manuscript sheaves, magazines, and old newspapers. The walls themselves were falling in at the corners, and the ancient parquet floor was barely discernible under decades of grime. A cot sat in the corner near the window; in the middle of the room were three chairs, two used for sitting and the third as a table. Andrei boiled water in an electric kettle and we had tea, along with some chocolates that I brought.

Andrei could have put himself in line for better housing years ago, and probably would have received at least a private one-room apartment, but he said that he chose to stay in this place because there were so many struggling artists whom he wanted to help, and a focus on his own lifestyle would take his attention away from his "apprentices' lives and the country's dire needs." "How can I possibly think about myself when our nation is so ill? When artists here struggle just to have a little bit of bread to eat so they can have the energy to write a story or a song? It is my duty to Russia and to the artistic spirit here to contribute my life, whatever little I can do."

In an interview published a few years after I visited his apartment, Andrei reflected the same sentiments:

> For many years I looked for a way to live. What do I tell my people and my children, through my poems, my songs, my articles? What must I say? I have found one answer: you must have a duty . . . I must do everything I can for all of those people who create. . . . It is my duty. It is my happiness to do something for one second for my people. I give all of my strength, all of my time, all of my rubles, everything, to the best people of this country and the last people of this country. (*Kyoto Journal* 1992, no. 20)

For the seven years that I have known Andrei, he has consistently lived by this cultural code, in which sacrifice for "his people" (sometimes identified as the *narod*, and sometimes as the narrower artistic community in which he is active) is the express value. He chooses not to smoke or drink as a rule, eats simply, spends little money on himself, instead using the money he earns from various projects to support his peers. In the years before glasnost, he organized underground venues for artists to share their work, despite harassment by the authorities; in the years since he has tirelessly promoted the work of young artists, often pulling off great feats of organization in the process.

Once I asked him about his early years, and his answer was: "I had a very, very difficult childhood, very difficult. But that is not important. What matters are the difficulties facing Russia. Though it is impossible and getting worse, we must try to redeem what is good here, what is beautiful, clean, honest."

Andrei, like Akhmatova, creates and sustains his identity through an ideal of transcending common suffering in order to help or express something for the *narod*. No doubt quite consciously (for he is nothing if not culturally astute), Andrei structures his life around traditions of asceticism and self-sacrifice that stem from Russian Orthodoxy; there is something of the "holy fool code" (Thompson 1987) mixed in too, however. Andrei frequently did and said things to defy certain standards of public decency; his forte sometimes seemed to be crossing lines, inverting logic, going to creative and self-sacrificing extremes. This going to extremes seems to be a significant part of the "saint's life" model in Russian culture, as the following story illustrates.

One Thousand Cookies

The genre of the saint's life was often used by ordinary people as well as artists, by people who were only narrowly famous (or not famous at all) but whose stories were shared and traded, explored and transformed in a variety of ways. One day I visited a Moscow school, to see its Great Patriotic War Museum. Many Soviet schools had one of these museums; the Soviet regime widely promoted memorialization of the war as a way to cement patriotic identity. Though their creation served official interests, however, those who had experienced the war found such museums (and all the other memorializations of the war) to be poignant and sacred places.

The main part of this school's museum was dedicated to photographs of veterans (male and female) taken in wartime and in the present, along with photographs of mothers holding up photographs of their dead sons. Beneath the photographs the stories of these people's lives and service were neatly typed on cards. The museum director showed me an album with snapshots from various reunions, student field trips, meetings, and memorial rituals with veterans who often visited the school. She told me that she herself had served on the front, that she was retired but that the museum was her passion and what kept her going in life.

After my tour of the museum, Natalia, a teacher and assistant principal, took me to her office for tea and crackers. In the quiet privacy of that space, we talked about the meaning of the war museum, and Natalia told me the following story.

There was a woman, Irina Ivanovna, who was connected to our school through the Veteran's Committee. She died in 1987 at the age of eighty-five, but before that she had constantly shared her life with our students and especially shared her tales of the war. Irina Ivanovna had two sons and a husband. After her husband and her elder son died at the front, she went with her second son, born in 1925, to the occupied territories; they became partisans working together against the Nazis. One day Irina Ivanovna was wounded and her son carried her for three weeks through dense forests to safety behind the front. [Here Natalia's voice rose into litany.] For three weeks, he carried her on his back, through woods, over small rivers, he fed her and tended her wounds—until finally, miraculously, they crossed into safe territory. Then he went back to fight. He was killed right before the end of the war.

At this point, Natalia took a large book down from her shelf. It was an album commemorating Irina Ivanovna's life, which had been put together by a group of schoolgirls. Elaborately embellished with calligraphic labels, arrows, and ribbons, it was like a sacred object in Natalia's hands. In the album were photos of Irina Ivanovna's natal family, Irina Ivanovna as a middle-aged woman before the war, Irina Ivanovna with her son during the war, dressed in improvised camouflage. After that came maps and charts of the front zone, one of them marked with an arrow and a ribbon to show the place where the son had died (now part of Poland). On the next page, surrounded by more ribbons, was a photographic copy of the son's last letter. A separate section held pictures of a visit Irina Ivanovna made in the late 1950s to her son's grave in Poland; living on meager means, she had only been able to make this trip because she studied Polish and placed first in a regional language competition, the prize for which was a four-day trip. After the war, Irina Ivanovna had adopted an orphaned teenager, and there were photographs of her with this daughter. The last image in the book showed Irina Ivanovna in a group picture with the children of the school, shortly before her death. As we looked at this photograph, Natalia said, with trembling voice:

Her life was so difficult, so unimaginably full of tragedy. But if you had ever seen her . . . she was such an energetic woman, and so kind. She loved our students. Every year for her son's birthday Irina Ivanovna baked *one thousand* cookies; she baked cookies for the whole school, and she came here and we held a birthday party. . . . The kids just ate the cookies, as you can understand, but to Irina Ivanovna they were cookies for her son.

Natalia concluded by saying, regretfully, that now that Irina Ivanovna was dead, the students who never knew her were somewhat indifferent to the album and to the whole story.[8]

But until Irina Ivanovna's death, Natalia's school had a marvelous, sacred "icon" of suffering and sacrifice, a woman whose life was an accrual of one loss upon another, one sacrifice on another, one sacrificial act of remembrance on another. Irina Ivanovna's life was iconic (rather than merely lamentable) because her own commemorative representation of her life, as least as it was described to me by Natalia, rejected the complex of victimization, achieving the saintly self-representation of someone who endures all manner of suffering without lament or complaint. The thousand cookies were a medium by which she deflected her own loss, valorizing instead the sacrifice of her son. Even the sacrifices she must have made to bake one thousand cookies (in a town where butter, eggs, and sugar were sometimes deficit commodities) became testimony not to *her* losses but to *his* self-sacrifice and *her* ability to transcend.

The Christian subtext in this story should be evident, although perhaps some of its specific Russian Orthodox elements are not. Without going into a long digression about the enormously rich topic of the Russian church and Orthodox tradition, I would like to mention two features of Russian Orthodoxy which have powerfully influenced Russian culture, and which are reflected in this account.

Russian Orthodox Traditions

The first pertinent feature of Orthodoxy is the kenotic tradition in Orthodox Christianity, defined by its emphasis on Christ's loving non-resistance in the face of death. Kenotic practitioners cultivated their own humility, poverty, suffering, sacrifice, and noniresistance. In the Russian tradition, the paradigmatic saint's life told of the martyrdom of Boris and Gleb, two young sons of Prince Vladimir, who adopted Christianity on behalf of the Eastern Slavs in 988. Boris and Gleb were murdered by their elder brothers in what was essentially a political struggle. After their deaths, Boris and Gleb were canonized, and an entire cult of religious orientation and practice developed around them. Its first adherent was the Kievan Saint Theodosius, through whose example of humility and poverty the tradi-

---

[8] Tumarkin (1991) and Dickinson (1995) have movingly described the widening split between the generations concerning memorials to the war and the active scorn that many children and teenagers have for war-related rituals and monuments. Tumarkin's essay also addresses the ways that the revelations of glasnost have changed people's feelings about the war.

"Feeding the Birds" (Photo by John Einarsen and Robert Kowalczyk)

tion was secured. George P. Fedotov (1975: 110) points out that the cult flourished (formally) for nearly nine hundred years. In monastic practice, the kenotic ideal was pursued through rigorous fasting and other mortifications and through deliberate self-impoverishment. The main virtues of kenoticism were "poverty, humility, and love, in their complete unity as one unseparable whole" (Fedotov 128).[9] Told with delectably poignant details about the beauty and purity of the two innocents, and their acceptance of painful and unwanted death, the story of Boris and Gleb stands as an emblem of Christ-like martyrdom or self-giving.

The Orthodox veneration of the "Mother of God" (*Bogomater'*) is the other important tradition to consider. By far the best known, best loved and most poignant of icons in the Russian church were icons of the Virgin. It was to icons of the Virgin that entreaties were made, and from her icons that miracles were said to flow. The hallmarks of the Mother of God—her own sorrowful sacrifice of her son, her tender sympathy for sufferers, and her intercession on their behalf—made her, arguably, the central figure in Russian Orthodox worship, and a central symbol of the sacred ethos of Orthodoxy.

The iconic stance rendered in depictions of the Virgin—her sorrowful, all-seeing, all-remembering, mindful compassion—were strongly suggested by Natalia's rendering of Irina Ivanovna's life story, which also had certain obvious parallels with Christian tradition (the school's possession and veneration of Irina Ivanovna's "relics," or the passing out of one thousand cookies to the schoolchildren which seemed to me hauntingly reminiscent of the sharing of sacramental wafers). I am not implying here that Irina Ivanovna or any other Russian modeled herself along Marian lines; what I am suggesting, rather, is that a certain sacred stance has endured in Russian culture: a stance of saintly acceptance of suffering, which appeared in its most intense forms in kenotic practices, and of which the Virgin has been the highest emblem. Older Russian women, whether Orthodox Christian or not, were especially inclined to adopt this stance.

Giving Blood

"Pain as an institutional, jural, and political idiom constructs a subject by fusing emotional/physical states with the ideological organization of the social structure," as C. Nadia Seremetakis noted (1991: 4). The official Soviet model for the heroic citizen borrowed much material and legitimacy from the available stock of cultural stances. Throughout socialist realist

---

[9] See Ingham (1984) on the genealogy of such a tradition. The original Life of Boris and Gleb can be found in *Izbrannie zhitiia sviatykh* (1992, vol. I) or in English in Zenkovsky (1963).

art and literature, especially that of the war years, the icon of the martyred saint (in Soviet terms, the citizen-soldier)—self-sacrificing, long-suffering, all-enduring—was valorized and modernized. The schoolgirl partisan, Zoia Kosmodemianskaia, who, although tortured and finally hanged by the Nazis, never confessed or gave out any information, was a perfect real-life model for this stance, and her life was effectively transformed into a useful Soviet saint's life.[10] In her life all the elements were clear and simple: the identity of the enemy, the kind of world that must come to be, the behavior required of a saint.

But in real life there was never such clarity. The following story shows the complications entailed by the contradictions of Soviet society, and the difficulties of self-construction in the face of the iconic model of the Soviet saintly life.

I went for an interview to the apartment of Tatiana Vasil'evna, seven bus stops away from a metro station in the south of Moscow. She had received this apartment five years before I met her; before that she had lived for forty years in one room of a communal apartment. Her new apartment, in a building no more and no less dilapidated than most Moscow apartment blocks, consisted of one room, a kitchen and a bathroom. The yellowed paint was peeling and some of the plaster was crumbling from the walls and ceilings, the parquet had lost its finish and pieces of it were coming up, leaving rectangular holes. The main room had huge, rough-hewn, homemade bookshelves spilling over with books and filing boxes, and a big desk and table for Tatiana Vasil'evna's botanical drawings; an antique dresser, cabinet, and her bed were in one corner, with a television set near the bed. The apartment seemed cozy and neatly organized but not particularly domesticated.

Trained as a biologist, Tatiana Vasil'evna had worked since the war as a botanical illustrator. Her labor of love involved sketching, cataloguing, and meticulously describing a certain genus of flowering plants.

Although in her late sixties, and quite hampered by cataracts, Tatiana Vasil'evna made her way by bus and subway to her academic institute two afternoons per week and on special occasions; she skied regularly and swam in the pond near her building even in cold weather. Her scientific work was her passion, and she used a magnifying glass to study drawings and photographs of the small flowers she had spent a lifetime collecting and cataloguing.

We sat in her kitchen, and Tatiana Vasil'evna fed me a midday dinner. She told me about her recent corneal operation, which had improved her

---

[10] See Stites (1992: 99 and 114) on the "canonization" of Zoia Kosmodemianskaia in Soviet popular culture.

eyesight; she told me the story of how she finally got her own apartment; she was cheerful and matter-of-fact. We went into her main room to talk. This was the second time I had interviewed her. She had previously given me the story of her girlhood and her college years, and the main outlines of her wartime experience working as a nurse on medical ships in the Baltic. She had asked me to come back to hear more of her wartime story. Before I had a chance to take out my tape recorder, she began to talk. Her story started with such momentum that I was loath to interrupt it in order to dig out my tape recorder, so this first part is reconstructed from notes which I jotted down later on the bus. The entire story was told in a calm, matter of fact manner, sometimes even lightly, although the experiences she was describing were painful.

> This week I was thinking it over, for some reason I was thinking it over a lot, could not get it out of my head, and I finally understood why twice in my life, during the war, I became hysterical, went into hysterics. I finally understood that both times it was on a day after I had given blood.
>
> I was in the Naval Base hospital corps. One morning I gave blood and then that afternoon I was off and I went to a concert with a couple of other nurses. On the way back from the concert, we were walking and talking and joking and I somehow failed to salute a senior officer whom we passed in the road. I was arrested and brought to the brig. They stripped me of my insignia—pulled the medical stars off my uniform shoulders and from my cap. They gave me an awful brown dress to put on instead of my uniform and then they gave me a mop and a floor to wash. A couple of other girls had been arrested and they made them wash floors as well. There were rifles and guns stacked in tepees at one end of the room. No one was watching us. One girl took a rifle, unnoticed by anyone, and she went into the bathroom where she propped the gun up and shot herself in the gut. I ran in and pressed myself up against her, trying to stop the blood which was gushing out of her aortal artery. An ambulance finally came but the girl was dead by that time. I started crying and crying, I could not stop crying. They put me in a cell for the night. I went into hysterics. All night I was crying and screaming. In the morning I demanded to be taken to a doctor and they were upset anyway and they let me go.
>
> The other time I went into hysterics was when one patient of mine died—a man who had been badly burned over most of his body. I would not have gone into hysterics but I had given blood that day, too. I just realized, because you were coming for this interview—why I went into hysterics those times. It was because I had given blood both days—I was not quite myself, you know how giving blood weakens you.

After the concert, we were in such a joyous mood. In the morning I had given blood and in the evening I went to the concert, in such a completely blissful state. Then the guardhouse, and the girl shot herself.

You know, Ostrovsky has a play, *The Hot Heart*. It is a remarkable play, of course, and there is a terrible merchant there, an awful, cruel, savage, despot . . . but he had a good daughter, devout, a remarkable girl. She was tired of it, so much oppression, so she went on a pilgrimage, and the father, sobering up, said, "Where is my daughter?" and went to the mayor, saying, "Return her to me! Have a soldier lead her back on a rope! Bring this daughter of mine to me on a rope." And the mayor said, "Listen, you have a daughter. She's a bride, a young girl, and you want me to have a soldier bring her on a rope. We Russian people, this is the extent to which we do not respect each other!" And so I remembered it, how they were taking me, and I was twenty-five years old, a big healthy woman, and they were leading me to the brig for no reason. There you have it. . . . Well, all these are just army rules.

Although this story contains many of the elements of litany—power and powerlessness, villains and victims, the idea of Russian cruelty and humiliation—it is much more in the vein of the saint's life, because it is ultimately framed by an attitude of acceptance rather than the implicit or explicit blame which is the frame of the litany.

In telling her story, Tatiana Vasil'evna seemed to want to exonerate herself from her own past lamenting. Several times in her narrative, Tatiana Vasil'evna made it clear how distraught she felt over her own slip, some four decades years earlier, into hysteria and despair. This was a woman who had lived by the tenets of socialist seriousness and science, and she signified her basic faith in these values through her no-nonsense, no-frills way of dressing, talking, living, and working. She had constructed herself around the paradigmatic signs of scientific and socialist dedication, reliability, and an androgyny that was a subtle dissociation from the traditional, elaborate sign system of Russian femaleness (though not uncommon for the wartime generation). Despite all this, Tatiana Vasil'evna had broken down on two occasions during the war, contradicting the expected public stance of unflinching stoicism, the saintly stance as filtered through wartime socialist realism. So this story was about this woman's sense of her own failure to respond in the proper "saintly," stoic manner to some terrible events.

Yet it was, of course, about those events themselves, and about Tatiana Vasil'evna's own long-held anguish over the abuses of power and acts of arbitrary cruelty to which she was witness. In this act of narration the speaker in effect told three nested and antithetical stories: the story of her own ultimate toughness and transcendence bracketed the story of her weakness ("hysteria"), which bracketed the story of arbitrary cruelty.

I regard this narrative as a saint's life because it showed the force of aspiration to that genre of speaking and being, a force that penetrated a person's memory of events with questions about her own identity that would not be quieted even after forty years. While remembering her story in order to tell it, Tatiana Vasil'evna formulated an answer to a nagging question she had about her fulfillment of the saintly/socialist realist ideal. She had given blood that morning, so that was why she cried after her friend died in her arms. Were it not for the physical effects of giving blood, she would have withstood all manner of humiliation and punishment from her fellow soldiers, thus living up to her internalized image of endurance.

Her narrative shows that she was not thinking of it in terms of external ideals or images. The ideal was within her in the form of a stance, a posture of the body which is the cultural signifier of transcendent composure in the face of horror and power. One thing this story reveals is how difficult it could be to maintain that stance. But in the present time, she still managed to project it; casting off the blaming paradigm, Tatiana Vasil'evna exonerated individuals, exonerated even power, attributing all the chilling events of her story to "army rules"—to structure.

The symbolism of one more detail in this story needs comment: the relationship between blood and belonging. Tatiana Vasil'evna's story explained her slips into hysteria as the result of her having given blood on the mornings before her "breakdowns." On both occasions, however, the immediate factor which precipitated her hysterics was her physical proximity to two people dying bloody deaths; in one case, another person's blood literally spilled all over her. With the invocation of her own giving of blood, Tatiana Vasil'evna's story merged her sacrifice with that of the two people who died in her arms.

The Cultural History of the Inverted World

Like the paradigm of power and powerlessness discussed in the previous chapter, the ideology of "mystical poverty" and the value of saintly endurance and witnessing quite probably originated in feudal society, specifically in the hierarchical, dualistic, and often brutal Russian social system. From the Kievan period on, there were two social worlds in Russia—the demographically infinitesimal but structurally "high" one of the elites (with their bureaucracies and retainers) and the demographically enormous but structurally "low" one of rural peasants and, later, of urban workers. For nearly a millennium, these two worlds have interacted with and been dependent on one another—and they remained, at least symbolically, in opposition, high to low, rich to poor, clean to dirty, noble to humble, exploiters to exploited, and dominant to dominated.

The significance of this long history is that it is a history of lasting and profound social duality—a relationship between two worlds. While they shared many cultural orientations and were quite interdependent, all aspects of these groups' existence were marked by the hierarchical relations between them, and all their social and economic practices reflected (and reproduced) the differences between them. If ultimately that difference appeared to be essential, natural, and real, it is because it was thoroughly hypostatized through the differentiating practices of both groups.[11]

In the process of the immediate and essential creation of self and other, peasants and elites both relied on common sets of cultural tools—props, materials, substances, objects, and symbols—but each class deployed them differently, and self-consciously so. A peasant riddle, one of the two thousand five hundred collected by the folklorist Sadovnikov in the 1870s, vividly capsulizes this familiar process of the creation of difference, while at the same time it is pierced through with irony at the entire practice of hierarchical differentiation; through such irony it forces a crucial (if minute and momentary) inversion in the hierarchy of values.

> The peasant throws it on the ground,
> The master collects it in his pocket.

The answer: "snot." In the invertive space of this riddle, cleanliness was made filth, politeness was made offensive, cleverness was made idiocy, and high was made low.[12] This was resistance in the field of identity, a regular form of discursive practice among peasants. Russian folklore provided crucial symbolic tools for defending the peasantry's sense of its own collective value. A line from one of the Russian Misery songs goes: "to walk naked without being ashamed" (Likhachev and Vaneeva 1985: 41), and this represents a central peasant concern: to maintain pride in peasant

---

[11] This kind of "network of oppositions," as Pierre Bourdieu puts it, "is the matrix of all the commonplaces which find such ready acceptance because behind them lies the whole social order" (1984: 468).

[12] As Robert Stamm writes, "the cheerful vulgarity of the powerless is used as a weapon against the pretense and hypocrisy of the powerful" (Stamm 1982: 47, cited in Stallybrass and White (1986: 18); see also Bourdieu (1977: 44), on the relation betweeen politeness and politics).

(or *narod*) identity in the face of poverty and the symbolic humiliations of a degraded social position.[13]

In an interesting study in cultural history, Ewa Thompson traced the provenance and habits of Russian "holy fools for Christ"—odd-looking, sometimes naked, bizarrely behaved religious wanderers who were revered and feared as prophets throughout prerevolutionary Russia, and who embodied the value-inversion process: acting foolishly to show their wisdom, impurely to show their purity, aggressively to show their meekness, and derisively to show their veneration (Thompson 1987: 16). Thompson's main argument is that the institution of holy foolishness brought about and then fostered the paradoxical structures of Russian mentality (184)—an unfortunately simplistic and deterministic conclusion to an otherwise rich and rewarding cultural history. The flaw that undermines Thompson's approach is that she never considers class, and the intricate and overwhelming practices of domination and exploitation, as playing any structuring part in the drama of Russian culture. She barely mentions the existence of serfdom in her entire study. This is an important lapse. While the logic of the value inversions that she describes certainly existed as a very significant structuring mechanism in Russian culture, its source was surely not voluntaristic—it could not have arisen in the behaviors of what was really a very small number of individuals. The holy fools were merely ritual practitioners of an inversion that was produced ubiquitously as part of the whole system of class domination, specifically in response to the symbolic violence (Bourdieu 1977: 190–197) which was a key practice in the construction and maintenance of hierarchy.

Symbolic violence is the violence rendered by the seemingly neutral, and seemingly natural, practices of classification and the evaluation concomitant to it. In Russia, a great deal of direct physical violence accompanied the domination of the peasantry by the upper classes and the state, but symbolic violence, which in the long run is far more efficient, was effected via every part of the social body: through laws that attributed different monetary values to different classes of people and laid out detailed systems of monetary valuation for peasant "souls"; through Orthodox religious practices and rituals, in which hierarchy was an omnipresent feature, as well as through the repression of pre-Christian practices by Orthodoxy; through the military draft (which set peasant family against

---

[13] Stallybrass and White's (1986) wide-ranging study of hierarchies of inversion and the complex "returns of the repressed" in the interpenetration of bourgeois and peasant culture should be mentioned here. They focus especially on the body, as the crucial site and source of symbolizations of social hierarchies, though their focus is largely on the ways that developing European bourgoisies used revulsion at peasant and proletarian practices in their own cultural constructions of self.

peasant family in an internal battle of valuation as all tried to avoid losing their own sons); through the logics of agricultural extraction and dietary differences, as seen in the peasant proverb, "The rye feeds everyone without exception, but the wheat makes distinctions" (Sokolov 1966: 269); through their use of peasants for "entertainment" (see Roosevelt 1991; Senelick 1991); and through other forms of manipulation and control of peasant family life or village communities—a manipulation in which the hierarchy of gender (and patriarchal practices in general) crossed paths with and abetted the hierarchy of classes.

In response to social and economic exploitation, as Rodney Bohac (1991) has shown, peasants developed numerous strategies of resistance: foot-dragging, deception, petitioning, pilfering, sabotage, obstruction, and so on (all of these notably similar to resistant practices in Soviet times). But what were their responses to the *symbolic* domination of social hierarchy?[14] What kinds of resistance did they put up to the *ritual* denigrations of their class?

The plethora of peasant songs, stories, laments, proverbs, ditties, riddles, divinations, and other folklore suggests two main points in answer to this question. First, the very enormity and variety of Russian oral lore demonstrates its importance in peasant social life. While it is true that all cultures produce stories, songs, sayings, and other orally transmitted texts, there is much variety in the scope of investment in the production of talk. In Russia talk has always been powerful. Numerous Russian texts, folkloric, literary, and historical, have attested to both the sacred and the sinister potential of the word in Russia. In the process of commenting on this power such texts, of course, also produce and reproduce it.

The second, but most crucial point to make about Russian folklore is that it reveals a primary mechanism of discursive resistance: the symbolic inversion of official hierarchies of value in Russian peasant culture. As Y. M. Sokolov observes, in reference to the large category of folk stories about "everyday life":

> The "positive" persons who take part in the action are found to be chiefly the clever or cunning common man, who is generally a poor peasant, a workman, soldier, barge hauler, potter, tailor, shepherd, son of a merchant, a simple country woman or girl, a cunning thief, a jester; while, on

---

[14] I do not know of any study that addresses this question directly, although it would be worthwhile to undertake such an investigation; in the process of exploring other things, however, several authors have suggested interesting manifestations of peasant "symbolic resistance": see Michael Cherniavsky's work, for example, on peasant myths about the tsar as their kindly benefactor (1961) and Mary Kelly's (1990) study of the hidden pre-Christian motifs in embroidery and other textiles.

the other hand, the "negative" element includes the nobleman or noble-woman, the general or the general's wife, the priest or the priest's wife, the rich merchant, the rich peasant kulak, the miser or stupid provincial person, the absolute fool, and his kinsman the peasant, or the devil, but stripped of every vestige of his miraculous quality, and what is more, of grandeur. (Sokolov 1966: 445–446)

A primary theme of folk tales is the inversion of the elite view of social stations and worth; folktales attribute spiritual good to the lowly and evil to the high. In addition, as Maureen Perrie (1989) has outlined, the tales feature various depictions of moral retribution, wherein clever peasants, tricksters, and often fools manage to get the better of their evil exploiters and level the social hierarchy. All these inversions take place in the relative safety of orally transmitted tales.[15]

I would argue that the resistant content of these oral productions reflexively infused the vehicle of that content—the world of talk—with magical importance, social significance, and sacred value: for in this communicative world justice (*pravda*) was the reigning principle and reciprocity existed between "low" and "high."

The "goodness" of the village world was constructed in relation to the "badness" of the encroaching outer world. The folktales valorized the local, native, restrained, impoverished peasant world through opposition to the foreign, impetuous, comfortable world of the elites. It should be noted that the peasant world was not powerless only in relation to the gentry. Representatives of the state, the priesthood, and the merchant class also impinged on it. In folktales, these groups too were often parodied and their social value inverted.

Such symbolic inversions by no means remained strictly in the peasant realm. Especially in the post-Enlightenment period, Russian writers and other members of the intelligentsia celebrated the moral piety of the peasant class and the wealth of peasant discourses. Pushkin, an ardent admirer

---

[15] Some genres of Russian *lubki* (woodblock prints) depict similar inversions, and at times they could have a threatening cast; James C. Scott describes prints of an ox slaughtering the butcher which were seized by tsarist officials (1990: 168). In terms of ritual activities, there were occasions on which inversion could be enacted physically; see Lotman 1984: 234, and Catriona Kelly (1990) on inversions in the Russian puppet theater. Stallybrass and White provide fascinating examples of "the world turned upside down" in European visual folklore, such as woodblocks and prints where "relations of power and dominance are reversed and the pig butchers the butcher; the ass whips its laden master; the mice chase the cat . . . the servant rides on a horse followed by the king on foot" (1986: 56–57). The anthropological literature is rich in examples of symbolic inversion; see, for instance, Marriot (1955) on the feast of Holi in India and the wide range of essays in Babcock (1978). Bakhtin's work on carnival has had an enormous influence on studies of symbolic inversion in general.

and student of peasant folklore, blended it into many of his works, producing numerous verses and stories based on the folklore he learned as a child from his nanny, or that he collected in his adult life. Dostoevsky's stories and novels often celebrate the virtue of the poor (although they certainly do not ignore the potential violence and cruelty of the peasantry); and, drawing the theme of inversion into other social contexts, much of his work centers on the transcendent powers of the meek, simple, or victimized (the examples of Sonia, and ultimately Raskolnikov, in *Crime and Punishment*, Myshkin in *The Idiot*, and Alesha in *Brothers Karamazov* are only the most obvious). Tolstoy's later work especially is characterized by an obsessive celebration of simple virtues, self-abnegation, suffering, and the ultimate triumph of the oppressed. Especially in the cases of Dostoevsky and Tolstoy, these logics are profoundly influenced by Christian philosophy, but that philosophy was always in dialogue with predominant cultural themes.

The latter half of the nineteenth century saw the burgeoning of the populist movement, in which Russians (largely from the socially dislocated gentry and intelligentsia) devoted themselves to studying and helping the peasantry, inspired (sometimes naively) by what they construed as the peasant way of life. At the same time, folklorists were fanning throughout the country, recording Russian folklore in great quantity and often demonstrating extraordinary scholarship.

The images, ideologies, patterns of symbolic inversion, and generic forms originating with the peasantry thus circulated widely throughout Russian society, permeating its literary, academic, and political culture in significant degrees. As Richard Stites (1989; 1992) has brilliantly and exhaustively demonstrated, many of the symbolic practices of the Russian revolution hinged around the elevation of the values and practices of peasant and proletarian Russia to sacred status; as he writes, "the moral superiority of the poor—very strong in folklore—became the central myth of the revolution" (1992: 23).

While the Russian intelligentsia has exalted the *narod's* ability to endure, romanticized its suffering, and in general promoted an image of the virtuous poor in both pre- and postrevolutionary times, nonetheless these values were an inherent (though no doubt as often subverted or parodied as celebrated) part of *narod* identity from the beginning. The suffering of loss, humiliation, cruelty, impoverishment, and restriction at the hands of the "other" world, frequently through arbitrary, absurd, and unpredictable applications of law and power—this was the context surrounding the Russian peasant world. From being the *context* of their social world, this suffering may have become a core *content* of peasant discourses, one of the foundations of peasant identity, one of the materials by which identity—both collective and personal—could be constructed. It is through operations such as these that suffering—contraintuitive though this may seem—might become a valuable thing in itself.

The sacralization of suffering has long stood at the heart of *narod* ideologies (and ideologies about the *narod*). Suffering, in all its forms, was both one of the peasant's few "possessions" (personally or collectively) and one of the sources of the peasant's moral authority. The solid tradition of Russian kenoticism no doubt sustained and sacralized these traits in the peasantry as it did among the other classes. Unlike many observers of Russia, however, I would not attribute peasant humility to Christianity; rather, I would argue that the particular style of Russian Orthodox practices and ideologies was created and constantly recreated in a dialectic interaction with other life patterns and experiences.

Industrialization and the upheavals of the Soviet period added new elements—new twists, new details, new intensity, new paradoxes—to the fabric of the *narod*'s suffering, but they barely altered the logic of it. Within a very short time following the revolution a new system of social hierarchy had developed. Although this system had brand new designations—Party, *nomenklatura, nachal'stvo* ("bosses")—it effectively reproduced many of the hierarchical structures and practices of prerevolutionary society. Along with these reassertions of power and hierarchy, which provided ample opportunity and need for fresh expressions of symbolic inversion and resistance, the twentieth century brought plenty of contextual material to sustain the abundance of suffering, which in turn sustained an identity system available to all classes. In dialectical fashion, the pre-existing system of identity served to sustain the population through all these crises, providing both a cognitive frame, a way to think about the traumas of history, and a mechanism for turning very real suffering into a sacred substance—sometimes even into a kind of sainthood—thereby subverting the value and identity structure of the dominant system.

In the shadow of the troublesome Russian material economy, a symbolic economy has thus existed, one in which suffering became a medium of exchange. In this symbolic zone, widespread hardship engendered shared abundance, through an operation of cultural logic whereby loss on the material or human plane could be made to create rewards or status on the sacred. This logic was actively reproduced through the complex cultural mechanisms of both personal and collective self-creation.

The Rituals and Paradoxes
of Perestroika

When the Soviet Union finally collapsed, Mother Earth quavered, erasing familiar street names, obliterating the addresses we used to know. All the Soviet man had left was song. We are living through extraordinary times today, when all the myths are dying. Witness all the sorcerers, astrologers, and witch doctors invading our TV screens. They have precise names and addresses, and their drivel doesn't seem to perturb us. Myths lend stability to the public mind; fairy-tale miracles happen suddenly, "all by themselves." At first we rejoiced when the myths began to fall by the wayside. Now that the floodgates of truth are open, we are desperately trying to stave off its tide, which threatens to engulf us. Even when we see through its deception, we do not want to see the myth explode and recoil from the sight of the mythological ruins.

—Zara Abdullaeva, "Popular Culture"

In the years since the collapse of the Soviet Union, the mood in Moscow has changed. The pitch and tenor of discussion are not what they were; conversations have become less intense, less focused. A certain fervor that was present during perestroika is gone, though there is now clearly an abundance of striving, bustle, anxiety and stress. What has changed is that a ritualistic transitional period has come to a close, and Moscow life, however drastically rearranged, now takes place on a plane of a strange kind of normalcy—a plane unimaginable during perestroika.

Many people's lives are more difficult than ever; some are working two or three jobs, some are hardly able to work at all, or are not paid for the work they do; and all have been struggling with the economic and psychological stress of inflation.[1] Meanwhile, the grand red brick houses and

---

[1] Richard Rose offers a telling overview of survival strategies in this new environment, using survey data to show the "multiplicity of economies" on which the majority of Russian households now rely, which include official and under-the-table paid labor, household produce, and exchanges of labor and favors with friends and relatives (1994: 48). During fieldwork in Moscow and Yaroslavl in 1992, 1994, and 1995 I was struck by the complexity and variety of strategies and schemes—legal, quasi-legal, and illegal—through which people are surviving or getting ahead economically; a full ethnographic study of these practices awaits doing.

dachas of the *nouveaux riches* have been springing up, Mercedes Benzes and Jeeps fill the streets, and bombs and gunfire go off around the city with no small regularity.

Despite all this, however, the fever pitch of questioning, wishing, and lamenting which characterized the perestroika years is muted. When I asked her about this in 1994, Olga remarked ironically, "All that lamenting was a luxury! Now we haven't got the time!" Diminished, too, is discourse stressing the radical, sacred unity of the *narod* in opposition to the overwhelming powers of the state. In its place, many people say that they are now the "masters of their own lives and destinies." This would seem to affirm the idea that litanies reflected a feeling of powerlessness in the context of rigid power relations. Many people, however, also express a growing sense of isolation in their private struggles. *Narod* identity is fragmented, on the one hand, because there seems nothing concrete and singular to oppose and, on the other, because the stable personal networks which characterized the Soviet period have disintegrated as some people have managed to leave behind the sphere of common economic and social difficulty which was its basis. Life is not normal in the sense of being easy or calm, but in many ways it seems to have achieved the level of the mundane: routine and predictable.

Transition, upheaval, revolution, restructuring, reform, crisis, collapse: these are the terms used to characterize perestroika. While perestroika was all those things and more, to characterize it in terms of ritual may provide a crucial perspective for understanding many of its processes and outcomes. This is not merely a matter of semantics. If we view perestroika as a period of intensely ritualistic activity, we can apply what we know of the phenomenology, structure, and efficacy of ritual to gain insight into both the transformative and the paradoxical effects of that period's practices.[2]

My interpretation of perestroika as a macro-scale rite of passage is, of course, largely shaped by the perspective from which I observed it: as a participant in conversations and social life among Moscow's intelligentsia. My focus is therefore on the ways that perestroika was ritually and symbolically lived, talked about, and enacted within this particular stratum of Moscow society. However, my attention to the broader cultural phenomena of the time, visible through the media and in coverage of major political events, convinces me that the concept of perestroika as a ritual

---

[2] For comparable accounts, see Kertzer (1988: 151–173) on the role of ritual in the French Revolution, the American Revolution, Nazi Germany, and the Iranian Revolution. Stites' study (1989) of utopian fantasy and experimentation in the Russian revolutionary period illuminates similarly "ritual" processes of liminality, *communitas*, anti-structure, and vivid symbolism.

process can be useful more generally. A study of ritual or symbolic discourse and interactions within, for instance, the Russian parliament, akin to M. J. Aronoff's detailed examination (1977) of Israeli party politics in the early 1970s, would certainly reveal a complex of symbolic and ritual practice which this study cannot encompass. Similarly, a close textual and ethnographic engagement with the rich output of the press and the intelligentsia in the perestroika years, modeled, for example, after Katherine Verdery's masterful (1991) study of the production of nationalist ideology in late Ceaușescu-era Romania, would be most valuable in our understanding of the discourses of perestroika and their political ramifications. What my own reflections may offer, instead, is a sense of the overall experience of perestroika from the perspective of the kitchen table, where perestroika rituals were both performed and pondered.

Ritual Phases

The anthropologist Victor Turner, working from Van Gennep's well-known definition of the phases of rites of passage, has discussed the tripartite structure of such rituals: breach or separation, liminality, and consummation (Turner 1967: 93–111). The perestroika era clearly traversed these phases, and the array of events and activities of that era exhibit many of the qualities associated with more conventional examples of rites of passage. While anthropology and other social science disciplines have often tended to consider as "ritual" only those discrete, localized, and cyclically repeated ceremonies and rites of passage typical of small-scale societies, and to apply a term such as "revolution" to macro-level events involving whole nations, I see this as a false dichotomy. Features of ritual such as inversion (what Turner calls "anti-structure" 1982: 44), the intensification of performative content and play, a heightened experience of unity or *communitas* among certain participants, and the symbolic presentation of social values, conflicts and cleavages, all were clearly visible in perestroika.

The Breach

The breach occurred during the years 1985–87 as the Gorbachev reforms were introduced and began to gain their social momentum. Glasnost was proclaimed, primarily as a way to open a critique of bureaucratic self-interest and Party privilege mongering, as well as to initiate a productive evaluation of the inefficiencies of the Soviet economy. This breach from past practices was real and effective. Instigated by Gorbachev's official activism, it provoked a spontaneous and effervescent rending of the Soviet social fabric until a broad liminal space was opened up, a space where, for the next few years, social norms and structures were turned inside out and upside down in dramatic fashion. The breach signified that the unsayable could finally be said, the undoable done, and the unchangeable changed.

Liminality

The study of the phenomenology of ritual liminality is a centerpiece of ethnography and anthropological theory. It is widely agreed that the core of rites of passage is a time out of time and out of structure, a period characterized by "conditions of uncertainty and indeterminacy" (Handelman 1990: 65) in which cultural systems are open to some degree of scrutiny, rearrangement, and transformation. Sacred ideologies are performed and sometimes inverted, and structural paradoxes and conflicts (such as those of gender, social status, power relations, etc.) are acted out and publicly interrogated (Turner 1967: 110; Turner 1977; Geertz 1973: 412–454). This is not to say, however, that ritual in any way resolves those issues; in many ways, even through inversion, the deep structuring forms of systems are replicated through ritual practice (Gluckman 1954; Handelman 1990: 52). While liminality produces a shared sense of *communitas*—brotherhood, egalitarianism, a symbolic leveling of status—this is only a temporary phenomenon, unsustainable when a system returns to some kind of normalcy (Myerhoff 1975).

The liminal period of perestroika lasted several years, from about 1988 through the coup of 1991. During this time, as in more typical examples of ritual, a number of key symbolic processes occurred widely throughout Russian (and all Soviet) society: the previously masked structuring principles, paradoxes, failures, and tragedies of Soviet society were publicly examined, lamented, and condemned; many people subverted the stable Soviet norms of political participation and reclaimed officially inviolable urban spaces by attending mass rallies or meetings (Istomin 1992); the sacred symbols, ideologies, and practices of Soviet society were thrown down, unmasked, and rejected wholesale; the sacred values of the *narod* were performed in unusually visible fashion; and millenarian themes and images of either utopian transcendence or ultimate cataclysm became prevalent.

Consummation

The consummation or closure of the perestroika period was rapid, distinct, and visible to the entire world: it clearly occurred at the time of the

August coup and the defense of Yeltsin and the Russian White House. During this event, perestroika's *finale*, the rituals of daily life were temporarily overturned, especially for members of the liberal intelligentsia (if only because they were glued to their televisions and radios); the key themes, new practices, and new identities of the perestroika era were condensed; and the cleavage between the official state and the *narod* (in its most inclusive sense) was ritually enacted. The *narod* seemed to gain a total victory over the most forceful institutions of the Soviet state (political, military, and security). When, a few months later, the Soviet Union itself was brought to an end, the perestroika era also closed and the next, as yet unnamed and perhaps unnamable, period of Russian social life began.

This book has focused on the discourses of the central, liminal phase of perestroika as performed among Moscow's intelligentsia during my field research. The following discussion views these discourses, and other cultural materials, within the conceptual framework of ritual, and suggests the ways in which their ritualistic quality made them both socially productive—i.e., revolutionary—but also, paradoxically, socially reproductive.

Glasnost: Talk Set Free

Gorbachev introduced the policy of glasnost primarily as a way to improve the efficiency and productivity of Soviet government and industry by increasing accountability and the flow of necessary information. In one of his early discussions of glasnost, the Soviet leader suggested the power that open communication was supposed to bear in social transformation. In his book *Perestroika*, he declaimed: "We want more openness about public affairs in every sphere of life. People should know what is good, and what is bad, too, in order to multiply the good and combat the bad" (1987: 75).

Here Gorbachev was suggesting that the verbal articulation of social successes and failures was a key to solving them. This was a kind of magical thinking about the power of social critique to change social ways. However, while Gorbachev may have taken advantage of the popularity of glasnost for political reasons and accepted its application to all spheres of Soviet life and history, the opening up for inspection of every single corner of that life and history had not been his original or ultimate intent. As Lewin describes it,

The coup from above, by Gorbachev, was followed by a chaotic anti-system urge from below. When the controlling mechanisms began to weaken, all the woes of the country that kept accumulating under the heavy cover of the regime's monopoly—all the wounds, neglect, and despair, and all that was in need of urgent mending—came up to the surface, with devastating effects and a multidimensional complexity. This was unavoidable, and actually indispensable, in the given situation: The country had to learn the full scope and depth of its problems, which it had not realized before. (Lewin 1995: 301)

Very rapidly, however, the reporting and absorbing of ever-darker truths became a central practice of glasnost, and the broad airing of these truths became a dominant mode of public discourse. What began as a necessary examination of the deep crises of the Soviet economy and the terrible history of that state, rapidly evolved into a ritualized practice of litanizing and lamenting *everything* about the past.

These genres became a central form of communication in the media, accompanying the appearance in print of long-suppressed works about the Stalin period, especially works about the *gulag* by Solzhenitsyn, Shalamov, Grossman, and others. The leading weekly journals *Moscow News* and *Ogonek* were dedicated to chronicling the suffering, loss, and brutality of the Stalin era. Many television and film documentaries and interviews were structured around litanies enumerating the many tragedies of Soviet history.

People responded by contributing their own chronicles of suffering. One indication of the intensity with which they did so was provided by Vitaly Korotich in his introduction to a translation of letters to the editor of *Ogonek*, the weekly magazine:

The art of pain—I have written and thought about this many times—is higher than the art of happiness. Pain is always concrete. Whether it is a tooth or an arm, leg or back that hurts, you understand the root of your suffering; you understand it not in some abstract way but precisely, concretely. Most of our letters are about pain. And about how to overcome the pain. Soon, there will be about 200,000 of them a year. At the beginning of 1986 there were barely twenty a day. Everything is different now. The openness of our society, its desire to have its say after decades of censorship, is stunning. People are writing letters, asking questions, and providing their own answers. (Cerf and Albee 1990: 14).

As Korotich noted, within a brief span the number of letters "about pain" to *Ogonek* swelled from about seven thousand to two hundred thousand per year. Many of these letters were concrete descriptions of the difficulty of existence—the scarcity of meat, sugar, housing, or medicines—

which lamented the lack of any sympathy or assistance or poignantly appealed for some redress. Many others were tragic stories of personal and familial tragedies attributable to Stalinism: repressions, executions, disappearances, long terms spent in the camps, exile, denunciations, and myriad other cruelties.

The sudden explosion of litanies in missive form to journals such as *Ogonek* reflects the explosion of such discourses in the population in general. Such litanies had always been spoken quietly in private conversation, but the opening up of these genres in the media recursively energized them in private as well, and private conversation became, at least for a while, an orgy of litany. It was as if glasnost had caused a huge seed-pod of stored memories to burst, spilling litanies into the public field, where they sprouted, were noticed, were listened to, and were consumed (even commodified) and where they generated other litanies in response, litanies that competed with, contradicted, or complemented and abetted the initial ones.

This eruption of litanies in its turn generated meta-litanies, which commented on the very fact of the public explosion of this genre. As a woman who was standing in the coat-check line behind me after a performance of a stage adaptation of Solzhenitsyn's *One Day in the Life of Ivan Denisovich*, said, "I lived through that time. Do I have to keep hearing about it?"

Litany and lament spread from the media and from the kitchen table into politics. To watch the televised sessions of the Congress of People's Deputies or the Moscow City Soviet in 1989 and 1990 was to hear endless litanies on one topic or another—actually an endless competition of litanies. The spokespersons for various regions and interest groups took turns occupying the podium and pouring forth their grievances, claiming their more elevated positions as victims relative to other supposedly more empowered (less suffering) groups. One evening in April 1990 during the broadcast of the Moscow City Soviet, a woman deputy got up to tell how she had been beaten on the street for her position on a certain issue. Hers was, unarguably, an important and terrifying story, but she went on at great length, describing all her injuries and the police non-response in vivid detail. Her allotted time had run out, but deputies wanted to hear more, fascinated by a tale which showed them how much danger they were in, how dangerous democratization was, how threatening the mafia could be. The deputies almost unanimously voted to hear the end of her story, even though the deputy mayor, Sergei Stankevich, clearly had an agenda he wanted to fulfill. It was hard for him to accomplish this when ritual discourse—litanizing—was more important to the members of the governing bodies than a reasoned discussion of the problems and possibilities facing their society. Michael Urban's (1994) discussion of the politics of identity is quite pertinent here. Perhaps it was not just the aesthetic or emotional intensity of such litanies which was most important, but the way that such stories could be used to construct particular political identities and assert the political purity of one's own side in opposition to the corruption of others. As Lewin points out: "The unmasking of past atrocities, iniquities, and corruptions had a liberating effect initially. The settling of accounts with an ugly past through condemnation and repentance might have delivered minds and souls from a national nightmare. Unfortunately, in many quarters the denunciation soon became a strategy and a way of thought that testified to an addiction to 'negationism.' An unending list of atrocities and injustices under Stalinism was not followed by analysis" (1995: 302).

The profusion of litanies revealing and lamenting the tragedies of the past had a paradoxical and quite disorienting effect, one contrary to that anticipated by Gorbachev when he launched the policy of glasnost. Instead of revitalizing Soviet society through openness, the deluge of revelations about the past contributed greatly to widespread derision of all the ideals of the socialist project, and this certainly abetted the deconstruction of Soviet social systems—those negative ones that people wanted to disappear, but also those they may have wanted to sustain. It was hard for many to avoid questioning the purpose and meaning of the suffering and sacrifice endured through the Soviet period. Many litanies invoked the now publicly named traumas of the past and led up to the lamenting question, "Why?" As one middle-aged woman asked bitterly, "Why did we have to go through all this, for it to end up like it has? Our country is in ruins, everyone is fighting everyone else, no one knows what will happen. . . . Did we sacrifice our entire lives for it to end up like this?"

Initially, the freeing of litanies into official, public space was part of the healthy, redressive ritual necessary to break out of and leave behind the myths of the past. The pouring forth of victim's tales was a ritual step toward moral healing. Litanies seemed to absolve the people of collective guilt, provide a vehicle for the expression of pent-up anguish, and destroy the authority of Soviet institutions, all of which were in some ways beneficial and transformative. But the sharing, spreading, and re-learning of victims' stories also reinforced social cleavages, deepened political apathy, and intensified a sense of despair and futility.

Absurdity and Negation

Alongside litanies and laments about the intense tragedy of the Soviet people, narratives and jokes about the surrealism of Soviet history and the absurdities and horrors of Russian life began to stream from private into public discourse. Because glasnost stimulated the airing of these stories, illusion and absurdism began to seem even more the primary context of Russian experience than they had previously; this became a key theme of Russian media and of Russian talk.

I use the term surrealism to refer to the sense my informants constantly described of living in a society where nothing was as it had been said to be. This situation had elements which could be termed paradoxes, ironies, inconsistencies, contradictions, discrepancies, deviations, unintended effects, or absurdities (my Russian informants' favorite word for it all). There were so many of these kinds of logical and social contradictions being discussed and displayed that they formed a tangle, nearly as hard to unravel discursively as politically.

Two broad categories of paradox filled both public and private conversation. The first was the paradox of the Soviet state and its massive internal contradictions; the second, which emerged gradually, was the paradox of perestroika and all the disappointments and unintended consequences perestroika entailed.

The first paradox emerged fully into public view and discussion at the very beginning of glasnost. Talk focused especially on the general contradiction between ideology and practice, the gap between the myths and actualities of Soviet society. The public drive to reveal and demystify drew attention to what at the time seemed a supreme paradox: the irony that the socialist revolution, with all its promises of equality and abundance, had resulted in a state that called itself socialist but where hierarchy and relative poverty were the norms. As perestroika continued, this paradox (this mass of multiple contradictions) became the focal, even fetishized topic of Russian media, scholarship, and conversation. The exquisite elaboration and lamentation of this paradox was the second key aspect of perestroika ritual.

For a brief interval in the late 1980s it was possible to watch this opening up of the ironies of Soviet history taking place alongside the continuing sacralization of socialism, Lenin, and 1917; the iconoclasm of perestroika operated concurrently with Soviet icon-maintenance for a while. So, as *Ogonek, Moscow News*, and *Novyi mir*, the leading, newly revisionist publications, printed the tragic biographies and stories of the Soviet damned, exposed the many levels of corruption, inadequacy, and deception of the Party and the *nomenklatura*, and bemoaned the destruction and suffering of the Soviet people, the orthodox part of the press tried hard to hold on to the symbols of communism, wielding images of the proletariat, the masses, and the Great Patriotic War as their weapons in this lofty debate. So, for example, on May 8, 1990, the eve of V-E day (Den' Pobedy), Gorbachev broadcast a memorial speech in which he poetically named the tragedies of the war not attributable to the German occupiers: the millions who died in famines, epidemics, and Soviet labor camps. The Soviet leader thus tried to appropriate for "his side" (the official side) the traumas and losses of the *narod*.[3]

By that time, however, such appropriations by the leadership of the *narod*'s losses could only seem hypocritical to listeners. The Soviet system itself had been fully moved into the conceptual slot of "the enemy," as revelations about Stalin's incompetence as leader and his willingness to sacrifice people's lives unnecessarily, along with vivid examples of the brutality of the contemporary Soviet army, had been extensively published and discussed. The rituals marking the war and personal memoirs (whether oral or written) about the war had become laden with a new dimension of lament, and the Soviet government was widely cursed for its role in the people's suffering.[4] Thus, however much Gorbachev may have tried to align himself with the *narod* on this issue, it was too late: discourses of blame had already entrenched an ideology negating the possibility of any good being accomplished by the government, including, crucially, its project of perestroika.

As part of this ritual of what Lewin aptly terms "negationism," all the various myths about Soviet socialism were overturned and deconstructed in the media. Myths about public order and safety were crushed by constant, explicit reportage about the most gruesome crimes; crime had previously been reported as a plague only of the West. Myths about the Soviet love of motherland were poisoned by exposés about the terrible pollution of Soviet lands. Myths about planning and control were contradicted by disclosures of the most absurd, ludicrous, and wasteful production and distribution practices. And the myth of the Party as the kindly elder brother, the repository of maturity, wisdom, and fairness, was blown apart by a barrage of media bombshells about abuses of power and privilege. Some of these myths had long been widely laughed at, parodied, and regarded as conspicuous lies. However, the public, ritualistic overturning of the official claims of the State made it impossible for many people to believe anything good about the Soviet regime. It entailed a "wholesale rejection of all the achievements of the post-October 1917 period" (Lewin 1995: 303), a period which had produced, despite all its terrors and afflictions, an educated, stable, modern society with a complex system of social

[3] See Tumarkin's wonderful discussion of the way the Great Patriotic War was reconsidered because of glasnost, and the effects that its desacralization had on different sectors of the populace (1994: 159–201).

[4] This new dimension, surprisingly, at the same time both dampened intense feelings about the sacredness of the Russian *narod*'s sacrifices in the war and reanimated them, as a previously unexplored (or previously repressed) layer of suffering was brought forward.

security and support, on which the populace had come to depend. And, as Lewin points out, "Making sweeping rejections without good knowledge is a prescription for destroying what works and replacing it with what does not. This happened after October 1917, for instance—and on a grand scale" (1995: 325).

Among many people, the widespread and rapid loss of faith in the Soviet system brought on by the assault of demystification led to an increase in the cynicism and passivity which had always plagued Soviet society; expressions of the impossibility of improvement and declarations of the powerlessness of individuals or of the *narod* became daily discursive fare, whether one listened to the media or to casual conversations. The final evaporation of the utopian dreams of the Soviet period brought on a state of discouragement summed up in the "dead end" metaphor which echoed all around Moscow in 1990.

Several years earlier, invoking the conventional metaphor of "the road of social life," Gorbachev had declared, referring to the pre-perestroika period, that "we thought we were in the saddle, while . . . the automobile was not going where the one at the steering wheel thought it was going" (1987: 23). It was Gorbachev's own ironic fate that perestroika did not go where he intended it to either; though called in to help "tune up" the automobile of state, glasnost seemed to make it go crashing into a "dead end." Talking with people in 1989 and 1990, I noticed the frequency of laments that although Gorbachev's perestroika was supposed to heighten social discipline, productivity, order, and efficiency ultimately it had resulted only in "chaos."

Perestroika Folklore

The media were full of stories that illustrated the multiple paradoxes and absurdities of the Soviet economy. Often, however, treatment of these was rather circular and vague; perhaps because they had little prior experience with "muckraking" journalism, writers often presented images of these absurdisms that failed to examine the concrete sources of the problems they revealed; of course, this could be said to characterize much journalism worldwide—especially in partisan publications. However, the particularly "folkloric" ways that this phenomenon manifested itself in perestroika journalism is worth illustration. Consider, for instance, a couple of samples from the press.

Two photographs stand juxtaposed in an issue of *Ogonek* September 2, 1989. In the upper one, a crowd of women waits in line in front of a tiny kiosk for milk; in the lower photograph, a grouchy-looking farm woman pours a pail of milk out as slop for pigs. The commentary reads:

Our agricultural mechanism is at times reminiscent of an absent-minded eccentric, who like the well-known hero set off on his travels in a sidelined wagon or took to the street wearing two different shoes. What kinds of astounding and mysterious wonders our amazing reality offers up! In the town of Apsheronsk of the lucky and well-tended Krasnodar region, long lines for milk form in the mornings. To each person, they will only give [literally, "let go of"] no more than three liters of the deficit product. The people are nervous, they complain. . . . In the very same Apsheronsk region in the Middle Tuva settlement they are feeding milk to the pigs. Because of the poor roads, the procurement officials avoid the out-of-the-way, distant settlements. For the same reason, the pigs also often have perfectly good fruit on their menu. . . . What is happening to us?

In an issue of *Moscow News* (September 24, 1989: 12), the following introduction to a story appeared:

"It is a bitter irony when a Tajik woman who lost her health in cotton fields poisoned by defoliants does not have the right to buy her grandson a cotton shirt at shops in Riga or Tallinn."

While it seems that these tales—and the many like them, for they were so common as to become a perestroika genre in and of themselves—addressed real problems, in terms of their structures and rhetorical details they were more like parables meant for popular consideration (parodies of the socialist realist representations of smiling milkmaids found in the *Ogonek* of years gone by) than calls to evaluate a problem or take action to resolve it.

The point of the first one would seem to be to underscore the absurdity of milk lines when milk is produced nearby. Yet its idiom was folkloric and its calculus of valuation traditional. It employed milk as a magical substance, cast the pig-feeding woman in the image of the archetypal "stubborn provincial person," and the local bosses as lazy and indifferent. The line "What kinds of astounding and mysterious wonders our amazing reality offers up!" was standard folktale language. The rhetorical question with which it ended ("What is happening to us?") was in the idiom of Russian laments.

Significantly, no hero appeared in either of these to save the day—nor were there many heroes to be found in other fables of perestroika. What was heroic in these images were the victims: the long-suffering *narod* standing in line in front of the milk store, the impoverished grandmother trying to buy a shirt.

There was more pathos in the second example, since it focused on one individual woman, and since she belonged to the least powerful social caste of all—cotton pickers. Was this tale apocryphal? Could it have been both true and apocryphal at once? In any case, it was characteristic of the type of story that circulated during the months when rationing grew tight and urban retail shops were keeping many of their allotted goods for their own people, and thus out of the hands of the many who came to cities from ill-served villages to get provisions.[5]

Again the folktale elements were clear—the protagonist was the poorest, most innocent, most long-suffering character imaginable—and she was not, of course, seeking to buy anything for herself, but to get a shirt for her little grandson—a paradigmatically unselfish folktale kind of quest. Implicitly, the villain in this tale was the merchant (here, Latvian) who would not sell the simplest shirt to the woman whose labor produced it. Also implicit in such tales was the promise of redress—the implication of salvation for the poor victim and punishment for the greedy (ethnic) hoarders. A higher justice was immanent in both of these tales. But for the time being (and the world at hand) the focus was clearly on the pathos of poverty, and the value that was marked, stressed, conveyed emotionally, reiterated, and reproduced was the value of that pathos, that suffering, located in the sacred condition of poverty and victimization, which was itself created from the larger context of supposedly impossible inefficiency, absurdism, stupidity, cruelty, exploitation, expropriation, and selfishness.

In these discourses, the question of rational provisioning which superficially seemed to be the main subject of concern, was in fact not on the agenda at all. Both stories posed the problem of agricultural production, processing, and distribution more as moral questions than as practical ones. In the first case, for instance, the root of the problem seemed to be the unwillingness of procurement officials to suffer the ignominy and discomfort of traveling on bumpy roads to distant settlements. The implication of the juxtaposition of the two pictures was that the farm woman's bucket of milk could provision the crowd of shoppers lined up at the kiosk (and the editor was probably counting on the fact that many readers had the frequent experience of standing in line for hours to get a liter of milk and would react viscerally to the sight of precious milk fed to pigs). In fact, what was wrong with Soviet agriculture was systemic, not local— milk was not exchanged between milkmaid and consumer in a direct way in a modern economy as this image and its commentary iconically suggest. This kind of discourse about production and distribution was not focused on the real, systemic source of the difficulty; it was not a utilitarian discourse but a mythical and moral one.

[5] Very common were rumors and stories about butter-producing collective farms with no butter for their own tables, and meat producers whose children get no meat. There is an old proverb in Russian—"*sapozhnik bez sapog*," a bootmaker who has no boots—which sums up this second paradox. The *Moscow News* story, and others like it, though probably "true," were basically illustrations of the proverb.

Solutions proposed were often mythical as well; that is, even the most obvious consequences of certain actions were all but ignored. One night in September 1989, a Moscow television program featured a long segment about a leather factory. In view of the camera, a group of experts toured the factory, pointing out for the camera pits full of gore, rooms and equipment covered with blood, and piles and layers of filth, buzzing with flies. A pair of workers, when questioned by the experts, revealed certain choice and gory facts for the viewing audience, after which they were asked how they could stand their work and the conditions of the factory. They explained that they received a high salary (more than 800 rubles per month) and that they had grown accustomed to the horrors of their work. Back in the television studio, one of the commentators asked, in an expressive, morally rich tone, whether human beings can really grow accustomed to such a life. He pronounced it "an inhuman kind of work," and declared "such factories must either be updated immediately or closed down!"

If the intention of journalists communicating in this fashion was to promote economic prosperity—ensuring there would be a chicken in every pot—their discourses were in many ways a tragic distraction from that goal, a distraction which became a significant social factor when multiplied a million fold. Obviously, the problems which faced the Soviet Union in 1980 or 1990 were of such complexity that few people could apprehend them, much less solve them. But in part because of the new freedom to speak out, in the perestroika era words seemed to have magical power to cure, and many journalists were occupied with lamenting problems or reveling in their familiar absurdity—rather than with the careful analysis of social crises.[6]

Ritual Inversion and Utopian Images of the West

Concomitant with the negation of everything Soviet came a celebration of everything having to do with the old capitalist nemesis, "the West." Where the Soviet media had regularly exhibited images of the cruelty, unfairness, and contradictions of capitalist systems, in perestroika this practice was inverted, and images of poor people receiving medical care in U.S. clinics were juxtaposed with interviews with Russian mothers who could not obtain medicines or services their children desperately needed. Thus mythical images of the West (as one-sided as the previous hellish

---

[6] Obviously, this is a problem with a great deal of public or media discourse in general.

images of Western life had been) were used in the assault on the mythos of socialism.

Numerous conversations brought this home to me. Discussing the problems of Soviet society, my friends and acquaintances often turned to me with questions about whether comparable problems existed in the United States. As much as I tried to explain the complexities and contradictions of U.S. society, and exemplify my abstractions about the problems of U.S. life through anecdotal illustrations, I could never really break through, and I felt as if my stories went unheard. Popular mythification of the bounty of the west had set up a form of ideological closure (Eagleton 1991: 194) which made reception of my arguments impossible. This was certainly not a new phenomenon; prior to perestroika, mythic images about the West were widespread, but they took the private form of rumors, jokes, and dissident discourses. What was new in the glasnost years was that these images gained an untouchable, almost official status. The ritualistic inversion of Soviet ideologies about Soviet life entailed the adoption of diametrically opposite ideologies. What is key here is that these were *ideologies*—as mystifying in their ways as their Soviet precursors had been. There was, thus, in private conversations as well as in public, an "uncritical acceptance of Western models, based on limited knowledge of them and an almost mechanical acceptance of positions that were the opposite of what the previous regime had done" (Lewin 1995: 303).

This remodeling of ideological positions was quite apparent in political and economic programs, but it was especially visible to me as an ethnographer in the sphere of identity formation. As stable Soviet-era social identities—personal, collective, and national—were deflated and questioned, new identities (beauty queen, hard-currency prostitute, businessman, mafia boss) were adopted; not surprisingly, these new identities were modeled after the archetypal images of American "bad guys" long used as emblems of capitalist evil by Soviet propaganda. Thus, instead of Gorbachev's fantasized "combating of the bad," glasnost unintentionally ushered in the adoption of the "bad" as emblems of "goodness" or at least of freedom. The extent of the attraction of the mafia for young Russian men (and some women), during and after perestroika, and the concomitant explosion of mafia activity and crime, seems to be due, in part, to the rapidity with which old identities were stripped of their social value and opposite identities invested with merit and meaning.

Of course, in the sphere of identity formation, the most significant adoption of all was that of people starting to do business, in whatever shape or form or degree of legality or legitimacy. In droves, the powerful denounced their Communist party affiliations and remade themselves as capitalist entrepreneurs (many of them transferring, secretly and not so secretly, the resources of their enterprises to their own private ownership). A new class of *biznesmeny* developed rapidly from its roots in the cooperative movement of 1988 to become the leaders of liberal economic reform. Small-scale trading went from being the illegal, underground activity of black marketeers to being the chosen profession of many young people. The mafia—a conglomerate of economic actors—rapidly increased its control of certain sectors and its influence and visibility expanded widely. While condemned for their spread of terror, there was a certain cowboy glory to be gained among mafia "tough guys"—whose iconic image and "mischievous," dangerous practices represented a kind of frontier of capitalist activity.

Capitalist ideologies—some of them already considered highly problematic in the West—were adopted wholesale. The marketization of all sectors of society was widely envisioned as a cure-all for the problems of the people, and socialist ideals were held by many to be the rubbish of long-term propaganda. Deluged with utopian images of Western lifestyles, many envisioned themselves "getting rich quick" and became ripe targets for pyramid schemes (such as the infamous "MMM"), which blossomed in 1992, and for investment in less-than-rational money-making ventures; this was also a magical solution for the problem of inflation and what to do with one's money so that it kept its value.

Amid all this, however, it must be said that the paradigm of mystical poverty, which I have described here in detail, remained the guiding ideology for many people, their way of seeing their own economic positions (and decline) as a sign of their morality in the face of social and economic transformations which they could not control and in which they could not participate.

The Ritual Renovation of Archaic Forms

There was another abundant source for the construction of "new," anti-Soviet identity: the pre-revolutionary Russian world. Many people invested in the revival of archaic, iconic identities. This is well exemplified by the widespread abandoning of Communist Party membership, which seemed rampant in 1990, and the simultaneous adoption by many former party members of Orthodox Christian affiliation and practice; it was as if they exchanged, overnight, one badge of legitimacy for another.

In Chapter 3, I described an Orthodox Christmas dinner that I attended in January 1990. That event marked, for all its participants, their first celebration of a religious holiday. I felt as if I had been invited to that dinner as a symbolic representative of religiosity, since my acquaintances knew

I had grown up in a Protestant family. Throughout the meal, they asked me about how Christmas was celebrated in my church and family; they seemed to gain confidence and a sense of the poignance and importance of religious practice from my presence and my stories. While the sincerity of their fascination with the religious life touched me, it was also clear to me that they were working hard to fill a recently opened ideological void in their lives, and that they were trying to fashion new identities for themselves by turning to the old.

Religious identity also became an object of commodification, as religious icons, first glorified on television and in museums, appeared in craft markets such as those in Izmailovsky Park and on the Arbat, and in kiosks citywide. Cheap replicas of icons began to be sold everywhere, supplanting the ubiquitous images of Lenin, in the form of pins, postcards, pocket calendars, and figurines.

There were some more hegemonic manifestations of this practice, however, as is clear in the fact that many educators, faced with the abandonment of Communist indoctrination in their schools, replaced it immediately and enthusiastically with new curricula stressing religious (Orthodox) practices and values. From being forbidden, religious education was suddenly instituted in some public schools, and it was argued by some that it should be mandated as part of all school curricula. Just as there had been, seventy years ago, a dictated transition from Christian to Communist veneration, now there was a forced transition from Communist to Christian. This was certainly problematic in that it was an unthinking replication of a reliance on a single ideology, one that allowed no room for a multiplicity of views or religio-cultural identities.

The spread of ethnic nationalism was the darkest manifestation of this inversion and substitution process, however. The Soviet ideological position of universalism and multinationalism was, for many people and groups, replaced by a celebration of national identities, and the assertion of particular ethnic interests within a highly blended polity. There were numerous quite positive manifestations of this—such as the development of opportunities for ethnic minorities to reassert their identities and revitalize their long-repressed cultural practices, including religious practices. However, ethnic nationalism has had a much darker side in recent years. Anti-Semitism emerged fully from the closet (where it had only been somewhat sequestered in any case); vicious anti-Jewish publications, including old Nazi tracts, began to be sold openly on the streets. Expressions of hatred for the so-called "blacks"—people from the Caucasus, mainly, many of whom bring produce to Russian cities to sell—became fervent, resulting in a number of policies designed to control their movements. I cannot do justice here to this enormously important problem, the causes of which are many and complicated. The main point I wish to make is that much Russian nationalism has been motivated by a desire to express disdain for Soviet internationalism (see Urban 1994 on this practice of creating political identities in opposition to Soviet forms).

Archaic gender identities were also massively resurrected as a way of overturning Soviet ideologies about gender equality. Many of my friends came to fetishize a mythic, bourgeois model of gender relations—one that the Soviet regime had propagandized against, in large part because it had so relied on the intense participation of women in the labor force (Lapidus 1978; Sariban 1984; Ries 1994). Under the new model, women would be able to return to their "natural roles" as homemakers and mothers and leave involvement in the workplace to men. While this bourgeois image was, for many Russian women, part of their fantasy of counteracting the famous "double burden" of Soviet women, it also encouraged the spread of intensely anti-feminist ideologies (cf. Erofeev 1993) and practices. The early 1990s witnessed an epidemic of assertions, in private discussion, in the media, and in politics, that women should be forcibly returned to their "natural" domestic roles as wives and mothers and that domestic patriarchy is necessary to restore the morality of women and families. The feminist philosopher Olga Voronina writes:

> This campaign began with Gorbachev's statement about the necessity of giving women back their true family purpose. The media picked up this statement and, as has long been their habit, evidently made note of it as a "valuable directive." The pages of the newspapers and magazines were full of articles on the topic of "women," yet only the statements made by the advocates of patriarchal values were printed. Even the "Domostroj" [a manual on household management from the sixteenth century] which, as is well-known, thinks that the best way of educating wives and children is to beat them, began to be propagated as a monument of national culture. (1993: 97–98)

As part of this reassertion of a range of patriarchal values, perestroika legitimated the growing segregation of the workplace, with many women—especially young women—being channeled into roles as secretaries, clerks, receptionists, and other servitors. Though this had, of course, always occurred, the selection of women for jobs on the basis of their physical attractiveness started to be an open practice (Khanga 1991). Many job advertisements in Russian newspapers sought stylish, attractive women with long legs, nice figures, and "without hang-ups" (*bez kompleksov*)—which meant a willingness to perform sexual as well as clerical functions.

Sexually titillating posters began to appear for sale in Metro underpasses and newsstands in 1990, and there quickly developed a large market for pornography, which was always totally forbidden in the Soviet era, though it was traded in unofficial ways. This "sexual glasnost" a popular expression of liberation from stodgy communism, has arguably contributed more to a reinstitutionalization of sexism and hierarchical gender relations than to any progressive exploration of previously suppressed sexual identities.

Although there were some significant developments in the sphere of feminist activity—the first feminist conference was held in Moscow in 1990, a Center for Gender Studies opened in Moscow that same year, numerous women's groups were founded, and many publications started featuring discussion of women's issues—as Goscilo writes in a recent essay, "these, however, are miniature pockets of revolutionary change, thus far more cosmetic than systemic. Isolated developments on a modest scale, they are virtually swamped by countercurrents, some new and imported from the West, others of immemorial domestic origin" (1993: 240).

The appearance of a tiny feminist movement in fact provoked and legitimated anti-feminist rhetoric on many fronts. The official Soviet ideology of female emancipation—which was, of course, never realized in day-to-day practice—was portrayed by women and men alike as having caused many of the ills of Soviet society, and thus had to be negated along with the rest. So, although many things Western were being adopted, ideas and practices associated with feminism were quite specifically berated and excluded.

With the cultural and social chaos wrought by perestroika, patriarchy as a political ideology also reasserted itself. Many began to clamor for "firm-handed" leadership. "Give me Stalin, but give me bread," read one poster at a political rally. This chilling sentiment, while not dominant, echoed widely enough in conversations, meetings, and the media to be a familiar refrain. Though largely a phenomenon of the suddenly disenfranchised elderly and working classes, it appeared in subtle ways among the intelligentsia as well.

Complaints were rampant, in the press and in private, about Gorbachev's hesitation and vacillation, and his seeming inability to maintain social order and control. While, on the one hand, they extolled the virtues of freedom, democratization, and the decentralization of power, many people cried out for Gorbachev to do whatever it would take to reduce crime, stop ethnic violence, restore economic stability, and prevent the crumbling of social welfare services. In their discourses, they thus unthinkingly rehearsed ancient ideologies about the magical power of paternalistic authority.

"Night-time Entertainments": Movie Billboard, 1992 (Photo by John Einarsen and Robert Kowalczyk)

Litanies of "total collapse" began to echo most widely. Their message was one of hopelessness, and they presented several images: images of the present time as a "dead end," and of the future, more darkly, as "civil war." The history of the civil war years (1918–21), its massive terror, violence, and famine, and dislocation made widely understood because of glasnost, became a kind of template for envisioning Russia's future. This was abetted by the terrible stories, relayed in the media and among friends, from the actual civil wars (ethnic cleansing) taking place in Armenia and Azerbaijan, and the influx to Moscow of thousands of refugees from those conflicts. Although there was, as yet, very little open civil conflict taking place in Russia, people widely imagined its possibility and even invoked that term to describe the crime and violence they heard about and experienced in their own milieu.

Magical, totalizing leadership was held by many to be the only way out of this chaos.[7] I call it imagined, because though events were turbulent, and the challenges of living under new social and economic conditions were immense, in fact, Moscow seemed quite peaceful. As Lewin writes, "for a crisis of this magnitude, it is the relative calm and the lack of massive disorder that are remarkable—although the continuation of the decline and growing despair may well lead to much more dramatic events" (1995: 302). Amid the growing despair of those days, only authority seemed to hold promise.

The revived fetishization of authority took several forms, some of them quite strange. In Chapter 3, I mentioned the appearance of the hypnotist Kashpirovskii on the cultural scene. Kashpirovskii's seances came out as a form of *orexis*, to use Turner's (1988: 91) term—a ritual willing of the reconstruction of social selves and institutions which could not be accomplished by rational bureaucratic planning procedures and initiatives. It is not coincidental that Kashpirovskii appeared at the moment when all the great dreams of a rational perestroika were beginning to disappear, when the more highly educated sectors of the bourgeoisie and the liberal intelligentsia were beginning to consider, openly and seriously, their prospects for emigration, and when the threat of total chaos or civil war seemed to loom larger all the time. In his hour-long presentations, Kashpirovskii would stand unblinking before the camera and chant: "As you listen to my words, you will be healed from whatever ails you. . . . Even if you are asleep, even if you are an unbeliever, even if you don't speak Russian . . . the healing will work. . . . You can be cured of diabetes, heart prob-

[7] This search for magical ways out of the complex problems of society obviously takes place everywhere. How much of American political rhetoric, for example, is based on rational analysis of problems and carefully thought-out proposals? Citizens anywhere are open to believe in magical solutions, such as Reagan's "Star Wars" or Gingrich's "Contract with America."

lems, myopia, depression, even baldness can be cured, and radiation sickness . . . you will quit smoking. . . . Alcoholics can be cured of drinking and our society restored to health." People of all social classes and persuasions, among them many of my educated, liberal friends, tuned into Kashpirovskii's show whenever it was on, and afterwards talk of his power to heal was heard everywhere.[8]

At the bread store one day, while I was waiting in line to pay, I heard a conversation. The young cashier was clutching her face as if ill. "What, are you sick?" asked a woman customer. "No, it's my tooth," said the girl. "Poor thing," said the woman, "you should watch Kashpirovskii." "I watched yesterday." "It didn't help?" asked the woman, amazed. "No," said the girl with a disappointed tone.

Another hypnotist, Chumak, appeared on television at about the same time, and he told people to put water near their televisions during his show and that it would become powerful. An acquaintance of mine, a young biologist, told me she put her skin creams there in hopes they would become more efficacious. One thing Chumak said was that his hypnotism would not work for any who drank alcohol—a strange confluence of magic and the ongoing anti-alcohol campaign.

The paradox in these rituals was that while they called for the healing of the body politic, the mode they offered for this healing was revival of a state of mass responsiveness to hypnotic power. At some level what Kashpirovskii's unblinking gaze on the television screen meant was: come back to the prior state of trance—nothing will happen, nothing will work, nothing will be well unless we are all hypnotized by whatever charisma is at hand. Kashpirovskii's current status as a deputy in the Russian Duma shows that the borders between mysticism and politics are rather permeable.

Even the figure of Sakharov was drawn into this realm of magical power. Having been transformed from his pre-perestroika place as a "nonperson" (as one woman said to me smugly in 1985, "he doesn't exist for us") into a symbolic representative of morality even before his death, when he died in mid-December 1989 people turned out in the tens of thousands for his funeral procession through Moscow, one of the great spontaneous public gatherings of the perestroika period. Marching miles through deep, slushy snow in an icy rain, people mourned the death of one who had become, through his dissidence, a great saint (see Tumarkin 1990). The eminent literary scholar D. S. Likhachev described Sakharov as a prophet, a man of the twenty-first-century, asking the great man to forgive the fact that so many had been only passive defenders of human

---

[8] His seances were in some ways similar to those of television preachers in the United States, although the practice of hypnosis via the airwaves was rather unusual.

rights; Academician Osipian called Sakharov a "great Russian person" and "a person like Tolstoy," "like Gandhi." Invoking a kinship metaphor, he said Sakharov was "our true older brother" and declared that "humanity will never forget him." A journalist from *Moscow News*, ecstatic at the expression of *communitas* she was experiencing, predicted that "this is the beginning of a great unification—all kinds of people are coming up to us and hugging us."

This ritual was a massive and meaningful celebration of the values of human rights and democracy, and its speakers and posters urged people to emulate Sakharov's dedication in their own lives. One poster, for instance, read "Andrei Sakharov gave his life for the *narod*. What will the *narod* give?" In the process of this celebration, however, they marked Sakharov as "the only one" who could have redeemed their society from all its ills. In so doing, they reinforced an ideological reliance on singular, charismatic power, the power of saints.

The Ritual of Political Rallies

Perhaps the most vivid of perestroika rites—and the most charged with ritual magic—was the public rally or demonstration. Among my friends and informants, participation in the *mitingi* (meetings) which supported democratization was like a necessary rite of passage from powerlessness to political participation. Hedged with a sense of peril (though there probably was no real danger), the rallies became a place for people to assert themselves as both courageous and moral. The largest one took place on Sunday, February 4, 1990, when thousands gathered in front of Gorky Park and marched to the Manezh, just outside of Red Square. The bulk of the crowd was made up of voters' clubs marching together under their various banners. Many slogans were extolled on signs and in speeches: they denounced Party privilege, demanded further freedom of the press, and called for an end to the human rights abuses which were still "legal" under Article 6 of the constitution; they decried the *Pamiat'* (proto-fascist) movement and ridiculed Gorbachev's conservative nemesis Ligachev (ironically, there have been some rumors that this and other rallies were covertly sponsored by Gorbachev himself). People were generally jubilant, amused, and excited, and reacted vigorously against the Communist and fascist "side-rallies" which were taking place around them, arguing fiercely with those on the margins, such as a crazyish old man who walked past chanting, "You're all a bunch of Jews and yids, Jews and yids."

A. A. Istomin, a Moscow anthropologist who took part in the mass demonstrations in 1990 and in the 1991 defense of the Russian White House, argues that the earlier meetings were a kind of mass practice for

the later, critical event. He notes their ritual feature of "a feeling of unification" of many segments of Moscow society, and even of previously
opposed parts of society, such as the *narod* and the police; he describes
the mood of meetings as being "a ceremonial atmosphere of a departure
from [normal] time and circumstance into another quality of existence"
in which barriers of daily and political practice were broken down; he
depicts the theatricalized, playful, ironic aspect of meetings, which, he
argues, were key in confronting the standard conditions of Soviet politics;
finally, he argues that meetings were key events in the flexing of new identities, allowing the "realization of the freedom of choice, opening the possibility of free, individual and collective creation of a variety of forms of
independent action" (Istomin 1992: 60–61).

The dramatic and moving defense of the Russian White House after
the coup was the magical apex of all perestroika ceremonies, clearly the
climactic finale of perestroika-as-ritual. It provided all the necessary elements for closure of these ritual years, and it offered a chance for the total,
visceral involvement of the "defenders," who stood in rain and cold and
under threat of danger for three days. It was an orgy of *communitas*—the
state of group sharing and mutual identification that is widely observed,
especially in rites of passage and ritual pilgrimages (Turner 1974: 231).
Anthropologists A. A. Borodatova and L. A. Abramian (1992) describe
the euphoric sense of unity and brotherhood that marked the occasion, the
open sharing of cigarettes, food, clothes, and other necessities among the
defenders, and the fact that, as was widely observed and celebrated in
conversation and in the media, the defenders came from every social level
and group and reveled in that fact; John B. Dunlop (1993: 218–234) gives
a detailed breakdown of the range of identities of the defenders. The defense was called "a moment of higher truth," "the birthday of the *narod*,"
an occasion of "honor," "brotherhood," and "achievement." Borodatova
and Abramian note that these terms, which had become empty of meaning due to their overuse in Soviet propaganda, regained a sincere meaning
for participants (1992: 56).

The extraordinary, courageous defense of the White House was without
any question the critical event in the final demise of hegemonic Soviet
power. But, as with so many historically momentous occurrences, participants and analysts of the event alike often remained frozen in the drama
and glory of these heroic moments in their personal and national lives.
Fetishizing the ritual in which they transcended their own fears, identities, and past habits, many have failed to realize the very difficult tasks
that followed.[9]

---

[9] Borodatova and Abramian point out that especially the young defenders of the White
House hung around after the event was over, not wanting to leave the site of their ritual

The celebration of the *communitas* of the defense obscures the fact that the actors came from diverse segments of Moscow society and represented extremely diverse interests; though all were focused around the sacred idea of "saving democracy," participants no doubt had enormously different visions of "democracy," some valuing in this key, symbolic term the freedom of the market, others freedom of speech, and still others total freedom from all social constraints. The ritual experience of several days of "total freedom"—of *carnival*—disguises the necessity, in any society, of balancing the divergent interests of different social strata and identities and creating a secure environment for a multiplicity of views, lifestyles, and human potentials (Myerhoff 1975). This problem is especially challenging in the aftermath of a totalizing state apparatus. The defense of the White House provided few models for working out ethnic conflicts or coping with the demands of the disenfranchised, demands that would become quite apparent in the parliamentary elections of 1993, when Zhirinovskii gained 24 percent of the popular vote by expressing (in his own bizarre and frightening ways) the resentment and despair many felt.

In the years since the abortive coup and the defense of the White House, I heard numerous first-hand reports from Russians (and Westerners) who were there for some or all of it. All these reports shared one crucial element: the narrators spoke of these days as the most important days of their lives, and expressed their deep pride in being part of "the defense of Russian democracy." In 1994 my university sponsored a lecture by two visiting Russian "democracy educators." The lecture was supposed to be about their grass-roots work in "building democracy in Russia today" but it consisted solely of a slide show illustrating the various ways that the speakers defended the White House: by standing in the rain, phoning their friends to come and join the defense, printing, posting, and handing out their own flyers about democracy—which, they claimed, "may have even been seen by Boris Yeltsin himself!" When asked for concrete details of their post-coup work in democracy building, they had nothing to say, and referred constantly back to their work on the barricades. They seemed to be as dumbfounded by our demand to know more about their work as we (faculty and students alike) were by their insistence that manning the barricades *was* the work.

This is, of course, only one example, and it may be an example merely of two young men capitalizing on their involvement in an historical event. There are many courageous, devoted, skilled individuals in Russia work-

---

"community," and that many decided "always to stay together" (1992: 47). The papers by Myerhoff and Turkle in Moore and Myerhoff (1975) describe similar feelings among young people after Woodstock and during the French student uprising of 1968, including the difficulty many felt in returning to "structured life" and their professed work of revising society.

ing for social change and the development of democratic practices. However, this story is representative of a more general mode (not only among Russians, but among many of those who take part in public rallies anywhere) of magical thinking about the ability of these ritual gatherings to alter a balance of power within society. In 1994 and 1995 I noted that people were already speaking of that ritual dismissively, having recognized that old patterns of power abuse and economic disparity were again (or still) the norm.

The ritualized defense of the Russian White House was certainly a key event in the dissolution of the Soviet state, but the question as to whether it has led to the creation of deeply democratic structures still remains. As Borodatova and Abramian write about the defense and its aftermath "the celebration is now long over, but if in traditional society the *narod* returned after their festivals to the routines of daily life, laid down by centuries, after our festival it is unclear, to what it returns: 'the old is destroyed, but the new has not yet been built'" (Borodatova and Abramian 1992: 57).

The Rituals of the Old and the Building of the New

In his recent book on cultural and national identities in the "two Berlins," John Borneman describes the reactions of Berliners to the opening of the wall in 1989:

> "We were speechless," so many of them said, the East and West Berliners; they said it over and over, describing their experience on November 9 of what they call *Verbrüderung*, an instant sense of kinship. "We were speechless," they said, making speech of their own silence. All Germans, who before the opening had coexisted in complex, tense, and carefully mediated relations, were suddenly, spontaneously loving brothers. And then they added, "It was all *Wahnsinn!*"—insane, or, more literally, crazy sense. (1992: 315)

When the wall came down, he writes, "old categories of East and West, communist and capitalist, friend and foe, lost their meaning, replaced by a speechless *Verbrüderung*" (1992: 316). In the *communitas* of this event, mythic constructs such as brotherhood, German cultural unity, and freedom captured the public imagination and were performed ecstatically as people shared, communed, and celebrated. With the impulse of this ecstatic mood, East Germans marched to the polls over the next year and reaffirmed their commitment to the notion of unity, thereby legitimizing the unified state which followed.

The aftermath of these momentous events was, of course, not so straight-forwardly simple. The myth of unification gave way under the weight of a series of social and economic transformations in which East Germans began to lose, both symbolically and materially. While the West German economy thrived on unification, East Germans found both their currency and their identity devalued, and the institutions and resources of their society "colonized" (though Borneman prefers the analogy of reconstruc-tion in the post–Civil War American South) by Western capitalism. In-stead of brotherhood and equal status, he writes, "it seems likely that well into the next century the East will be permanently demarcated as the in-ferior, the less valuable, the garbage dump (literally and figuratively) not only of Germany but of Western Europe" (1992: 332).

The parallels between the two Germanies and Russia are striking. The perestroika years saw an extended telling and retelling of experiences of victimization, loss, and suffering under the Communist regime. This gradually built up into a public narrative—a very coherent narrative—of Russian (Soviet) existence, characterized as an opposition between "us and them," *narod* and state. The coherence of this narrative, this national story, and the ideology of mystical, moral, sacred poverty which formed the crux of it, allowed people to fantasize its inversion, a systemic trans-formation that would restore moral order and provide economic secu-rity. This fantasy was finally enacted at the barricades around the Russian White House, and the singular moment of jubilation which followed seemed to mark a moment of victory, in which the *narod* had finally tri-umphed and all the oppositions and structures of the past had been erased.

It very soon became clear, however, that such was not the case. Though radically transformed and opened up, in many ways Russian society is the same society it was during Soviet times—and before; while acknowl-edging the profound reforms in legal, political and economic spheres, many of the cultural and social institutions of the old state—the very institutions that my informants decried—remain. Russia is still as hierar-chically divided between rich and poor, powerful and powerless, elites and masses, as it ever was, though the ideologies promoted to mystify these divisions now appear in new, capitalistic guises. Terror remains a vital weapon of social control though it now asserts itself in the economic sphere (via the ubiquitous mafia) rather than in the political one. Corrup-tion is still a crucial tool for self-enrichment, as enterprise managers and their new cohorts transfer formerly state-owned resources into their pri-vate control and pad their overseas bank accounts and domiciles—often quite legally, since they have played an invisible hand in writing the laws that allow them to do this. And survival, for many, still depends on both utilizing and circumventing the official system, earning income or bartering "on the side," pilfering materials from workplaces, accepting "gifts" for services rendered on the job, carving out an existence in the margins, whether those of semi-legal trade or dacha gardening.

Systems have a way of replicating themselves; this we know from widespread observation of revolutions in large societies and ritual rebellions in smaller ones. I constantly wonder: was there a time, during perestroika, when truly meaningful transformation to an egalitarian, democratic society was possible? This was what most of the people I spoke with in those years dreamed of; when they could articulate their visions, what they imagined was a community of relative equals, living not the lavish lifestyles of the Western middle class, but something simpler, more in line with their own modest ways, but with greater security, opportunity, and openness. Perhaps this was a utopian vision, never achievable even under the best of circumstances.

However viable such a vision might have been, many of the practices and discourses of the perestroika era were insufficient or even contradictory to its realization; as cultural mechanisms and responses they were unlikely to produce positive transformations. Bourdieu calls this the "hysteresis of *habitus* . . . the structural lag between opportunities and the dispositions to grasp them which is the cause of missed opportunities and, in particular, of the *frequently observed incapacity to think historical crises in categories of perception and thought other than those of the past, albeit a revolutionary past* (1977: 83; emphasis mine).

It is the irony of all societies, not just Russia, that strategies for coping with trouble, including the discursive mythification of trouble, may also cause or allow the toleration of more trouble. In Russia in the time of perestroika, this has meant the submerging of an intended goal—the goal of liberation from oppressive practices and ideologies—in the deep waters of ritualistic signification.

In essence, the rituals of perestroika were a public marking and lamentation of the opposition between power and powerlessness, or, in a different valence, the battle between hierarchical and egalitarian impulses in Russian society. This opposition was hardly resolved or canceled by perestroika. If anything, it was culturally validated and reproduced, as systematic, rational modes of social transformation were excluded from imagination and practice. By uttering their litanies and mystical poverty narratives, many people rehearsed themselves in the very stances of passivity, ironic detachment, and victimization that have helped to ensure their continuing vulnerability to power and pain.

Ethnographic Notes, 1994 and 1995

That nothing turns out as was intended and expected—this banal expression of the reality of life here asserts itself in each individual case so inviolably and intensely that Russian fatalism becomes comprehensible.
                                                    —Walter Benjamin, "Moscow," 1927

Russian talk has changed significantly since the time of perestroika, but the changes in this talk are like the plot developments in a long novel, or the poetic permutations in an epic cycle. People's narratives mark the social and cultural transformations which have occurred; however, their stories and commentaries on contemporary reality reference the past in a multitude of ways. Here I offer a medley of narratives and fragments of conversations recorded during fieldwork in Russia in the summers of 1994 and 1995, leaving them to stand on their own as reflections of both continuity and change.

There are no politics nowadays, only clothes. That's what is most important for Russia today. Clothes are people's theater, the internal expression of their internal souls.
                                    —Vladimir, a theater critic (Moscow, 1994)

In general, the life to observe now is in the "bazaars"—the world of kiosks and *tolkuchki* [flea-market]. That's where it is really interesting, where you really see the fantasies of our people, fascination with commodities. But do *not* go without a man. It's very dangerous out there.
                                    —Pavel, an historian (Moscow, 1994)

The service in the stores is terrible, not like in America. Our government should decree that better service be provided in the stores. And they should also control the ads on TV: they all try to manipulate, deceive people. That should not be. In America, that's never the case. I never saw such lies when I was in America.
                                    —Misha, a computer programmer (Moscow, 1994)

"Browsing the Kiosks, 1992" (Photo by John Einarsen and Robert Kowalczyk)

They drove the vegetable market out of our neighborhood. It was filthy; nobody cleaned up after a day's selling. But it is much harder now; we have to go much farther to shop.

—Sveta, a kindergarten teacher (Obninsk, 1994)

The richest man in town is a young guy, who used to be a black-marketeer. In the 1980s, he was kicked out of his apartment and fired from his job for "speculating." Now, he's the town's richest businessman, with a dacha, a house, several cars, and his own bodyguards; he drives around in an armed car, with armed guards.

—Sveta (Obninsk, 1994)

My nephew . . . he's really small and charming, but he smokes and trades already, at the age of ten. Kids today only seem to think about money. When I asked him what he thought of a pretty girl in his class as a possible future wife, he said, "No, she's too poor."

—Sveta (Obninsk, 1994)

I worked forty years, for this minimal pension, which is often two months late. It is insulting, that some who have worked only eight months get as much as those who worked forty years. My pension is not nearly enough to live on. I can't buy *tvorog* [a staple Russian dairy product]—it is out of the question. A lot of this was to be expected, though. I voted for Zhirinovskii though at first I didn't like him. After last year, I lost all faith in politics. It is insulting and stupid that the other countries broke away from us, after all that Russia did for them. We all like this new freedom, but some kind of conscience is needed. I like Prime Minister Chernomyrdin—he is from the working class and understands us. What Russia is going through now is like the American depression of the 1930s.

—Irina Sergeevna, Sveta's mother (Obninsk, 1994)

There's no future for Russia, it's twenty or thirty years away. The government does not serve the people, it just wrings them dry and steals from them. Our mayor, our governor, what do they do? They just travel to exotic lands supposedly to make "deals"—they go to Portugal, Japan, Europe, on money from our taxes, and stay in fine hotels, eat fancy meals, buy presents for their mistresses. They live like tsars already, but they want more. Our own factory director, who already has piles of money of his own, demanded that a shipment of wood for the factory be put aside, so he could use it in his own dacha. They have everything, but they want more. And we, who have worked all our lives, have nothing.

—Anatolii Anatolievich, a retired auto factory machinist
(Yaroslavl, 1995)

Women are just being put down nowadays, given bad jobs, ignored for jobs in their professions, let go from long-time professional jobs, spat on right and left. Young marriage is now the fashion, because there is nothing else for girls to do, and they think they may have a chance to marry a business-man and be happy housewives with rich husbands. Girls used to wait until they were in their twenties, but now I see a lot of my friends, getting married and having babies at eighteen. And then they really start to suffer, because their husbands lose their jobs, or don't make enough money, because if you try to work like a normal person, you can't make it. Some of my friends are really proud of themselves, because they are going out with bandits, who have lots of money to buy them presents and take them to fancy clubs. There is no normal life. Who would want to do anything for themselves in this situation?

—Anna, a young artist and would-be fashion designer (Yaroslavl, 1995)

Before, I hated my job. I just fulfilled designs handed down from the top. But I lived well, had enough to eat, went to the sea every summer. . . . Now I love my work, there are interesting projects to work on. But there's no money, and life is very insecure. I know I could be a homeless person like anyone else.

—The chief designer in a large shoe factory (Yaroslavl, 1995)

Discussion with clerks in a semi-private produce shop (Moscow, 1994):

Female worker 1: I worked for thirteen years in another shop; it was like paradise there, we were all such friends. But it closed. I got this new job through my acquaintances. We're working for the future here. I want to stay here and work a long time. But it is very scary; what will be is not clear. The same people are in power as before—they just gave up their party cards.

Female worker 2: The *narod* is disappointed. They want something else. The youth can reconstruct itself but for older people. . . . In two generations, only in two generations will it be okay here.

Female worker 1: It is hardest now for older people and children. Especially with health care—you just have to have lots of money to pay for it now.

Female worker 3: No, it's better than before. The regulations are looser.

Female worker 1: No, it was better then. Then we had security, a perspective on the future, stability.

Female worker 3: Our store is an island of stability. The boss is demanding but not severe. The store has its own dormitory.

Female worker 1: The situation in the country is terrible. People are so poor, and it just gets worse. It is especially bad because our best young people are just leaving; there's no future for them here, and private farmers continue to have a hell of a time.

Male worker: We want to work and get rich, so we can get a house, a dacha, a car, and *women*.

Female worker 3: You have enough woman problems!

Male worker: Yes, but if I could just take care of my women better. . . .

Nancy: Why is there no self-service in your store?

Female workers together: No! Impossible! Everything would be stolen.

Female bookkeeper 1: The problem with business and government is that so many people simply have no morals. Money poisons morality.

Female bookkeeper 2: Outside Moscow, people are much poorer in a material sense, but they are much kinder, and much more honest.

We try to "control the press" so the public does not get scared about their investments; they are very nervous right now after MMM and everything. This is easy, since there is no free press here, no fourth estate. We just pay journalists to write what we want them to, and the *narod* believe anything in print. Although it is hard when you have investments from regular people. They have the strange habit of coming to collect their interest and then turning around and cursing the bankers, calling us "scoundrels" because they are sure we are getting very rich off their money. They are earning 300 percent a year from us and calling the bankers scoundrels.

—Alexei, a bank public relations director (Yaroslavl, 1995)

You know how my father taught me to swim? He rowed me out to the middle of the river and threw me overboard. I was five years old: "swim or drown." He quickly rowed away from me. Of course I moved my arms and kicked my feet, and somehow made it to the shore, while all the adults standing on the bank just laughed. They were all drunk. And this is how Russians do everything. They are impatient to do anything gradually, just do everything in a moment, just like they now await financial miracles, instantaneous success, and don't want to work gradually to build something up. Everybody waits for a miracle, like in a fairy tale. That's why people still believe in MMM, for instance; they can't not believe. They even believe in the government somehow, that miraculously order will be restored and everybody will become rich. That's why so many believe Zhirinovskii's insane promises. They all think our problems can be solved in one day, magically.

—Kolia, an artist in his forties (Yaroslavl, 1995)

Russians don't really want to work, anyway. It is too hard. A friend of mine went to Florida, and stayed with a Russian émigré there. He said it was beautiful and everybody was rich, but he couldn't stand it. Life there was too crazy, the phone was always ringing, there were always dozens of messages on the answering machine, business calls to answer, too much bustle, exhausting. Russians don't need that kind of insanity. Though we are living in poverty now, we wait for miracles, like always. All poor Russians wait for miracles, like Ivan the Fool from Russian fairy tales, who always did everything wrong but married the princess in the end anyway. But miracles do happen nowadays. One artist I know brought some paintings to Moscow to sell in a park. An Italian wandered by, fell in love with his work, brought him to Italy, toured him around, lavished millions on him. He came back loaded with money and bought himself an apartment in Moscow!

—Anna (Yaroslavl, 1995)

Why should we vote, when the elections are totally rigged and political offices are just bought and traded? It is nothing but a giant mafia up there. We must simply try to live on our own down here and get by without politics.

—A young bread-factory worker (Yaroslavl, 1995)

People are afraid to vote a new party into power today, because the existing bureaucracy has already enriched itself, and it is getting hard for those people to imagine having *more* than they already have. They have stolen whatever they could possibly need in the way of money and luxury for their whole lives. They are comfortable. But a new party in power—would just have to start all over, enriching themselves. People prefer to keep the current government in power, not to pay another round of taxes just so a new party can build fancy dachas for themselves.

—Galina, a labor economist (Yaroslavl, 1995)

We honest people are still as poor as ever. It is no wonder that nobody wants to live honestly anymore. If you live honestly, you starve. Regular workers are just starving nowadays. The minimal sum required for living is now officially one and a half million rubles per month per person, and we get 150,000 each as pensioners, so we live *one hundred times worse* than the minimum standard. While the big guys and the criminals get rich, resting on our backs.

—Viktoria, a semi-retired schoolteacher (Yaroslavl, 1995)

There always was, and is still and always will be, power and *narod* and a huge gap in between, no interconnection; the *narod* is meaningless to power. They do nothing in the parliament but joke around and the *narod* gets by on its own, like always.

—Anna (Yaroslavl, 1995)

The communists knew everything that would happen in advance. They knew in 1990 what was coming, the coup and the fall of the Soviet Union and everything. They had it all planned, and were totally poised for things to change course, ready to grab everything for themselves and become rich. They had it all in their pockets, well before the people had any inkling what was going on. It was always this way. At the top, they "held their noses to the wind," which means to be in the course of things, to know what is going on. They held all the information, and could always use that information to take care of themselves and each other. The hell with the people, who never had a clue and never had a chance.

—Kolia (Yaroslavl, 1995)

I think people have to make their own ways, and not depend on others, nor on the government. I never liked how my parents lived, how they trusted and believed in the system. They always played by the rules, and now they have very little. So they complain about how hard it is, but then they give everything away. They get their miserly pensions, a ridiculously small amount of money. And even now, having nothing, really, my mother constantly buys things for my sister, even though she has a good job as a dance teacher and her husband is a military man with a decent salary. My parents spend their last money to buy some presents or food for my sister and her kids. I can't stand it, it makes me sick.

—Pasha, a small-scale soap distributor (Yaroslavl, 1995)

The poor will just get poorer, the old people will die off from poverty or illness, and with them, their old ideas. Those who have the motivation or willingness to do whatever it takes to get ahead will survive these times and prosper; the weak ones will just die off or retreat to the villages and grow their potatoes and become irrelevant. And eventually, slowly, after a generation or so, Russia will mature, will be a normal country, like yours, where people work honestly and obey the laws because the laws will protect them.

—Pasha (Yaroslavl, 1994)

Conversation with Alesha, a cheerful mafia *"bandit"* in his mid-thirties:
Nancy: So what does it mean to be a bandit? What you do?
Alesha: I build "roofs" (*kryshi*)—covers. The traders and speculators are always cheating each other. They borrow money and disappear with it. They take goods on consignment and don't pay for them. They are always out to cheat each other, to make money however they can. Goods get stolen out of warehouses and stores. We protect the businessmen

from each other. We ensure the collection of debts and recover stolen goods. Our clients' partners know who's protecting them, whether our clients have good "roofs" or not. A good roof means good business.

Nancy: Does every business have a roof? Even the old ladies selling potatoes and mushrooms on the sidewalks? Do schools and hospitals have roofs?

Alesha: We don't make a point of "covering" the old ladies. But they are constantly hassled by street criminals and alcoholics. So they ask our guys to protect them. They pay maybe twenty, thirty bucks a month, and we watch over them. The hoodlums know they better not mess with the old ladies because our guys are watching out for them. And schools don't have roofs because there's no money involved. It's only when there is some kind of money being made that people need protection. Understand, Nancy, we don't go out and seek our clients: they come to us, our clients approach us to provide them a service which they need.

Nancy: But you seem like a nice guy, how do you feel about being a *bandit*?

Alesha: Bandits are known for their honesty. We protect our clients from being cheated, we enforce their contracts, collect their debts for them, ensure some kind of normal business relations. They know they can count on us. Eventually, this will become, I would like to have it become a legitimate business, a regular kind of collection agency like you have in America.

Nancy: Do you, have you ever had to . . . kill anyone?

Alesha: No. There are few killings; it isn't necessary. Although sometimes there are fights among the different gangs in town. We try to keep our men out of trouble. We enforce a policy of discipline. Our soldiers shouldn't drink too much, or smoke even. They should be family men, decent, orderly people.

Nancy: And what about the police?

Alesha: The police know us. They know all the bandits in town, who works for whom, whom we protect, etc. They know everything. And they rely on us to provide order, which they can't; they don't have the resources. There would just be chaos were it not for us, because the businessmen are incapable of running their affairs in an orderly way. Most of them are uncivilized! You know, the Russian *narod*. . . . You know, it's not the decent businessmen who are driving around in Mercedes. They live in a more modest way; they have family values and don't need the show-off of fancy homes and cars; it's only those from the working-class backgrounds who need to show off their new wealth.

We tried to buy another apartment. We found some agents, and they showed us a place, and we put a deposit down on it. Then they refused to give us the apartment or our money back; the whole thing was just a huge swindle. We tried to get some guys to help us get the money back, we had our own roof, but the agents' roof was stronger, and our roof couldn't break through theirs.

—Olga, a schoolteacher, and her husband Yuri, a well-paid bookkeeper
(Yaroslavl, 1995)

My ex-wife and her gangster boyfriend threw her daughter out of their apartment. They told her they would toss her in the frozen Volga if she didn't leave. Women today are totally warped. Lilia just doesn't want to deal with her daughter; she wants to drink and have sex and travel and have fun with her new gangster friends. So I went to her apartment and banged on the door. I said to Lilia, "we have to work this out" (*nado razo-brat'sia*). But that was a big mistake, I forgot that in gangster jargon that means "to fight it out." Her boyfriend heard me say that and started to threaten me with his gun. It took me four hours to get out of there alive. I had to calm him down by apologizing and admitting that I found him threatening. That's all they care about, they want you to show that they are bigger than you are, and that you know it. *Znai nashikh*—that's an important phrase which means "know that I am higher than you are." So I showed him. In the end, we drank a bottle together, and he put his arm around me and said, "Kolia, I respect you. You are an okay guy." That's how I got out of there alive.

—Kolia (Yaroslavl, 1995)

You're an anthropologist, huh? Oh yeah. Look deeply into my eyes . . . don't look away! I want to see if you are telling the truth. If you're not who you say you are, we're going to put concrete on your feet and throw you into the Volga.

—A Belorussian gangster boss (Yaroslavl, 1995)

A "joke" on me: Walking in the evening with a teenage friend, I stop to photograph a casino. Two workers, a bit drunk, pass us, and one intones, humorously: "At the next corner, they're waiting to arrest you."

(Moscow, 1994)

Everyone is now purveying myths. They say the Russian government is working for the CIA, or that it is all a Masonic plot against Russia, that the Jews are taking over the country. My first childhood memory is of Kirov's murder and the ensuing terror. We had to sing a song in school: "We killed, are killing, and will kill our enemies." I used to put the word "not" in all these lines. Another boy heard me one day, and said he would write a report and have my parents investigated. Then our phone was cut off, which was always a sign of impending arrest. We were scared, and I thought it was my fault. It was just a coincidence and nothing happened. But such terror implants a very deep emotion in you which lasts a lifetime.

—Aleksandr Mikhailovich, retired physicist (Moscow, 1994)

You have to just *accept* Russia. You must not even try to understand Russia. It's impossible to understand. If you do try, you'll go nuts.

—Ilia, a retired grammar school director (Yaroslavl, 1995)

I totally love my country, my motherland. I don't want to live anywhere else. This place nourishes my soul, with all its craziness, mysteriousness, and unpredictability. I would die anywhere else, couldn't live. But I can't stand the corruption. Everyone who has power or money is corrupt. The politicians—that is our true mafia, each and every one of them: the *real* mafia. The street bandits, whom you have met, they are basically honest, hard-working guys. The real corruption is at the top, and it is the politicians, from top to bottom, who are the real criminals. I think they should all be taken out and shot. That is the only way for Russia to become a clean and civilized place: like Stalin did, we should just round our leaders up and destroy them. We pay our taxes to them and it just goes in their pockets. I am not against supporting the poor, the elderly, but I think the best way is for us to do this independently: give me three old ladies to support and I will happily, joyously support them! Directly! Without the intervention of the fucking mafia government which takes the largest percent just for themselves. This is the way our country should be arranged. I am an honest businessman, and I pay my taxes diligently, but I resent it, because I see the poor old women on the street and I know I could do a better job of taking care of them, just assign me three old ladies and I will take care of them until they die. Another thing that is really pathetic: the way the old people believe in and give their last kopecks to the Church. They are totally happy to give their last kopecks for the reconstruction of the local churches. But then you see the priests driving around in Mercedes, really! And living it up on the money the poor believing old ladies give them. The priests today, are also the real mafia. Getting rich from two directions, from the contributions of the people, who want to believe in something again, and from the huge investments of the government, which is trying to prove its spirituality by rebuilding the Church. And wherever you have such money pouring in, there is corruption and evil.

—Pasha (Yaroslavl, 1995)

Nobody cares. Everybody is just trying to get by. And if you try to do something you will just be frustrated and give up. It is impossible. The system is too corrupt, and those with power are happy for it to remain as it is, they profit from the system as it is. The only thing that matters now is the cult of money.

—Kolia (Yaroslavl, 1995)

There is no mafia, we are all mafia now.
—Olga, a social scientist, referring to the fact that there seems to be no way to survive if one is honest (Moscow, 1994).

We are morally damaged. Look at how men these days are glued to their televisions, and what are they watching? All the American films so long denied them, but especially the martial arts films. Our old Soviet films all had some moral base, which wasn't bad. In fact the philosophy of communism corresponded to Christian philosophy. The only problem then was at the top, with the officials. They gave us those moral messages but we didn't mean anything to them, we "little people," and they lived their comfortable lives behind a curtain; that was the *real* iron curtain, hiding their happy lives from us. Now it is all out in the open, and *nobody is ashamed*. Now we all know what it is about, and everybody wants to get rich and live like our leaders once lived, even the children are already totally damaged, totally warped.

—Viktoria (Yaroslavl, 1995)

A conversation with Andrei, the writer and supporter of young artists. Andrei related quite a magical story about how a businessman, valuing the work Andrei had done for years to help fledgling, underground artists, had given him this nice one-room apartment to get him out of the communal flat he had lived in for decades (described in Chapter 4). After a while, I asked Andrei to explain to me why conversations in Moscow in 1994 had fewer of the litanies I had heard in years before:

Suddenly, into this life, in which the Russian people has been conditioned to perceive poverty an accomplishment, a sign of cleanliness, morality, you understand, suddenly into this life, flies a sixteen-year-old boy behind the wheel of a Mercedes Benz, or a Lincoln, a sixteen-year-old! And the question arises: when did he succeed in earning enough for a Lincoln? A Lincoln is an expensive car! Any fool understands what it means: He killed somebody, he robbed somebody, participated in a racket, kidnapping, and so on. Everyone understands. Where did he manage to earn it? This sixteen-year-old kid with hardly anything on his face to shave? The people see this and go into wild shock. All understand: hard work, honest labor now means nothing. There's a guy, he's served in, survived the army, the war, everything, and here he is working, and he earns a minimal salary, nowadays 20,000 rubles—what is 20,000 now? It means one breakfast. Per month. That is the minimum wage, what people earn who are washing floors, working their hands raw, and these people see the kid with the Mercedes. . . . Philosophers, scientists, make 60,000 a month. That's three breakfasts. To express this in the Russian language is impossible. That is why people are so quiet now. They can only express themselves in silence or in cursing or in drinking. Even artists can't describe this contrast of two Russias. Even our humor is dying. What can you say about this new world of ours? Nobody can say anything. But I'll tell you: When the big companies let out at night, the new rich pour into the street, and they are all drunk. They have been drinking all day. I have seen it with my own eyes, on the main streets, in front of the fancy new buildings. Our new wealthy class files out of their gleaming skyscrapers, wearing their Armani suits, and they are all falling down drunk, falling into puddles in their Armani suits. All they can do at work is drink. They know there's no future, for them or for us. They live in mortal fear, in mortal shame, and to forget about it they drink until they fall down. This is the world we live in now.

—Andrei (Moscow, 1994)

I traded icons for a while, buying them up from old women in the countryside who didn't know how valuable they were. But then I realized that everyone who sold icons ended up dead. So I began to give them away instead.

—Kolia (Yaroslavl, 1995)

In an attempt to find the best, most ecological ways to utilize the natural resources in the countryside near Yaroslavl, we gather all the concerned parties, from top government officials to the poorest old ladies. We want to get them talking, and try to help them find some common ground. The very experience is strange for all involved, because none of the officials ever paid the smallest heed to the "complaints" of old ladies, and the old ladies never saw these officials in real life. The meetings go on for hours, and everyone has a chance to speak. The Germans taught us techniques for holding these kinds of meetings. At one meeting, after a long series of laments and accusations from the old ladies and serious pronouncements from the government side, we finally achieved some kind of calm. People realized that they weren't so violently opposed. And one old woman stood up and, with tears in her voice, said she was astonished to discover that her concerns were shared by a top regional official. That was the first time in her life such a thing had happened.

—Marina, an anthropologist (Yaroslavl, 1995)

Enlivened with the familiar magic of cultural detail, these narratives capture the flavor of Russian talk a few years after perestroika. Contradictory, paradoxical, and impassioned, they reveal a world transformed and yet unchangeable. They reveal a world where the schism between the people and the powerful endures, and where, for most people, struggle and privation continue to be the realities of day-to-day life. At the same time, they illustrate the power that absurdism and mystical poverty still hold, as ways to conceptualize that life, as frames for expressing that life in talk.

References

Abdullaeva, Zara. 1996. "Popular Culture." In *Russian Culture at the Crossroads: Paradoxes of Post-Communist Consciousness*, ed. Dmitry Shalin. Pp. 209–238. Boulder, Colo.: Westview.

Abu-Lughod, Lila. 1986. *Veiled Sentiments: Honor and Poetry in a Bedouin Society.* New York: Oxford University Press.

———. 1991. Writing against Culture. In *Recapturing Anthropology*, ed. Richard Fox. Pp. 137–162. Santa Fe: School of American Research Press.

Afanas'ev, A. N. 1973. *Russian Fairy Tales.* New York: Pantheon Books.

———. 1985. *Russkie narodnye skazki.* Moscow: Nauka.

———. 1991. *Russkie zavetnye shazki.* Moscow: Mif.

Alexiou, Margaret. 1974. *The Ritual Lament in Greek Tradition.* Cambridge: Cambridge University Press.

Almond, Gabriel A. 1983. Communism and Political Culture Theory. *Comparative Politics*, 16 (1): 127–138.

Anderson, Benedict. 1983. *Imagined Communities: Reflections on the Origin and Spread of Nationalism.* London: Verso.

Anderson, Richard D., Valery I. Chervyakov, and Pavel B. Parshin. 1995. Words Matter: Linguistic Conditions for Democracy in Russia. *Slavic Review* 54 (4): 869–895.

Anikin, V. P. 1975. On the Origin of Riddles. In *The Study of Russian Folklore*, ed. Felix J. Oinas and Stephen Soudakoff, pp. 25–37. The Hague: Mouton.

Appadurai, Arjun, Frank J. Korom, and Margaret A. Mills, eds. 1991. *Gender, Genre, and Power in South Asian Expressive Traditions.* Philadelphia: University of Pennsylvania Press.

Aronoff, M. J. 1977. *Power and Ritual in the Israel Labor Party: A Study in Political Anthropology.* Assen/Amsterdam: Van Gorcum.

Aslund, Anders. 1989. *Gorbachev's Struggle for Economic Reform.* Ithaca: Cornell University Press.

Attwood, Lynne. 1990. *The New Soviet Man and Woman: Sex Role Socialization in the USSR.* Bloomington: Indiana University Press.

Austin, J. L. 1962. *How to Do Things with Words.* Oxford: Oxford University Press.

Babcock, Barbara A., ed. 1978. *The Reversible World: Symbolic Inversion in Art and Society*. Ithaca: Cornell University Press.

Bakhtin, Mikhail. 1981. *The Dialogic Imagination*, ed. Michael Holquist. Translated by Caryl Emerson and Michael Holquist. Austin: University of Texas Press.

———. 1984. *Problems of Dostoevsky's Poetics*, edited and translated from the Russian by Caryl Emerson. Minneapolis: University of Minnesota Press.

———. 1986. *Speech Genres and Other Late Essays*. Austin: University of Texas Press.

Balashov, D. M. 1985. *Russkaia svad'ba: Svadebnyi obriad na Verkhnei i Srednei Kokshen'ge i na Uftiuge (Tarnogskii raion Vologodskoi oblasti)*. Moscow: Sovremennik.

Balzer, Harley, ed. 1996. *Russia's Missing Middle Class: The Professions in Russian History*. Armonk, N.Y.: M. E. Sharpe.

Balzer, Marjorie Mandelstam, ed. 1992. *Russian Traditional Culture: Religion, Gender, and Customary Law*. Armonk, N.Y.: M. E. Sharpe.

Baranskaia, Natal'ia. 1969. Nedelia kak nedelia. *Novyi mir* 1969 (11): 23–55.

Bataille, Georges. 1985. *Visions of Excess*. Translated from the French by Allan Stoekl. Minneapolis: University of Minnesota Press.

Bauer, Raymond A. 1952. The Psychology of the Soviet Middle Elite. In *Personality in Nature, Society, and Culture*, ed. Clyde Kluckhohn, Henry A. Murray, and David Schneider, pp. 633–650. New York: Alfred A. Knopf.

Bauman, Richard. 1986. *Story, Performance, and Event: Contextual Studies of Oral Narrative*. Cambridge: Cambridge University Press.

Bauman, Richard, and Charles L. Briggs. 1990. Poetics and Performance as Critical Perspectives on Language and Social Life. *American Review of Anthropology* 19: 59–88.

Bazanov, V. G. 1975. Rites and Poetry. In *The Study of Russian Folklore*, ed. Felix J. Oinas and Stephen Soudakoff, pp. 123–134. The Hague: Mouton.

Belknap, Robert, ed. 1990. *Russianness: Studies on a Nation's Identity in Honor of Rufus Mathewson*. Ann Arbor, Mich: Ardis.

Ben-Amos, Dan. 1976. *Folklore Genres*. Austin: University of Texas Press.

Benjamin, Walter. 1978. Moscow. In *Reflections: Essays, Aphorisms, Autobiographical Writings*, translated by E. Jephcott, ed. Peter Demetz, pp. 97–131. New York: Schocken Books.

Bock, Philip K. 1980. *Continuities in Psychological Anthropology*. San Francisco: W. H. Freeman.

Bohac, Rodney. 1991. Everyday Forms of Peasant Resistance: Serf Opposition to Gentry Extractions, 1800–1861. In *Peasant Economy, Culture, and Politics of European Russia, 1800–1921*, ed. Esther Kingston-Mann and Timothy Mixter, pp. 236–260. Princeton: Princeton University Press.

Borneman, John. 1992. *Belonging in the Two Berlins: Kin, State, Nation*. Cambridge: Cambridge University Press.

Borodatova, A. A., and L. A. Abramian. 1992. Avgust 1991: Prazdnik, ne uspevshii razvernut'sia. *Etnograficheskoe obozrenie* 3: 47–58.

Bourdieu, Pierre. 1977. *Outline of a Theory of Practice*. Translated from the French by Richard Nice. Cambridge: Cambridge University Press.

———. 1984. *Distinction: A Social Critique of the Judgement of Taste*. Translated from the French by Richard Nice. Cambridge: Harvard University Press.

———. 1991. *Language and Symbolic Power*, ed. John B. Thompson. Translated from the French by Gino Raymond and Matthew Adamson. Cambridge: Harvard University Press.

Bourdieu, Pierre, and Loïc J. D. Wacquant. 1992. *An Invitation to Reflexive Sociology*. Chicago: University of Chicago Press.

Boym, Svetlana. 1994. *Common Places: Mythologies of Everyday Life in Russia*. Cambridge: Harvard University Press.

Brenneis, Donald. 1988. Telling Troubles: Narrative, Conflict, and Experience. *Anthropological Linguistics* 30 (3): 279–291.

Brenneis, Donald, and Fred R. Myers, eds. 1984. *Dangerous Words: Language and Politics in the Pacific*. Prospect Heights, Ill.: Waveland Press Inc.

Briggs, Charles L. 1992. "Since I Am a Woman, I Will Chastise My Relatives: Gender, Reported Speech, and (Re)production of Social Relations in Warao Ritual Wailing."*American Ethnologist* 19 (2): 337–361.

Briggs, Charles L., and Richard Bauman. 1992. Genre, Intertextuality, and Social Power. *Journal of Linguistic Anthropology* 2 (2): 131–172.

Brown, Archie, ed. 1984. *Political Culture and Communist Studies*. Armonk, N.Y.: M. E. Sharpe.

Buckley, Mary. 1992. *Perestroika and Soviet Women*. Cambridge: Cambridge University Press.

Burant, Stephen R. 1987. The Influence of Russian Tradition on the Political Style of the Soviet Elite. *Political Science Quarterly* 102 (2): 259–272.

Burke, Peter. 1993. *The Art of Conversation*. Cambridge: Polity Press.

Bushnell, John. 1985. *Mutiny amid Repression: Russian Soldiers in the Revolution of 1905–1906*. Bloomington: Indiana University Press.

———. 1988. Urban Leisure Culture in Post-Stalin Russia: Stability as a Social Problem? In *Soviet Society and Culture: Essays in Honor of Vera S. Dunham*, ed. Terry L. Thompson and Richard Sheldon, pp. 58–86. Boulder, Colo.: Westview.

Caraveli-Chaves, Anna. 1980. Bridge Between Worlds: The Greek Woman's Lament as a Communicative Event. *Journal of American Folklore* 93 (April–June): 129–157.

Cerf, Christopher, and Marina Albee, eds. 1990. *Small Fires: Letters From the Soviet People to Ogonyok Magazine, 1987–1990*. New York: Simon and Schuster.

Cherniavsky, Michael. 1961. *Tsar and People: Studies in Russian Myths*. New Haven: Yale University Press.

Chistov, K. 1984. *Russkaia narodnaia poeziia: Obriadovaia poeziia*. Leningrad: Khudozhestvennaia literatura.

Clark, Katerina. 1977. Utopian Anthropology as a Context for Stalinist Literature. In *Stalinism: Essays in Historical Interpretation*, ed. Robert C. Tucker, pp. 180–198. New York: W. W. Norton.

Colton, Timothy J. 1995. *Moscow: Governing the Socialist Metropolis*. Cambridge: Harvard University Press.

Conrad, Joseph L. 1989. Russian Ritual Incantations: Tradition, Diversity, and Continuity. *Slavic and East European Journal* 33 (3): 422–444.

Cruikshank, Julie. 1990. *Life Lived Like a Story: Life Stories of Three Yukon Native Elders*. Lincoln: University of Nebraska Press.

Cushman, Thomas. 1995. *Notes from Underground: Rock Music Counterculture in Russia*. Albany: State University of New York Press.

Daniels, Robert V. 1962. *The Nature of Communism*. New York: Random House.

———. 1985. *Russia: The Roots of Confrontation*. Cambridge: Harvard University Press.

Degh, Linda. 1976. Symbiosis of Joke and Legend: A Case of Conversational Folklore. In *Folklore Today: A Festschrift for Richard M. Dorson*, ed. Linda Degh, Henry Glassie, and Felix J. Oinas, pp. 101–123. Bloomington: Indiana University Press.

Denich, Bette. 1994. Dismembering Yugoslavia: Nationalist Ideologies and the Symbolic Revival of Genocide. *American Ethnologist* 21 (2): 367–390.

Dickinson, Jennifer. 1995. Rebuilding the Blockade: New Truths in Survival Narratives From Leningrad. *Anthropology of East Europe Review* 13 (2): 19–23.

Dicks, Henry V. 1960. Some Notes on the Russian National Character. In *The Transformation of Russian Society*, ed. Cyril E. Black, pp. 636–651. Cambridge: Harvard University Press.

Dostoevsky, F. M. 1971. The Meek One. Translated by Olga Shartse. In *Fyodor Dostoevsky: Stories*. Moscow: Raduga.

——. 1980. *Polnoe sobranie sochinenii*. Vol. 21: *Dnevnik pisatelia 1873*. Leningrad: Nauka.

Draitser, Emil. 1982. The Art of Storytelling in Contemporary Russian Satirical Folklore. *Slavic and East European Journal* 26 (2): 233–238.

——. 1989. Soviet Underground Jokes as a Means of Popular Entertainment. *Journal of Popular Culture* 23 (1): 117–126.

Drakulić, Slavenka. 1993. *The Balkan Express: Fragments from the Other Side of War*. New York: W. W. Norton.

Dundes, Alan. 1972. Folk Ideas as Units of Worldview. In *Toward New Perspectives in Folklore*, ed. Americo Paredes and Richard Bauman, pp. 93–103. Austin: University of Texas Press.

——. 1980. *Interpreting Folklore*. Bloomington: Indiana University Press.

Dunham, Vera. 1960. The Strong-Woman Motif. In *The Transformation of Russian Society*, ed. Cyril E. Black, pp. 459–482. Cambridge: Harvard University Press.

——. 1990. *In Stalin's Time: Middleclass Values in Soviet Fiction*. Durham, N.C.: Duke University Press.

Dunlop, John B. 1993. *The Rise of Russia and the Fall of the Soviet Empire*. Princeton: Princeton University Press.

Dunn, Ethel. 1992 .They Don't Pay Attention to Us: The Russian Peasant Today. *Russia and Her Neighbors: Facts and Views on Daily Life* 6: 1–25.

Eagleton, Terry. 1991. *Ideology: An Introduction*. London: Verso.

Edmondson, Linda, ed. 1992. *Women and Society in Russia and the Soviet Union*. Cambridge: Cambridge University Press.

Einarsen, John. 1992. Voices from Moscow. *Kyoto Journal* 20, pp. 13–25.

Epstein, Mikhail. 1991. *Relativistic Patterns in Totalitarian Thinking: An Inquiry into the Language of Soviet Ideology*. Washington, D.C.: Kennan Institute Occasional Papers.

Erofeev, Venedikt. 1980. *Moscow to the End of the Line*. Translated by H. W. Tjalsma. New York: Taplinger.

Erofeev, Viktor. 1993. Ochen' zhenskoe 'Chto delat''? *Moskovskie novosti* 93 (3).

Evans-Pritchard, E. 1937. *Witchcraft, Oracles, and Magic among the Azande*. Oxford: Oxford University Press.

Fairclough, Norman. 1989. *Language and Power*. New York: Longman.

Fedotov, George P. 1975. *The Russian Religious Mind*. Vol. 1:. *Kievan Christianity*. Belmont, Mass.: Nordland.

Field, Mark G. 1987. The Contemporary Soviet Family: Problems, Issues, Perspectives. In *Soviet Society Under Gorbachev*, ed. Maurice Friedberg and Heyward Isham, pp. 3–29. Armonk, N.Y.: M. E. Sharpe.

Finnegan, Ruth. 1992. *Oral Traditions and the Verbal Arts: A Guide to Research Practices*. New York: Routledge.

Fitzpatrick, Sheila. 1994. *Stalin's Peasants: Resistance and Survival in the Russian Village after Collectivization*. Oxford: Oxford University Press.

——.1996. Supplicants and Citizens: Public Letter-Writing in Soviet Russia in the 1930s. *Slavic Review* 55 (1): 78–124.

Foster, George M. 1965. Peasant Society and the Image of Limited Good. *American Anthropologist* 65 (2): 293–315.

Frierson, Cathy A. 1993. *Peasant Icons: Representations of Rural People in Late Nineteenth-Century Russia*. New York: Oxford University Press.

Gakov, Vladimir. 1989. *Ul'timatum: Iadernaia voina i bez'iadernyi mir v fantaziiakh i real'nosti*. Moscow: Izdatel'stvo politicheskoi literatury.

Gal, Susan. 1989. Language and Political Economy. *Annual Review of Anthropology* 18: 145–167.

Geertz, Clifford. 1973. *The Interpretation of Cultures*. New York: Basic Books.

——. 1983. *Local Knowledge*. New York: Basic Books.

Gibian, George. 1956. Dostoevskij's Use of Russian Folklore. *Journal of American Folklore* 69: 239–253.

——. 1990. How Russian Proverbs Present the Russian National Character. In *Russianness: Studies on a Nation's Identity in Honor of Rufus Mathewson*, ed. Robert L. Belknap, pp. 38–43. Ann Arbor, Mich.: Ardis.

——. 1991. The Quest for Russian National Identity in Soviet Culture Today. In *The Search for Self-Definition in Russian Literature*, ed. Ewa M. Thompson, pp. 1–20. Houston: Rice University Press.

Giddens, Anthony. 1984. *The Constitution of Society*. Berkeley: University of California Press.

Glazov, Yuri. 1985. *The Russian Mind since Stalin's Death*. Dordrecht, Holland: D. Reidel Publishing Company.

Glickman, Rose. 1984. *Russian Factory Women: Workplace and Society 1880–1914*. Berkeley: University of California Press.

Gluckman, Max. 1954. *Rituals of Rebellion in South-East Africa*. Manchester: Manchester University Press.

Goldman, Irving. 1950. Psychiatric Interpretations of Russian History. *American Slavic and East European Review* 9: 151–161.

Goldman, Marshall I. 1992. *What Went Wrong with Perestroika*. New York: W. W. Norton.

Goldstein, Judith L. 1986. Iranian Jewish Women's Magical Narratives. In *Discourse and the Social Life of Meaning*, ed. Phyllis Pease Chock and June R. Wyman, pp. 147–168. Washington: Smithsonian Institution Press.

Gorbachev, Mikhail. 1987. *Perestroika: New Thinking for Our Country and the World*. New York: Harper and Row.

Gorer, Geoffrey, and John Rickman. 1950. *The People of Great Russia*. New York: Chanticleer.

Goscilo, Helena. 1993. *Domostroika* or *Perestroika*? The Construction of Womanhood in Soviet Culture Under Glasnost. In *Late Soviet Culture: From Perestroika to Novostroika*, ed. Thomas Lahusen and Gene Kuperman, pp. 233–256. Durham, N.C.: Duke University Press.

Gossen, Gary H. 1972. Chamula Genres of Verbal Behavior. In *Toward New Perspectives in Folklore*, ed. Americo Paredes and Richard Bauman, pp. 145–167. Austin: University of Texas Press.

Grant, Bruce. 1993. Dirges for Soviets Past. In *Perilous States: Conversations on Culture, Politics, and Nation*, ed. George E. Marcus, pp. 17–52. Chicago: University of Chicago Press.

——. 1995. *In the Soviet House of Culture — A Century of Perestroikas*. Princeton: Princeton University Press.

Gray, Francine du Plessix. 1989. *Soviet Women: Walking the Tightrope*. New York: Doubleday.

Grillo, Ralph. 1989. Anthropology, Language, Politics. In *Social Anthropology and the Politics of Language*, ed. Ralph Grillo, pp. 1–24. London: Routledge.

Grima, Benedicte. 1991. The Role of Suffering in Women's Performance of Paxto. In *Gender, Genre, and Power in South Asian Expressive Traditions*, ed. Arjun Appadurai, Frank J. Korom, and Margaret A. Mills, pp. 81–101. Philadelphia: University of Pennsylvania Press.

——. 1992. *The Performance of Emotion among Paxtun Women*. Austin: University of Texas Press.

Hammer, Darrell P. 1986. *The USSR: The Politics of Oligarchy*. Boulder, Colo.: Westview Press.

Handelman, Don. 1990. *Models and Mirrors: Towards an Anthropology of Public Events*. Cambridge: Cambridge University Press.

Hanks, W. F. 1987. Discourse Genres in a Theory of Practice. *American Ethnologist* 14: 668–692.

Harvey, David L. 1993. *Potter Addition: Poverty, Family, and Kinship in a Heartland Community*. New York: Aldine.

Hellberg, Elena. 1986. Folklore, Might, and Glory: On the Symbolism of Power Legitimation. *Nordic Journal of Soviet and East European Studies* 3 (2): 9–20.

Hingley, Ronald. 1977. *The Russian Mind*. New York: Scribner's.

——. 1981. *Nightingale Fever: Russian Poets in Revolution*. New York: Alfred A. Knopf.

Holst-Warshaft, Gail. 1992. *Dangerous Voices: Women's Laments and Greek Literature*. London: Routledge.

Hosking, Geoffrey. 1991. *The Awakening of the Soviet Union*. Cambridge: Harvard University Press.

Howe, Jovan E. 1991. *The Peasant Mode of Production*. Tampere, Finland: University of Tampere.

Hubbs, Joanna. 1988. *Mother Russia: The Feminine Myth in Russian Culture*. Bloomington: Indiana University Press.

Humphrey, Caroline. 1983. *Karl Marx Collective: Economy, Society, and Religion in a Siberian Collective Farm*. Cambridge: Cambridge University Press.

——. 1991. "Icebergs," Barter, and the Mafia in Provincial Russia. *Anthropology Today* 7 (2): 10–13.

Hymes, Dell. 1964. Introduction: Toward Ethnographies of Communication. In *Directions in Sociolinguistics*, ed. John Gumperz and Dell Hymes, pp. 1–34. *American Anthropologist Special Publication* 66(6): pt. 2.

——. 1974. *Foundations in Sociolinguistics: An Ethnographic Approach*. Philadelphia: University of Pennsylvania Press.

Ingham, Norman W. 1984. The Martyred Princes and the Question of Slavic Cultural Continuity in the Early Middle Ages. In *Medieval Russian Culture*, ed. Henrik Birnbaum and Michael S. Flier, pp. 31–53. Berkeley: University of California Press.

Irvine, Judith T. 1989. When Talk Isn't Cheap: Language and Political Economy. *American Ethnologist* 16 (2): 248–267.

Isenberg, Charles. 1987. The Rhetoric of Nadezhda Mandelstam's *Hope against Hope*. In *New Studies in Russian Language and Literature*, ed. Lisa Crone and Catherine V. Chvany, pp. 168–182. Columbus, Ohio: Slavica Publishers.

Istomin, A. A. 1992. Revolutsiia, kotoraia byla prazdnikom. *Etnograficheskoe obozrenie* 3: 58–66.

Ivanits, Linda J. 1989. *Russian Folk Belief*. Armonk, N.Y.: M. E. Sharpe.

Izbrannye zhitiia russkikh sviatykh X–XV vekov. 1992. Moscow: Molodaia gvardiia.

Jakobson, Roman. 1966. Grammatical Parallelism and Its Russian Facet. *Language* 42 (2): 399–422.

Jowitt, Ken. 1992. *New World Disorder: The Leninist Extinction*. Berkeley: University of California Press.

Kan, Sergei. 1989. *Symbolic Immortality: The Tlinget Potlatch of the Nineteenth Century*. Washington: Smithsonian Institution Press.

Kelly, Catriona. 1990. *Petrushka: The Russian Carnival Puppet Theatre*. Cambridge: Cambridge University Press.

Kelly, Mary. 1990. *Goddess Embroideries of Eastern Europe*. Winona, Minn.: Northland.

Kerblay, Basile. 1989. *Gorbachev's Russia*. New York: Pantheon Books.

Kerby, Anthony Paul. 1991. *Narrative and the Self*. Bloomington: Indiana University Press.

Kertzer, David I. 1988. *Ritual, Politics, and Power*. New Haven: Yale University Press.

Khanga, Yelena. 1991. No Matryoshkas Need Apply. *New York Times*. November 25, 1991.

Kingston-Mann, Esther, and Timothy Mixter, eds. 1991. *Peasant Economy, Culture, and Politics of European Russia 1800–1921*. Princeton: Princeton University Press.

Kleinman, Arthur. 1992. Pain and Resistance: The Delegitimation and Relegitimation of Local Worlds. In *Pain as Human Experience: An Anthropological Perspective*, ed. M. DelVecchio Good, P. E. Brodwin, B. J. Good and A. Kleinman, pp. 169–197. Berkeley and Los Angeles: University of California Press.

Kluckhohn, Clyde. 1962. Recent Studies of the 'National Character' of Great Russians. In *Culture and Behavior*, ed. Richard Kluckhohn, pp. 210–243. New York: Free Press.

Kon, Igor S. 1989 The Psychology of Social Inertia. In *New Directions in Soviet Social Thought*, ed. Murray Yanowitch, pp. 241–254. Armonk, N.Y.: M. E. Sharpe.

Korotich, Vitaly, and Cathy Porter, eds. 1990. *The New Soviet Journalism: The Best of the Soviet Weekly Ogonyok*. Boston: Beacon Press.

Kotkin, Stephen. 1991. *Steeltown, USSR: Soviet Society in the Gorbachev Era*. Berkeley: University of California Press.

Kravchenko, Maria. 1987. *The World of the Russian Fairy Tale*. Bern, Switzerland: Peter Lang.

Kuipers, Joel C. 1986. Talking about Troubles: Gender Differences in Weyewa Speech Use. *American Ethnologist* 13 (3): 448–462.

Lane, Christel. 1981. *The Rites of Rulers: Ritual in Industrial Society—the Soviet Case*. Cambridge: Cambridge University Press.

Lapidus, Gail W. 1978. *Women in Soviet Society: Equality, Development, and Social Change*. Berkeley: University of California Press.

Lapshov, B. A. 1992. Between the Philosophy of Poverty and the Philosophy of Misery. *Herald of the USSR Academy of Sciences* 62 (1): 35–46.

Lavie, Smadar. 1990. *The Poetics of Military Occupation*. Berkeley: University of California Press.

Leibovich, Anna Feldman. 1995. *The Russian Concept of Work: Suffering, Drama, and Tradition in Pre- and Post-Revolutionary Russia*. Westport, Conn.: Praeger.

Lempert, David. 1996. *Daily Life in a Crumbling Empire: The Absorption of Russia into the World Economy*. New York: Columbia University Press.

Lévi-Strauss, Claude. 1966. *The Savage Mind*. Chicago: University of Chicago Press.

Lewin, Moshe. 1988. *The Gorbachev Phenomenon: A Historical Interpretation*. Berkeley, Calif.: University of California Press.

——. 1995. *Russia—USSR—Russia: The Drive and Drift of a Superstate*. New York: New Press.

Likhachev, D. S.. 1981. Notes on the Essence of Russianness. *Soviet Literature* 2: 126–162.

Likhachev, D. S., and E. I. Vaneeva, eds. 1985. *Povest' o Gore-Zloschastii*. Leningrad: Nauka.

Lomonosov, M. V. 1952. *Rossiiskaia grammatika*. In *Polnoe sobranie sochinenii*, vol. 7. Moscow: Izdatel'stvo Akademii Nauk SSSR.

Lotman, Juri, and Boris Uspenskij. 1984. *The Semiotics of Russian Culture*, ed. Ann Shukman. Ann Arbor: Michigan Slavic Contributions.

Luthi, Max. 1976. Goal-Orientation in Storytelling. In *Folklore Today: A Festschrift for Richard M. Dorson*, ed. Linda Degh, Henry Glassie, and Felix J. Oinas, pp. 357–369. Bloomington: Indiana University Press.

Mandel, David. 1994. *Rabotyagi: Perestroika and After Viewed from Below*. New York: Monthly Review Press.

Maranda, Pierre, and Elli Kongas Maranda. 1971. *Structural Analysis of Oral Tradition*. Philadelphia: University of Pennsylvania Press.

March, Kathryn. 1987. Hospitality, Women, and the Efficacy of Beer. *Food and Foodways* 6: 351–387.

Marriott, McKim. 1966. The Feast of Love. In *Krishna: Myths, Rites, and Attitudes*, ed. Milton Singer, pp. 200–212. Honolulu: East-West Press Center.

Matthews, Mervyn. 1978. *Privilege in the Soviet Union: A Study of Elite Lifestyles under Communism*. London: Allen and Unwin.

McAuley, Mary. 1984. "Political Culture and Communist Politics: One Step Forward, Two Steps Back."In *Political Culture and Communist Studies*, ed. Archie Brown, pp. 13–39. Armonk, N.Y.: M. E. Sharpe.

Mead, Margaret. 1951. *Soviet Attitudes toward Authority*. New York: McGraw Hill.

——. 1954. The Swaddling Hypothesis: Its Reception. *American Anthropologist* 56: 395–409.

Mead, Margaret, and Rhoda Metraux. 1953. *The Study of Culture at a Distance*. Chicago: University of Chicago Press.

Mikheyev, Dmitry. 1989. The New Soviet Man: Myth and Reality. In *The Soviet Union and the Challenge of the Future*. Vol. 2. *Economy and Society*, ed. Alexander Shtromas and Morton A. Kaplan, pp. 634–647. New York: Paragon.

Millar, James R. 1987. *Politics, Work, and Daily Life in the USSR: A Survey of Former Soviet Citizens*. Cambridge: Cambridge University Press.

Moerman, Michael. 1988. *Talking Culture*. Philadelphia: University of Pennsylvania Press.

Moore, Sally Falk, and Barbara G. Myerhoff, eds. 1975. *Symbol and Politics in Communal Ideology*. Ithaca: Cornell University Press.

Moskoff, William. 1990. *The Bread of Affliction: The Food Supply in the USSR during World War II*. Cambridge: Cambridge University Press.

————. 1993. *Hard Times: Impoverishment and Protest in the Perestroika Years*, Armonk, N.Y.: M. E. Sharpe.

Motyl, Alexander J. 1990. *Sovietology, Rationality, Nationality: Coming to Grips with Nationalism in the USSR*. New York: Columbia University Press.

Munn, Nancy D. 1986. *The Fame of Gawa: A Symbolic Study of Value Transformation in a Massim (Papua New Guinea) Society*. Cambridge: Cambridge University Press.

Myerhoff, Barbara G. 1975. Organization and Ecstasy: Deliberate and Accidental Communitas Among Huichol Indians and American Youth. In *Symbol and Politics in Communal Ideology*, ed. Sally Falk Moore and Barbara G. Myerhoff, pp. 33–67. Ithaca: Cornell University Press.

————. 1978. *Number Our Days*. New York: Simon and Schuster.

————. 1986. "Life Not Death in Venice": Its Second Life. In *The Anthropology of Experience*, ed. Victor W. Turner and Edward M. Bruner, pp. 261–287. Urbana: University of Illinois Press.

Nove, Alec. 1989. *Glasnost' in Action: Cultural Renaissance in Russia*. Boston: Unwin Hyman.

Ochs, Elinor. 1992 Indexing Gender. In *Rethinking Context: Language as an Interactive Phenomenon*, ed. Alessandro Duranti and Charles Goodwin, pp. 335–358. Cambridge: Cambridge University Press.

Oinas, Felix J. 1984. *Essays on Russian Folklore and Mythology*. Columbus, Ohio: Slavica.

Ong, Walter J. 1981. *Fighting for Life: Contest, Sexuality, and Consciousness*. Amherst: University of Massachusetts Press.

————. 1982. *Orality and Literacy: The Technologizing of the Word*. London: Methuen.

Ortner, Sherry B. 1973. On Key Symbols. *American Anthropologist* 75: 1338–1346.

————. 1995. Resistance and the Problem of Ethnographic Refusal. *Comparative Studies of Society and History* 37(1): 173–193. Cambridge: Cambridge University Press.

Parker, Tony. 1991. *Russian Voices*. New York: Henry Holt.

Parkhomov, L. 1984. Bessmertnye sueveriia. *Novoe russkoe slovo*, 8.

Parthé, Kathleen. 1997. The Empire Strikes Back: How Right-Wing Nationalists Tried to Recapture Russian Literature. In *Nationalities Papers* (forthcoming).

Peletz, Michael G. 1997. "Ordinary Muslims" and Muslim Resurgents in Contemporary Malaysia: Notes on an Ambivalent Relationship. In *Islam in an Era of Nation States: Politics and Religious Renewal in Southeast Asia*, ed. Patricia Horvatich and Robert Hefner, Honolulu: University of Hawaii Press.

Perrie, Maureen. 1989. Folklore as Evidence of Peasant Mentalité: Social Attitudes and Values in Russian Popular Culture. *Russian Review* 48 (2): 119–143.

Pesmen, Dale. 1995. Standing Bottles, Washing Deals, and Drinking "For the Soul" in a Siberian City. *Anthropology of East Europe Review* 13 (2): 65–75.

————. n.d. Suffering, Public Transportation, Depth, and 'The Russian Soul.'

Petrochenkov, Valery. 1990. Christian Patterns in Contemporary Soviet Prose. In *Christianity and Russian Culture in Soviet Society*, ed. Nicolai N. Petro, pp. 119–142. Boulder, Colo.: Westview.

Pilkington, Hilary. 1994. *Russia's Youth and its Culture*. London: Routledge.

Pipes, Richard. 1974. *Russia Under the Old Regime*. London: Weidenfeld and Nicolson.

Porokhniuk, V., and M. S. Shepeleva. 1982. How Working Women Combine Work and Household Duties. In *Women, Work, and Family in the Soviet Union*, ed. Gail Lapidus, pp. 267–276. Armonk, N.Y.: M. E. Sharpe.

Propp, Vladimir. 1968. *The Morphology of the Folktale*. Translated from the Russian by Laurence Scott. Austin: University of Texas Press.

Rancour-Laferriere, Daniel. 1995. *The Slave Soul of Russia: Moral Masochism and the Cult of Suffering*. New York: New York University Press.

Redl, Helen B., ed. 1964. *Soviet Educators on Soviet Education*. New York: Free Press.

Ries, Nancy. 1991. The Power of Negative Thinking: Russian Talk and the Reproduction of Mindset, Worldview, and Society. *Anthropology of East Europe Review* 10 (2): 38–53.

——. 1994. The Burden of Mythic Identity: Russian Women at Odds With Themselves. In *Feminist Nightmares: Women at Odds*, ed. Susan O. Weisser and Jennifer Fleischner, pp. 242–268. New York: New York University Press.

Riordan, Jim, and Sue Bridger, eds. 1992. *Dear Comrade Editor: Readers' Letters to the Soviet Press under Perestroika*. Bloomington: Indiana University Press.

Roosevelt, Priscilla. 1991. Emerald Thrones and Living Statues: Theater and Theatricality on the Russian Estate. *Russian Review* 50 (1): 1–23.

Rosaldo, Renato. 1986. Ilongot Hunting as Story and Experience. In *The Anthropology of Experience*, ed. Victor W. Turner and Edward M. Bruner, pp. 97–138. Urbana: University of Illinois Press.

——. 1989. *Culture and Truth*. Boston: Beacon Press.

Rose, Richard. 1994. Getting By without Government: Everyday Life in Russia. *Daedalus* 123 (3): 41–62.

Rzhiga, V. 1931. *Povest' o Gore Zloschastii i Pesni o Gore*. Moscow: Slavia.

Sakharov, I. P. 1991. *Russkoe narodnoe chernoknizh'e*. Moscow: Evrika.

Sangren, P. Steven. 1987. *History and Magical Power in a Chinese Community*. Stanford: Stanford University Press.

——. 1991. The Dialectics of Alienation: Individuals and Collectivities in Chinese Religion. *Man* 26 (1): 67–86.

Sariban, Alla. 1984. The Soviet Woman: Support and Mainstay of the Regime. In *Women and Russia*, ed. Tatiana Mamonova, pp. 205–213. Boston: Beacon Press.

Saussure, Ferdinand de. 1959. *Course in General Linguistics*. New York: Philosophical Library.

Scarry, Elaine. 1985. *The Body in Pain: The Making and Unmaking of the World*. New York: Oxford University Press.

Scott, James C. 1985. *Weapons of the Weak: Everyday Forms of Peasant Resistance*. New Haven: Yale University Press.

——. 1990. *Domination and the Arts of Resistance: Hidden Transcripts*. New Haven: Yale University Press.

Seidel, G. 1985. Political Discourse Analysis. In *Handbook of Discourse Analysis*, vol. 4, ed. T. Van Dijk, pp. 43–50. London: Academic Press.

Senelick, Laurence. 1991. The Erotic Bondage of Serf Theatre. *The Russian Review* 50: 24–34.

Seremetakis, Nadia. 1991. *The Last Word: Women, Death, and Divination in Inner Mani*. Chicago: University of Chicago Press.

Shalin, Dmitri N., ed. 1996. *Russian Culture at the Crossroads*. Boulder, Colo.: Westview.

Shanin, Teodor. 1972. *The Awkward Class: Political Sociology of Peasantry in a Developing Society: Russia 1910–1925*. London: Oxford University Press.

Sherzer, Joel. 1983. *Kuna Ways of Speaking: An Ethnographic Perspective*. Austin: University of Texas Press.

———. 1987 A Discourse-Centered Approach to Language and Culture. *American Anthropologist* 89 (2): 295–309.

Sinyavsky, Andrei. 1976. *A Voice From the Chorus*. Translated from the Russian by Kiril Fitzlyon and Max Hayward. New York: Farrar, Straus and Giroux.

———. 1984. The Joke Inside the Joke. *Partisan Review* 51 (3): 356–366.

Slobin, Greta A. 1992. Revolution Must Come First: Reading V. Aksenov's *Island of Crimea*. In *Nationalisms and Sexualities*, ed. Andrew Parker, Mary Russo, Doris Sommer, and Patricia Yaeger, pp. 246–263. New York: Routledge.

Smith, Barbara Herrnstein. 1982. *Contingencies of Value: Alternative Perspectives for Critical Theory*. Cambridge: Harvard University Press.

Sokolov, Y. M. 1971. *Russian Folklore*. Translated from the Russian by Catharine Ruth Smith. Detroit: Folklore Associates.

Solzhenitsyn, Aleksandr I. 1970. Matryona's Home. In *Stories and Prose Poems*. Translated from the Russian by Michael Glenny, pp. 3–52. New York: Farrar, Straus and Giroux.

Stahl, Sandra Dolby. 1989. *Literary Folkloristics and the Personal Narrative*. Bloomington: Indiana University Press.

Stallybrass, Peter and Allon White. 1986. *The Politics and Poetics of Transgression*. Ithaca: Cornell University Press.

Stites, Richard. 1989. *Revolutionary Dreams: Utopian Vision and Experimental Life in the Russian Revolution*. New York: Oxford University Press.

———. 1992. *Russian Popular Culture: Entertainment and Society since 1900*. Cambridge: Cambridge University Press.

Taussig, Michael. 1987. *Shamanism, Colonialism, and the Wild Man: A Study in Terror and Healing*. Chicago: University of Chicago Press.

Thompson, Ewa M. 1987. *Understanding Russia: The Holy Fool in Russian Culture*. Lanham, Md.: University Press of America.

Thompson, John B. 1984. *Studies in the Theory of Ideology*. Berkeley: University of California Press.

———. 1990. *Ideology and Modern Culture*. Stanford: Stanford University Press.

Thurston, Robert W. 1991. Social Dimensions of Stalinist Rule: Humor and Terror in the USSR, 1935–1941. *Journal of Social History* 24: 541–562.

Tolstaya, Tatyana. 1992. Is There Hope for Pushkin's Children? *Wilson Quarterly*, Winter 1992: 121–130.

Tucker, Robert C. 1977. Stalinism and Comparative Communism. Introduction to *Stalinism: Essays in Historical Interpretation*, ed. Robert C. Tucker. New York: W. W. Norton.

Tumarkin, Nina. 1983. *Lenin Lives! The Cult of Lenin in the Soviet Union*. Cambridge: Harvard University Press.

———. 1990. Truth Teller. *World Monitor*, February 1990: 22–23.

———. 1991. The Invasion and War as Myth and Memory. *Soviet Union* 18 (1): 277–296.

———. 1994. *The Living and the Dead: The Rise and Fall of the Cult of WWII in Russia*. New York: Basic Books.

Turner, Victor. 1967. *The Forest of Symbols: Aspects of Ndembu Ritual*. Ithaca: Cornell University Press.

———. 1974. *Dramas, Fields, and Metaphors: Symbolic Action in Human Society*. Ithaca: Cornell University Press.

———. 1977. *The Ritual Process: Structure and Anti-Structure.* Ithaca: Cornell University Press.

———. 1982. *From Ritual to Theatre: The Human Seriousness of Play.* New York: PAJ Publications.

———. 1988. *The Anthropology of Performance.* New York: PAJ Publications.

Urban, Gregory. 1991. *A Discourse-centerd Approach to Culture: Native South American Myths and Rituals.* Austin: University of Texas Press.

Urban, Michael. 1994. The Politics of Identity in Russia's Post-Communist Transition: The Nation Against Itself. *Slavic Review* 53 (3) 733–765.

Varlamova, Inna. 1989. A Threesome. In *Balancing Acts: Contemporary Stories by Russian Women.* Translated by Helena Goscilo. Bloomington: Indiana University Press.

Verdery, Katherine. 1991. *National Ideology under Socialism: Identity and Cultural Politics in Ceauşescu's Romania.* Berkeley: University of California Press.

Voronina, Olga. 1993. Soviet Patriarchy: Past and Present. *Hypatia* 8 (4): 97–112.

Wada, Haruki. 1979. The Inner World of Russian Peasants. *Annals of the Institute of Social Science* 82: 61–93.

Weiner, Annette B. 1976. *Women of Value, Men of Renown: New Perspectives on Trobriand Exchange.* Austin: University of Texas Press.

Wierzbicka, Anna. 1985. Different Cultures, Different Languages, Different Speech Acts. *Journal of Pragmatics* 1985 (9): 145–178.

———. 1989. Soul and Mind: Linguistic Evidence for Ethnopsychology and Cultural History. *American Anthropologist* 91 (1): 41–58.

Willis, David K. 1985. *KLASS: How Russians Really Live.* New York: Avon.

Willis, Paul E. 1981. *Learning to Labor: How Working Class Kids Get Working Class Jobs.* New York: Columbia University Press.

Wosien, Maria-Gabriele. 1969. *The Russian Folk-Tale: Some Structural and Thematic Aspects.* Munich: Otto Sagner.

Yanowitch, Murray, ed. 1989. *New Directions in Soviet Social Thought.* Armonk, N.Y.: M. E. Sharpe.

Yevtushenko, Yevgeny. 1990. A Nation Begins with Its Women. In *Perestroika: The Crunch Is Now,* ed. Lena Krishtoff and Eva Skelley, pp. 313–321. Moscow: Progress.

Zand, Arie. 1982. *Political Jokes of Leningrad.* Austin, Texas: Silvergirl, Inc.

Zemtsov, Ilya. 1985. *Private Life of the Soviet Elite.* New York: Crane Russak.

Zenkovsky, Serge A. 1963. *Medieval Russia's Epics, Chronicles, and Tales.* New York: E. P. Dutton.

Zhirinovskii, Vladimir. 1993. *Poslednyi brosok na iug.* Moscow: Liberal'no-Demokraticheskaia Partiia.

Index

Nancy Ries is Assistant Professor of Anthropology at Colgate University in Hamilton, New York. She received her B.A. in Russian and Slavic Studies from Boston College in 1976 and her Ph.D. in Anthropology from Cornell University in 1993.